Learn LabVIEW™ 2012 Fast:

A Primer for Automatic Data Acquisition

Douglas Stamps, Ph.D.

Department of Mechanical and Civil Engineering
University of Evansville

Publications

Schroff Development Corporation

www.SDCpublications.com

Table of Contents

Preface

This primer is written with the expectation that one has no experience with LabVIEW and a limited understanding of automatic data acquisition. The primer was written for new LabVIEW users using feedback from new users to help guide the format to best learn LabVIEW. The primer would be suitable, for example, as an introduction to the use of LabVIEW in an undergraduate course on experimental methods that covers instruments and measurement techniques or for courses that focus on the control and operation of practical electrical devices.

Although this primer is written specifically with LabVIEW 2012 in mind, different LabVIEW versions are relatively stable. For example, LabVIEW 8.5 was used to test some of the example problems in this primer. While there may be some minor variations between LabVIEW versions in the screen shots or detailed steps of the primer, the concepts will remain invariant to any differences.

The primer is divided into two parts. You are introduced to the general concepts of LabVIEW in the first part through the development of a general program to acquire analog input data in Chapter 1. The second part introduces you to general concepts of data measurement and generation using LabVIEW's configuration approach for automatic data acquisition.

The goal of this primer is to introduce you to LabVIEW for hands-on use in automatic data acquisition and controls applications. Most LabVIEW books do not discuss data acquisition in any depth and this primer uses a number of practical real-life examples to provide both breadth and depth to the topic. If the examples in the primer are directly applicable to you…great! If not, the hope is that you can modify one of the current examples, modify one of the examples provided by LabVIEW, or write your own program using the concepts covered in this primer. At the very least, you should be able to use other more advanced texts on LabVIEW more efficiently after using this primer as your introduction to LabVIEW.

Philosophies Incorporated Into This Primer

The primer is developed based on the premise that the best way to learn and retain key concepts in LabVIEW is to develop and execute programs as you are learning them. This experiential approach to learning is one of the quickest ways to learn and retain new material. As such, LabVIEW concepts are introduced as they are needed within problems used to develop skills and proficiency in LabVIEW. Consistent with this philosophy, a general program to acquire analog input data is developed in Part 1 to learn some basic concepts of LabVIEW. The sole chapter in this part of the primer, Chapter 1, contains a detailed step-by-step guide in one section. The format of the guide to develop the general analog input program is as follows. An overview of a new LabVIEW concept is first introduced followed by a set of steps to implement the new concept into the example program that is being developed. The overview is brief by design but provides enough information to understand how it is used in the subsequent steps. Following the steps, general information about the concept may be provided. The information may or may not pertain directly to the example program but helps develop a general understanding of LabVIEW and allows the user to try out the newly described features in their program. While the analog input program in Chapter 1 has practical application and may be used for your basic data acquisition needs, the main purpose of the program is to introduce the majority of LabVIEW concepts that you will need throughout the remainder of the programs in the primer.

Another premise is that the best way to become proficient at programming with LabVIEW is through practice. As such, every section in the remaining part of this primer introduces a new data acquisition topic, a problem to develop skills within the new topic, and a number of practical application problems at the end of each chapter to help develop proficiency. The skill-development problems are generally limited to a single data acquisition mode, like analog input or digital output, and provide a step-by-step guide to develop the program. The proficiency-development problems may include mixed mode data acquisition, like digital output that depends on an analog input signal. The data acquisition program is given, but the detailed steps of the program's development are left to you. The primer progresses from a very detailed step-by-step guide to develop the first program in Chapter 1 to limited guidance with the proficiency-development problems at the end of each remaining chapter. It is hoped that this progression will help you develop confidence in your abilities to create your own application programs.

Example problems were selected so as to be both practical and pertinent to real-life applications. It is hoped that the real-life examples demonstrate the value of LabVIEW and provide motivation to learn it. Furthermore, it is hoped that you will find the examples fun to program. The example problems show many aspects of analog input, such as hardware and software timing, buffered and triggered acquisition, and examples with common sensors, such as thermocouples and strain gages. Examples from other acquisition modes show how to drive many common output devices, such as stepper motors, servo motors, and DC motors, as well as software control programs, such as the PID compensator and pulse width modulation. Each problem describes example hardware that is needed to perform the problem. However, the function of the program can be demonstrated for many of the problems without any additional hardware beyond the PC, data acquisition board, and the terminal block connector.

This primer has a modular structure to learn LabVIEW fast. Most books on LabVIEW present topics in a serial fashion. In such books, a topic that is of interest to you but located in the middle of the book requires that previous chapters must be read to provide the background to the chapter of interest. This is especially true when discussing material on data acquisition in most LabVIEW books. This primer assumes that everyone unfamiliar with LabVIEW has read Chapter 1. Beyond that, you may proceed with any other section without regard to the order of occurrence in this primer. This creates some redundancy in the topics covered if you read the entire primer; for example, some topics may be covered in more than one section. However, the beneficial effect of this built-in redundancy allows you to select only those topics of interest. It is anticipated that your needs may focus on only one or two of the sections. This introduction to learning LabVIEW should be much faster than reading a text where topics are built upon one-by-one in a serial fashion until you learn the topics of interest to you.

How to Use This Primer

Part 1 introduces you to basic LabVIEW concepts that are used throughout the remainder of the primer. First-time LabVIEW users need to complete Chapter 1 before proceeding to any other chapter. You are introduced to some of the general concepts of LabVIEW in this chapter through the development of a program to acquire analog data. The other chapters assume you know the concepts discussed in Chapter 1.

If the primer is used as part of a course, the material in Part 1 may be delivered in one of the following approaches. One approach can be used if data acquisition using LabVIEW is taught in a class or computer lab but time is limited. In this approach, material in Sections 1.1-1.3 can be assigned for reading before class, students can then develop the example VI to take analog input measurements following only the material under **Steps** in Section 1.4 during the class or lab with the assistance of an instructor and, finally, students can be assigned the background material in Section 1.4 for reading after the class. The development of the VI will take one to two hours if only the steps in Section 1.4 are followed. This example VI will give the student experience to better understand and retain the background material at a later time since they already have the experience of working through the LabVIEW concepts. Another approach is to have the students read the material in Chapter 1 and develop the VI independently, since the guide to the development of the VI was written with detailed step by step instructions.

Part 2 introduces concepts of data acquisition for different modes of data measurement and generation. Separate chapters are devoted to analog input and output, digital input and output, and counters, which can generate or measure a series of digital pulses and their associated periods and frequencies. The reader may select any chapter of interest without regard to order. Basic concepts associated with each mode of data acquisition are discussed in the beginning of a chapter or section followed by a program to develop skills in the new topic. Part 2 demonstrates the configuration-based approach to programming found in the Express functions, such as the DAQ Assistant. It is an approach often taken by those relatively new to LabVIEW. The relative simplicity of the configuration approach allows for rapid LabVIEW startup, especially in the development of simple programs for single mode data acquisition. However, the attempt to develop ease of use through the configuration approach can also make a function less flexible and limit the ease of using functions for multi-mode data acquisition.

Part 1 Introduction to LabVIEW

The purpose of Part 1 is to introduce many of the basic LabVIEW concepts used in programs to measure or generate data that are developed throughout the remainder of the primer. LabVIEW concepts are introduced as you develop a general analog input program using a step-by-step guide. The general structure of the guide is to give an overview of a new concept, provide a detailed set of instructions to implement the new concept into the example program, and then provide additional information that can be tested on the newly incorporated concept. The best way to learn and retain LabVIEW concepts is to incorporate the concept in the development of a program while the material is read.

Part 1 is written for the first-time LabVIEW user and, as such, the concepts and steps are described in detail. Programs developed in the remainder of the primer assume a familiarity with the material introduced in this part, and the steps to developing the remaining programs are not as detailed. If you are already familiar with the basic concepts of LabVIEW and interested primarily in how to use LabVIEW for data acquisition, you may skip Part 1 and proceed directly to Part 2.

A general analog input program that can acquire either a finite set of measurements or collect measurements continuously was selected to develop your skills for a number of reasons. It contains many of the concepts that you will use throughout the remainder of the primer. It has practical application and may be used for acquiring voltage signals that do not vary quickly with time. It will also be used to show the similarities with hardware-timed finite and continuous data acquisition programs introduced in Chapter 2.

The focus of the general analog input program is to introduce you to basic concepts and develop the reader's LabVIEW skills. Because of this focus, a detailed discussion of data acquisition concepts will be deferred until Part 2. Likewise, since the purpose of the program is to cover different LabVIEW concepts, the execution efficiency was not a key consideration in developing this program.

The material discussed in this primer assumes that LabVIEW Professional Version or Student Version software, NI-DAQ software, and a data acquisition board have been installed on your computer.

Notes:

Chapter 1   LabVIEW for Data Acquisition

1.1   What is Automatic Data Acquisition?

In a broad sense, data acquisition (DAQ) is the measurement or generation (control) of a physical phenomenon. It may be performed manually by a person or automatically by a computer. There are numerous reasons to automate your data measurement and generation.

Automatic data acquisition has advantages over manual data acquisition when changes occur either very quickly or very slowly in the physical phenomenon or when there are many inputs and/or outputs associated with the phenomenon. For example, a person would not be able to record the pressure inside an airbag during deployment or the strain in the structural members in the frame of the car during an automotive test crash because the event would occur too quickly to record any data. Likewise, events that occur over a long period of time, like measuring meteorological data, are better performed automatically with a computer. Even if the event occurs at a manageable pace and period of time for a human, a person would be limited in the number of switches or relays that could be controlled or the number of sensors from which data could be recorded simultaneously. Automatic data acquisition also has the advantage over manual acquisition in that the data can be recorded without the possibility of human error and be viewed as it is collected, which permits experimental methods to be corrected if problems arise before the experiment is completed. Otherwise, with manual data acquisition, the experiment is typically completed before the data is entered and plotted in a spreadsheet.

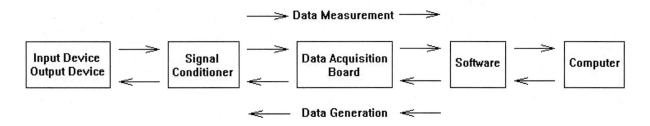

Figure 1.1.1   Components of a data acquisition system

A data acquisition system is composed of several components as shown in Figure 1.1.1, which may take on different configurations depending on the type of system used, but perform similar functions regardless of the system. A typical data acquisition system would have an input or output device, a signal conditioner, which, for the purposes of this introduction, will be broadly interpreted as a device that alters, modifies, or manipulates a signal, a data acquisition (DAQ) board that can convert analog to digital signals or vice versa, a computer, and software to allow the computer to communicate with the DAQ board. The specific components used depend on the type of data and the flow of data, that is, if data is measured or generated.

For data measurement (data direction defined by the arrows pointing towards the computer in Fig. 1.1.1), the input device could be a sensor or transducer, like a thermocouple or pressure transducer, that is detecting a physical phenomenon, like temperature or pressure, and outputting an electrical signal, such as a voltage or current. The signal may pass through a signal conditioner, which is a device that may, among other things, attenuate, amplify, filter, or linearize a signal. Signal conditioners are needed, for example, when the sensor's output is outside of an acceptable range of the other DAQ hardware, the signal has too much electrical noise relative to the output associated with the physical phenomenon, or it is convenient to have the signal in a linear form for unit conversion. The signal is then read by a DAQ board and converted into a digital signal that can be interpreted by a computer. Sometimes DAQ boards are called A/D boards since they are often used to measure an analog input signal and convert it into a digital signal. Software is required for the computer to communicate with the DAQ board. LabVIEW software interfaces with the computer to analyze, store, and display data and with driver software, called NI-DAQmx, which configures data channels and measures data.

Data generation (data direction defined by the arrows pointing away from the computer) operates in the opposite direction as to data measurement. In this case, data is typically generated by LabVIEW to control an output device, such as a switch or motor. LabVIEW works with the NI-DAQmx software to configure the DAQ board to generate the proper electrical signal based on the data generated by LabVIEW. If the output device requires an analog signal, the DAQ board must convert the digital signals used by the computer into an analog signal required by the output device, that is, a digital to analog conversion. In some cases, the DAQ board can provide sufficient current within an acceptable voltage range to drive the output device. However, this is normally not the case as the DAQ boards are typically limited to a voltage range of ±10V and a few milliamps of current. To prevent damage to the DAQ board, another device, such as a solid state relay or an integrated circuit hardware driver, must be connected between the DAQ board and the output device to condition the signal that drives the output device. Loosely speaking, it is analogous to the signal conditioner used during data measurement. Examples of output devices used in example programs found in this primer include stepper motors and DC motors.

Components of a data acquisition system are shown in Figure 1.1.2 for a desktop PC. LabVIEW and driver software are installed on the computer. A data acquisition board is fitted into a PCI slot in the computer. However, the pins on the data acquisition board are too small to make direct connections with sensors or signal conditioners. A terminal connector block is attached by cable to the data acquisition board to provide room to connect the signal conditioners or the input/output devices. A close up of a terminal connector block connected to a data acquisition board is shown in Fig. 1.1.3. The connector block has screw slots for all channels on the data acquisition board and system grounds.

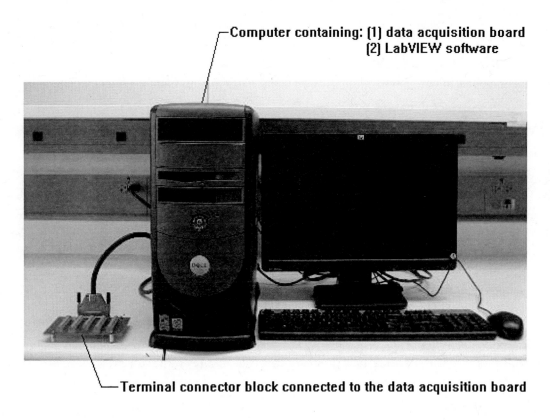

Figure 1.1.2   Components of a data acquisition system

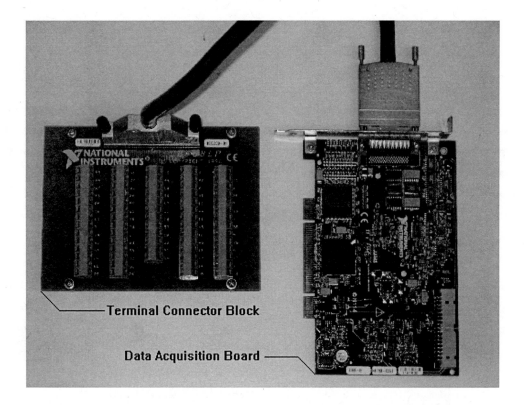

Figure 1.1.3   Terminal connector block connected to a data acquisition board

1.2   What is LabVIEW?

LabVIEW is a software development environment created by National Instruments that allows your computer to interface with data acquisition hardware with appropriate hardware drivers. Early in its development, a focus of LabVIEW was to allow the user to develop virtual instruments to acquire and display data without the aid of an equivalent hardware instrument, like an oscilloscope or a multimeter. The software's name, LabVIEW (**Lab**oratory **V**irtual **I**nstrument **E**ngineering **W**orkbench), and the name given to programs developed by LabVIEW, which are called Virtual Instruments (VI) and have a ".vi" file extension, are a result of this early focus of the software. LabVIEW programs are still typically referred to as VIs even though the purpose of the program may not relate to a virtual instrument.

LabVIEW has traditionally been used for automated measurement and control of hardware and processes, which continue to be important application areas. LabVIEW software permits the quick development of VIs to measure, process, analyze, display, and store data as well as to generate data (voltages or currents) to control instruments and hardware, such as motors, valves, or switches. Continued development of the LabVIEW software by National Instruments has allowed it to become a general programming tool, permitting the development of algorithms, mathematical analyses, and communication tasks that extend beyond data acquisition.

LabVIEW is software built on a graphical programming language, known as G code, and the concept of data flow to control program execution. The G programming language is represented by function icons connected by virtual wires, which permit data to flow between the function icons. Functions can have any number of input and output terminals. A function does not execute until data arrives at all input terminals. The execution of the program, therefore, is controlled by the flow of the data. This is conceptually different from text-based programming languages where the execution of the program is determined primarily by the order of the program statements.

1.3   The LabVIEW Environment

The purpose of this section is to introduce you to the LabVIEW environment, which includes the main LabVIEW windows, called the front panel and block diagram, menus and shortcuts that provide options for working with LabVIEW VIs, toolbars to manage objects within the LabVIEW windows, and the palettes that contain the objects that will be used to develop your programs and the user interfaces of the programs. A detailed discussion of all of the features will not be provided in this section as it is difficult to remember the details without actually applying them. However, the hope is that you will become aware of features that exist and where they are located so as to be familiar with them when they are discussed in more detail throughout the examples. So launch LabVIEW and explore the LabVIEW environment as you read this section.

1.3.1   Starting LabVIEW

If your version of LabVIEW was installed using the default installation procedure, launch LabVIEW by selecting **All Programs>>National Instruments>>LabVIEW 2012>>LabVIEW 2012** from the Start menu. Or, if available, double click on the LabVIEW shortcut icon on the desktop. A LabVIEW window will appear as shown in Figure 1.3.1. Click on "Create Project" and select "Blank VI" to open a new file for this exercise. Later, you may select a previously used file in the panel located under "Open Existing" or click on "Open Existing" to browse for an existing file not shown.

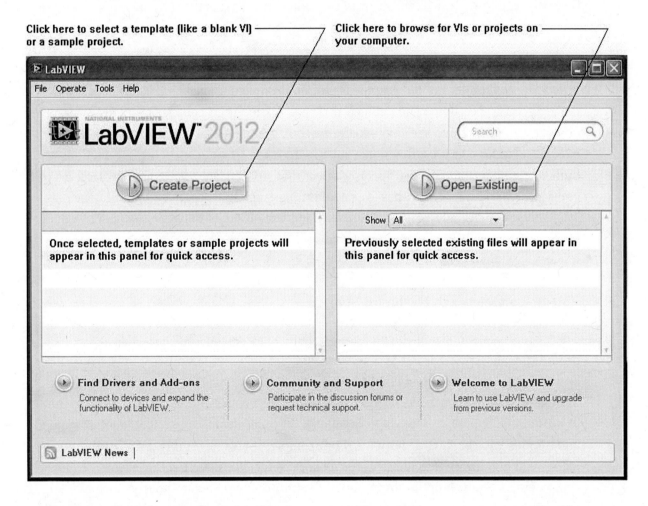

Figure 1.3.1   LabVIEW startup window

1.3.2 Front Panel and Block Diagram

Your first view will be two overlapping windows: the gridded front panel on top and the plain block diagram beneath it.

The front panel window displays controls (user input) and indicators (data output). It can be configured to appear like the instrument panel on measurement equipment. For example, you can place virtual knobs and switches (controls) and display charts, graphs, or virtual LEDs (indicators) in this panel. It is the graphical user interface. This panel provides input to the block diagram through the controls and displays the output of the block diagram through the indicators. The controls and indicators also appear as terminals in the block diagram. Terminals pass data between the front panel and the block diagram, either from the controls or to the indicators. This is the only panel you need to see when your VI is running.

The block diagram window contains the source code of the program and displays the interconnected objects of the graphical programming language. This is the panel where the program is developed and debugged. The block diagram consists of nodes, which are objects that have inputs and outputs and perform some type of operation when the VI executes. Nodes comprise functions, subVIs, Express VIs, and structures. Functions are built-in elements that perform specific operations, subVIs are self-contained sections of code like subroutines in text-based programming languages, Express VIs are configurable VIs, and structures control VI execution. Wires transfer data between the nodes in the block diagram. Wires take on different color, thickness, and texture depending on the type of data they carry.

1.3.3 Pull-Down Menus and Keyboard Shortcuts

There are a number of pull-down menus to help you manage your files, edit your program, manage the LabVIEW windows, and get help, among other things. The pull-down menus are located just under the title of each window. Specific pull-down menu options will be introduced as needed throughout the primer although this is a good time to browse the options to see what is available on each menu. Notice that some commands and options have keyboard shortcuts. For example, if you select the "Edit" pull-down menu, you will notice that <Ctrl+B> is a shortcut for "Remove Broken Wires". If you find yourself using an option from one of the pull-down menus regularly, such as removing broken wires, you can reduce program development time using the keyboard shortcuts listed to the right of the command or option.

You may find it easier to work with the LabVIEW examples in this primer if you click on "Window" in the menu bar and then select "Tile Up and Down" from the pull down menu as shown in Figure 1.3.2. LabVIEW will place the front panel window on the top half of the screen and the block diagram window on the bottom half.

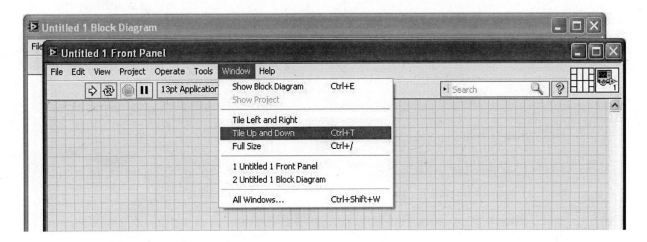

Figure 1.3.2   Untitled VI showing the "Window" pull-down menu options

1.3.4   Toolbars

The front panel and the block diagram have toolbars that contain commands, some of which are in the pull-down menus, that manipulate the objects to provide good housekeeping, provide means to debug the VI, get information on VI objects, and run the VI.

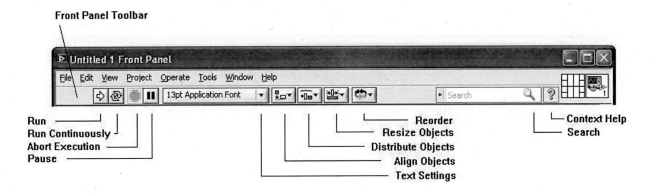

Figure 1.3.3   Front panel toolbar

The front panel toolbar is shown in Fig. 1.3.3. The four buttons on the left of the toolbar control program execution. The "Run" button takes on different appearances depending on the status of the VI, as shown by the top four buttons in Fig. 1.3.4. The other buttons control the execution of the program. When selected, the "Run Continuously" button runs the VI over and over again until you abort or pause the execution. For example, one could write a program to take one data measurement and then select the "Run Continuously" button to take multiple measurements. However, there are LabVIEW structures, such as the While Loop, that perform this type of task more efficiently. The "Run Continuously" button should not be a substitute for this type of programming. Likewise, the "Abort Execution" button stops the VI but a better practice is to include a stop control in the front panel. The next five buttons in Fig 1.3.3 provide options for general housekeeping for front panel objects and labeling. A VI is easier to operate if the controls and indicators in the front panel are aligned and grouped according to common functions. The last two buttons provide information on LabVIEW objects.

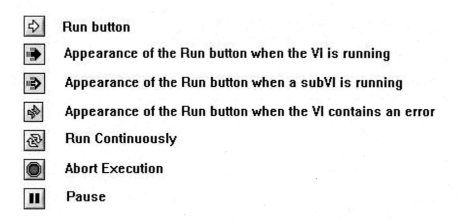

Figure 1.3.4   Buttons that control the execution of the VI or show it's status

Many of the buttons in the block diagram toolbar, shown in Fig. 1.3.5, perform the same functions as described for the front panel toolbar. However, the block diagram toolbar also contains buttons to help debug the VI. The "Highlight Execution" button and the "Step" buttons animate the data flow, provide step-by-step control over program execution, and provide the means to see data values at each node. The middle set of buttons on the toolbar provides options for general housekeeping. A neat and organized set of objects in the block diagram, especially when it pertains to new LabVIEW users, reduces the chances for wiring errors and makes debugging easier.

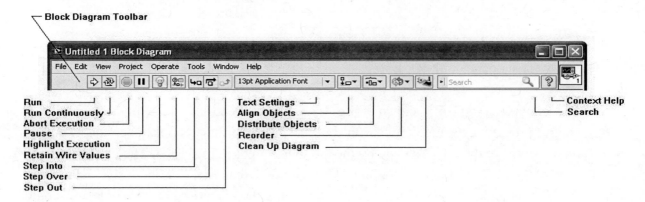

Figure 1.3.5   Block diagram toolbar

1.3.5 Palettes

There are three important palettes: "Tools", "Controls", and "Functions". The "Controls" palette is available only in the front panel, the "Functions" palette is available only in the block diagram, and the "Tools" palette is available in both.

The "Tools" palette, as shown in Fig. 1.3.6, contains special cursors that enable you to perform different functions, like typing alphanumeric characters, entering values, and wiring, selecting, resizing, and positioning objects. A functional name for each tool is given in Fig. 1.3.6 along with the name assigned in the "Tools" palette in parentheses. This palette may already be displayed in the front panel. If not, click on "Tools Palette" from the "View" pull-down menu. At the top of the "Tools" palette, there is an automatic tool selection button. When this button is highlighted green, LabVIEW tries to anticipate what cursor you will need. You may find that this feature improves your programming efficiency although use of the automatic tool selection is a personal preference. If you find that you don't like it, you can disable the feature by clicking on any of the buttons in the "Tools" palette and the automatic feature will be disabled. You will then need to manually select the tool needed until you click on the "Automatic Tool Selection" button at a later time.

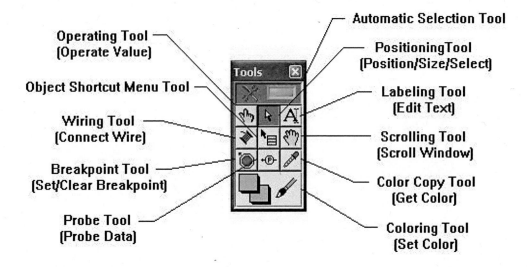

Figure 1.3.6   The "Tools" palette

Four of the tools that you will frequently use in this primer include:

- Operating
- Positioning
- Labeling
- Wiring

The "Operating" tool allows you to enter data or change the value of a control. The "Positioning" tool allows you to select, move, or resize an object. The "Labeling" tool allows you to create a free label or edit an existing one. The "Wiring" tool allows you to establish data flow between nodes in the block diagram by wiring them together.

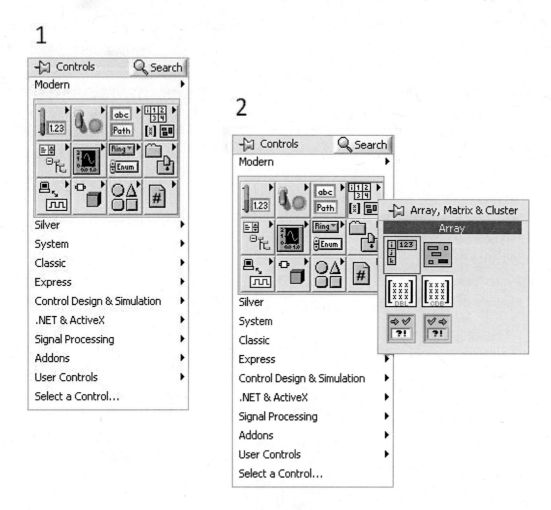

Figure 1.3.7   The "Controls" palette

The "Controls" palette contains different controls and indicators for the front panel (virtual instrument panel). If the "Controls" palette is not visible in the front panel, there are two options to retrieve the palette. One option is to select "Controls Palette" from the "Views" menu and the "Controls" palette will remain with the front panel as you use the selected icons. You may have to expand the palette by clicking on the button with the right facing arrow if a view similar to the one in Fig. 1.3.7 does not appear. The other option is to place the mouse over an open area in the front panel and right click. Using this approach, a view similar to the first image in Fig. 1.3.7 should appear. The "Controls" palette disappears after the icon is selected, which frees up space on the front panel. If you retrieve the palette by right-clicking on the front panel and want the palette to remain, you may also tack down the palette by clicking on the thumbtack in the upper left corner. Whether the palette remains on the front panel for ready access or disappears to free up working space is a matter of personal preference.

Since there are a number of different styles and categories of controls and indicators, most of the palettes are collapsed showing only the category heading name. To expose other palettes, place the cursor over the palette category name or click on it. You can expose subpalettes the same way, as shown in steps 1 and 2 in Fig. 1.3.7. You may have to expand the palette by clicking on the button with the right facing arrow. You may then click on the object of interest and drag it to the front panel.

The "Functions" palette contains all of the graphical programming functions that may be used to develop your program in the block diagram. The term function is applied loosely to functions, VIs, and Express VIs found in the Functions palette. Functions have inputs and outputs to perform specific tasks, like arithmetic or logic operations. VIs on the "Functions" palette are typically LabVIEW programs with a specific purpose that are referred to as subVIs when used in another VI. VIs whose parameters can be configured through a dialog box are referred to as Express VIs. An advantage of the Express VI is that input parameters can be configured interactively, which is usually a benefit for new LabVIEW users. The three functions palettes that will be used primarily in this primer are shown in Fig. 1.3.8. The "Programming" palette contains the building blocks for developing source code. Data acquisition Express VIs in the "Express" palette will be used in Part 2 of this primer to measure and generate data.

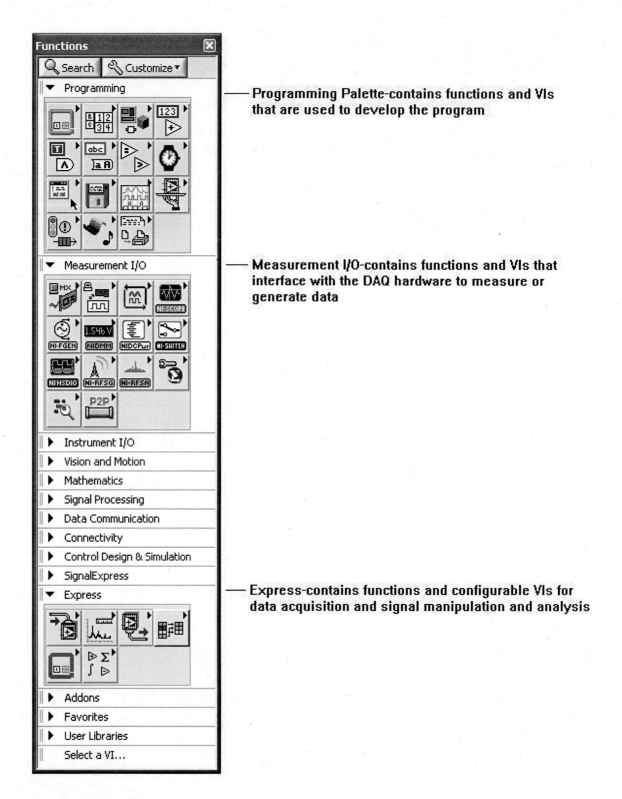

Programming Palette-contains functions and VIs that are used to develop the program

Measurement I/O-contains functions and VIs that interface with the DAQ hardware to measure or generate data

Express-contains functions and configurable VIs for data acquisition and signal manipulation and analysis

Figure 1.3.8   The "Functions" palette

1.4   An Experiential Introduction to LabVIEW

This section describes how to write a relatively simple analog input VI to introduce LabVIEW and develop your skills. The VI can be used to record either a finite set of analog measurements or record measurements continuously from multiple channels. The idea is that it will be easier to learn and retain key LabVIEW concepts by applying the concepts as you learn them. Analog input means to acquire data from devices with voltages that vary continuously. This VI is most appropriate when you acquire data at relatively low sampling rates and the length of time to record data is uncertain. For example, this VI would be appropriate to measure strain sensed by a strain gage affixed to a structural member with a time-varying load or to measure the temperature, as sensed by a thermocouple, of a cooling object.

This VI employs non-buffered data acquisition and software timing. Non-buffered data acquisition means that samples are acquired one at a time and are stored temporarily within memory on the DAQ board. LabVIEW can then read the sample from the DAQ board and use it in the VI or store the sample on a permanent storage device, such as a hard drive or flash drive. Software-timed intervals are controlled by LabVIEW software timing functions, which depend on the computer's CPU clock. Software timing can produce irregular sample intervals while data is collected, especially if the requested time intervals are small or the CPU has large demands for resources, such as a graphic-intensive task like moving a window on the screen. From a practical point of view, this VI can sample at rates up to approximately 200-500 samples per second, although the maximum rate is limited by the ability of the computer's hardware to execute the LabVIEW software. This VI could also be used to sample at very low rates, such as one sample per hour.

Within this section, guided steps are interwoven among concepts that allow you to learn LabVIEW while you are developing a practical VI. The section is formatted as follows:

- A new LabVIEW concept is first introduced and a brief overview is provided to familiarize you with its function
- Steps are then provided to help you implement the new concept into the development of the VI
- Additional information about the new concept may follow the steps so that you may explore more general features of LabVIEW using your VI, which will provide a better foundation for subsequent VI development

The material discussed in this section assumes that LabVIEW Professional Version or Student Version software, NI-DAQ software, and a data acquisition board have been installed on your computer.

Goals

1. Become acquainted with basic LabVIEW concepts that will be used throughout this primer.
2. Become acquainted with the LabVIEW DAQ Assistant, a means to create tasks to acquire and generate data.
3. Learn about ways to display data including charts and graphs and the ability to write data to a spreadsheet.
4. Develop the software-timed analog input VI shown in Figs. 1.4.1 and 1.4.2, which can acquire either a finite set of measurements or acquire measurements continuously until stopped by the user.

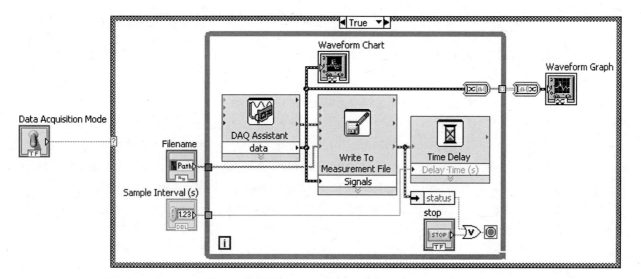

Figure 1.4.1   The general analog input VI showing the option to measure data continuously

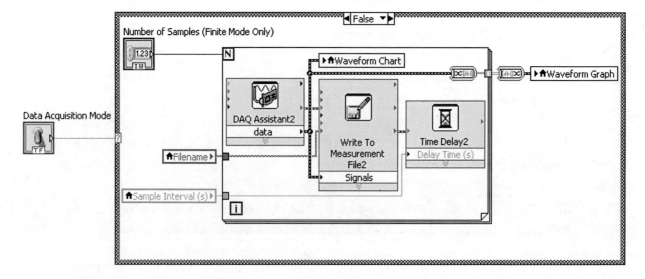

Figure 1.4.2   The general analog input VI showing the option to measure a finite set of data

1.4.1   Case Structures

Overview of Case Structures

The Case Structure executes a portion of code contained within its borders that corresponds to a condition, or case, among two or more possible case options. The Case Structure consists of a border, which encompasses the code, a selector label on the top of the border, and a selector terminal on the left side of the border. The case is identified in the selector label. The portion of code that executes is determined by the case input to the selector terminal. The case may be determined by the user through a control or by other code in the block diagram that is external to the Case Structure.

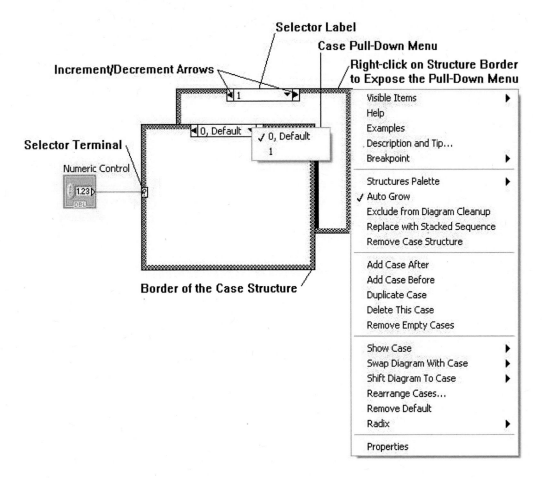

Figure 1.4.3   LabVIEW Case Structure

Two cases of a Case Structure are shown in Figure 1.4.3. The sub diagram, or code, that is to be conditionally executed is contained within the border of each case of the Case Structure. Each case will have a different sub diagram. Cases are stacked and show only one sub diagram at a time, unlike Fig. 1.4.3, which includes an offset second case for illustration purposes.

The case is determined by the data type wired to the selector terminal. A numeric control is wired to the example shown in Fig. 1.4.3, which shows two number cases, 0 and 1. The number case "0" has been selected as the default case. The default case will be executed if a wired value does not match any of the other cases. The default case might include an error message, for example. The example in Fig. 1.4.3 shows that a control is wired to the selector terminal, which would allow the user to directly select the case.

Input and output data may pass through tunnels in the border of the Case Structure. The tunnels are depicted by squares on the border. Input data that passes through tunnels is available to all cases. If output data is wired to the border of one case of the Case Structure, all cases must output a value or else the "Run" arrow on the toolbar will remain broken. An output tunnel appears as a hollow square until data is provided from all cases, at which point the tunnel appears as a solid square.

Steps 1-5: Creating a Case Structure

The general analog input VI that is to be developed in this problem is designed to allow the user to select finite or continuous measurement of data. For this VI, the user will provide input through the front panel to select a measurement case for data acquisition: either continuous or finite. A Case Structure (represented by the outermost border in Figs. 1.4.1 and 1.4.2) will be used to determine what case will be executed. When the data acquisition mode is set to "True", data is taken continuously. Likewise, when the data acquisition mode is set to "False", a finite set of data is taken. Two cases (True and False) of the same Case Structure are shown in Figs. 1.4.1 and 1.4.2.

1. If you haven't already done so, launch LabVIEW by selecting **All Programs>>National Instruments>>LabVIEW 2012>>LabVIEW 2012** from the "Start" menu.

Note: Read Section 1.3 to get the necessary background on the LabVIEW environment, if you haven't already done so.

2. Select "Blank VI" to open a new file for this exercise.

Tip: Use the keyboard shortcut <Ctrl T> to tile the windows with the front panel above and the block diagram below.

3. In the Functions palette, place the cursor over the Express palette and then over the Execution Control subpalette. Depress the left mouse key on the Case Structure icon in the Execution Control subpalette and drag the structure to the block diagram. This

procedure will be referred to as **Express>>Execution Control>>Case Structure** in the remainder of this primer. If you have problems with this or any other step, you can remove the Case Structure and start over using the "Undo" feature on the "Edit" pull-down menu.

Note: The Case Structure can also be found in **Programming>>Structures>>Case Structure**.

4. Resize the Case Structure to be large enough to contain the functions, structures, and VIs shown in Figs. 1.4.1 and 1.4.2.

Tip: The initial size is not critical since the Case Structure can be resized at any time by clicking on the border and dragging the border with the mouse on one of the blue "handles."

5. Place the cursor over the selector terminal (box containing the question mark on the left border), right click, and select "Create Control."

Note: A Boolean push button control appears simultaneously in the front panel and a terminal appears in the block diagram. This control will allow a user to determine if a finite set of data will be measured or if the data will be measured continuously.

Additional Information about Case Structures

Different data types, such as Boolean (True or False) and string (text), can be wired to the selector terminal and case values will be shown at the top of the border in the selector label area. You can select a case by cycling through the available cases using the increment and decrement arrows or by using the pull-down menu by selecting the down arrow in the Selector label.

A number of options for the Case Structure are available if you right-click on the structure border, as shown in Fig. 1.4.3. For example, you can add or delete a case. If you add a case, you can change the value in the selector label using the Edit Text (letter A) cursor.

Case Structures are part of a larger class of structures that control the execution of data flow in a VI. Some of the other structures used in this primer are listed below:

- The While Loop continuously executes of a portion of code within its borders, called a sub diagram, until a condition is met.
- The For Loop executes a sub diagram a finite number of times.
- The Sequence Structure executes one or more sub diagrams in a sequential order.

1.4.2 Data Acquisition: The DAQ Assistant

Overview of the DAQ Assistant

The DAQ Assistant is a configurable Express VI that can create, edit, or test a data measurement or generation task. A task contains information on the timing, triggering, and configuration of one or more channels. The DAQ Assistant graphical user interface allows the user to configure channels and set data acquisition timing and triggering conditions. An advantage of the DAQ Assistant is that the graphical user interface guides the user to properly configure data acquisition tasks, which is beneficial for new users.

Figure 1.4.4   Using the DAQ Assistant to configure an analog input measurement task

The DAQ Assistant guides the user through a series of windows to configure the data acquisition task as shown for an analog input measurement task in Fig. 1.4.4. The DAQ Assistant automatically launches when placed in the block diagram. The "Create New…" window sets up the measurement type for the data acquisition task. You select if the data will be acquired or generated for the measurement type (this view is not shown in Fig. 1.4.4). If you expand the list, you can see that analog, digital, and counter modes are available for both "acquire" and "generate". By further expanding the list, you can see what types of measurements are supported for each mode. For example, the different types of analog input measurements are shown in the first view of Fig 1.4.4. Once you select the type of measurement you want, for example, a voltage analog input measurement was selected in Fig. 1.4.4, the DAQ Assistant then lists the channels that are available for that type of measurement based on the DAQ board in your computer. This is the second view in Fig. 1.4.4. After you select the channel(s) that you want, a DAQ Assistant window opens, as shown in the third view of Fig. 1.4.4, which allows you to configure the channel(s).

Steps 6-9: Creating a Measurement Task using the DAQ Assistant

In the following steps, you will create an analog input measurement task to sample data from two different channels when called by the software. You will use the DAQ Assistant to create the measurement task.

6. Select **Express>>Input>>DAQ Assistant** from the Functions palette in the block diagram and drag it inside the Case Structure.

7. Click on "Acquire Signals", "Analog Input", and "Voltage" as shown in Fig. 1.4.4 to create a measurement task that can sample a continuously varying voltage signal.

8. Click on the hardware device to show the channels that are available to measure analog input signals on your DAQ board. Select analog input channel 0 ("ai0") and channel 1 ("ai1") by depressing the control key, <Ctrl>, on the keyboard while selecting the channels with the left mouse key. After you select "Finish", the DAQ Assistant window appears.

Note: All of the default settings are acceptable for this example problem except the timing settings of the acquisition mode. The default signal input range is ±10 V, the maximum range allowed by the data acquisition board. You may modify this parameter at a later time if you measure a signal having a different voltage range. Differential mode is the default configuration of the input terminals. This means that positive and negative leads must be connected to the data acquisition board. Other types of terminal configurations are described in Section 2.1.1. No custom scaling is selected but this feature allows you to create a scale that converts voltage data into physically meaningful units, like temperature or pressure. Without any custom scale, the "Scaled Units" parameter shows "Volts."

9. Since this VI uses software timing, select "1Sample (On Demand)" from the "Acquisition Mode" pull-down menu and then OK at the bottom right corner of the window.

Tip: You can double-click on the DAQ Assistant icon to edit the configurations at a later time, if needed.

Note: The DAQ Assistant can be displayed as an icon or an expanded node by dragging the icon by the "handle" at the bottom of the icon.

Additional Information about the DAQ Assistant

The DAQ Assistant can, among other things:

- Create and edit data measurement and generation tasks
- Create and configure channels in the tasks
- Create and edit scales that convert voltages into physically meaningful units
- Test and save your data measurement or generation configuration

Specifications in the data measurement or generation task include the acquisition mode and timing. As seen at the bottom of the window in Fig. 1.4.5, there are four acquisition modes: two of which take single samples, a finite set of N samples, and continuous acquisition by repetitively taking blocks of a finite set of N samples. The timing can be either software timing controlled by the computer's CPU clock, which occurs when the LabVIEW software calls a subVI to acquire data, or by hardware timing, which occurs when a clock on the DAQ board or an external hardware device controls the data acquisition.

The first acquisition mode, "1 Sample (On Demand)", employs software timing since the sample is not acquired until a LabVIEW subVI demands the sample. It is referred to as software timing since the execution of the LabVIEW software is controlled by the CPU clock. This sample mode can also permit continuous data acquisition if the calling subVI is placed in a loop. However, the time spacing between VI calls depends on the execution time of the program and the CPU clock, which has other priorities as well as LabVIEW. This can result in uneven time spacing, especially for fast sampling rates, and ultimately limits how fast data can be acquired.

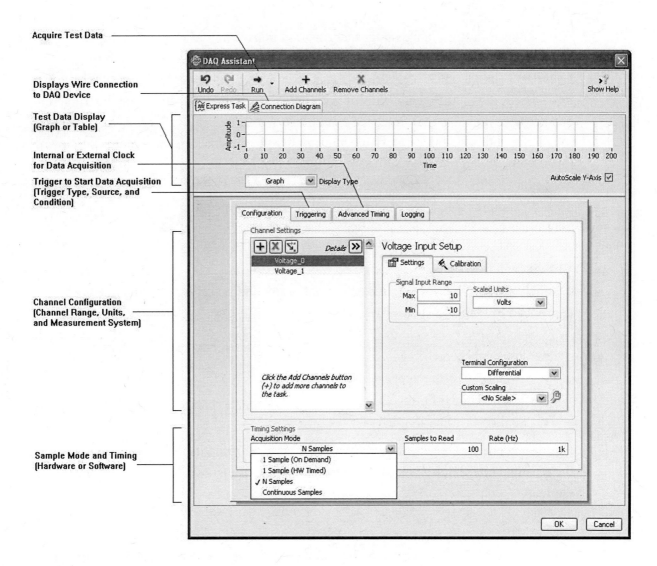

Figure 1.4.5 DAQ Assistant features

The second acquisition mode, "1 Sample (HW Timed)", takes one sample, whose acquisition is controlled through a clock on the DAQ board or an external timing device. Multiple samples can be taken by repetitive triggers, typically using a train of digital pulses from an external timing device.

The last two acquisition modes use hardware timing via a clock on the DAQ board or an external hardware timer. You can specify which one through the "Sample Clock Type" on the "Advanced Timing" tab. "Internal" and "External" refer to the DAQ board or external hardware device, respectively. The control of data acquisition is transferred to the DAQ board when using hardware timing. It ensures uniform time spacing and offers the possibility of significantly higher sampling rates compared to software timing, depending on the DAQ hardware installed on your computer.

Another specification in a data measurement or generation task includes triggering. The data measurement or generation task will be executed as soon as it is called by the LabVIEW subVI, unless triggering is employed using options listed in the "Triggering" tab. Depending on the capabilities of your hardware, data acquisition may be triggered by an analog or digital signal from, for example, a sensor or a relay. Triggering is essential to acquire data when an event will occur rapidly yet the onset of the event is unknown. A rapid event would dictate a high sampling rate, yet copious quantities of data would need to be stored if the data measurement was not triggered. The rupture of a pressure vessel is a good example since a high sampling rate is required to capture the pressure history yet the timing of the rupture is unknown.

Virtual channels can be created and configured using the DAQ Assistant. Virtual channels are required for data measurement or generation tasks. A virtual channel is comprised of the following:

- Physical channel
- Type of measurement or generation system
- Voltage range for the channel
- Scaling information

A physical channel is part of the DAQ board and manifests itself as a terminal or pin at the terminal connector block that can make a wired connection to an input or output device.

You specify how the input or output device is connected using the "Terminal Configuration" options, shown in the middle of the window in Fig. 1.4.5. The option shown, a differential measurement system, reads the potential difference between two terminals. The other two options (not shown in Fig. 1.4.5) include both referenced and non-referenced single-ended measurement systems. The referenced single ended (RSE) measurement system measures the signal with respect to the DAQ hardware (system) ground. The non-referenced single ended (NRSE) measurement system measures the signal with respect to a common reference, for example, a shared power supply ground that is not the system ground. A description of these measurement systems is given in Section 2.1.1. Depending on the measurement system selected, the DAQ Assistant shows how to connect the wires of the input or output device to the DAQ board's terminal connector block through the "Connection Diagram" tab, shown near the top of the window in Fig. 1.4.5.

The "Signal Input Range" determines the voltage range accepted by the DAQ board for that channel and is based on the anticipated minimum and maximum voltages for the input signal. A physical channel can also be scaled to convert a voltage to a physically meaningful unit. A sensor's calibration curve, typically a linear relationship, can be entered through the "Custom Scaling" options.

Finally, once the data measurement or generation task has been created and configured, the DAQ Assistant allows test data to be taken using the "Run" button, which is shown at the top of the window in Fig. 1.4.5. You can display the data in tabular or graphical form. This is a very useful feature of the DAQ Assistant since you can check data from your measurement system with an independent method, such as a multimeter or an oscilloscope, to verify that everything is connected and configured correctly.

1.4.3   Writing to a Measurement File

Overview of the Write to Measurement File Express VI

The general analog input VI that we are developing collects data continuously, one data point per channel per iteration. Since the data measured through a measurement task (created and configured by the DAQ Assistant) is stored in temporary RAM memory, it must be written to a permanent file to archive it. This can be accomplished through the "Write to Measurement File" Express VI.

The Write to Measurement File Express VI writes numerical data to a text-based measurement file with a ".lvm" (**LabVIEW M**easurement) extension. The data in a text-based file is human readable, separated by a delimiter like a tab or comma, and can be read by a spreadsheet or word processing application for later analysis, plotting, or printing.

This Express VI is an expandable node as are most Express VIs, such as the DAQ Assistant. The VI appears as the icon shown in the first view of Fig. 1.4.6 when placed in the block diagram. The VI may also be expanded by placing the "Position" (arrow) cursor over one of the top or bottom blue "handles" and dragging the handle until the VI appears as the second view in Fig. 1.4.6. This has the advantage of making it easier to wire the input and output terminals although at the expense of space in the block diagram.

Steps 10-19: Writing Data to a Measurement File

In the following steps, you will configure a file for permanent storage of the measurement data. For this to be completed, you will use the Write to Measurement File Express VI.

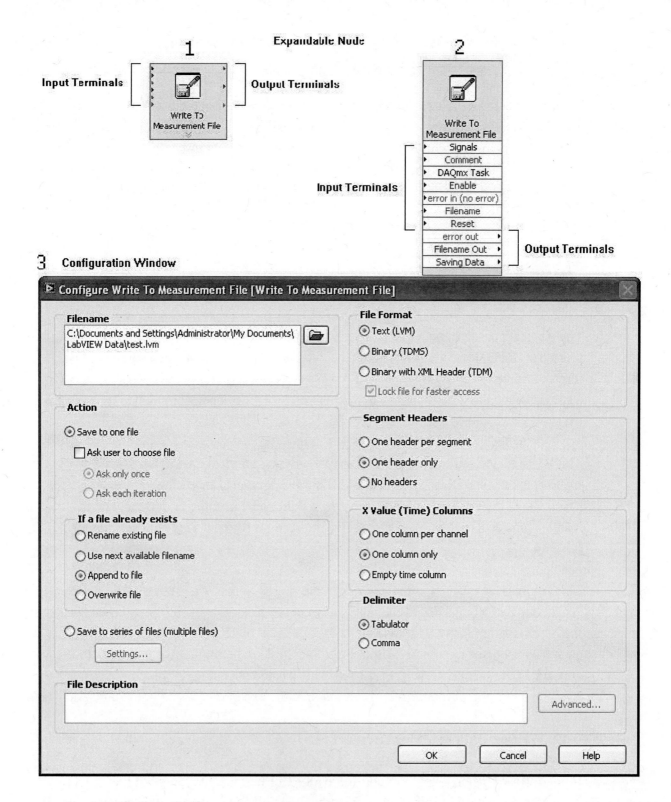

Figure 1.4.6 Write to Measurement File Express VI

10. Select **Express>>Output>>Write to Measurement File** from the "Function" palette in the block diagram and drag the icon inside of the Case Structure and to the right of the DAQ Assistant.

Note: You may skip the next step if the default filename provided by LabVIEW is acceptable.

11. Type the path of a file in the "Filename" dialog box or select an existing one by clicking on the folder to the right of the default file path to browse the directory on your computer or external storage device. LabVIEW will create the file if the filename does not exist.

12. Make sure the action is to "Save to one file" but *do not* check the box "Ask user to choose file.

Note: The user was not asked to choose a file to avoid the potential of delaying data acquisition. Based on the execution of the block diagram in Fig. 1.4.1, the Write to Measurement File Express VI executes after the measurement task is created and samples are taken. If the user was asked to choose a file, the execution of the program would be suspended until a filename was provided by the user. Potential measurements could be missed if the physical event occurred quickly.

13. Select "Append to file" under the heading "If a file already exists."

Note: Since the VI will take data continuously in the current example, a file will be created on the first iteration and data should be appended to that file on subsequent iterations. Otherwise, a different file name would be required every iteration. Any of the other options may be suitable if a finite number of data points are taken and data are recorded after the measurement task is complete.

14. Select "Text (LVM)" under "File Format."

Note: A text format is chosen so that the data can be viewed in a spreadsheet at a later time. Binary measurement files cannot be read by humans and are used to transfer data efficiently between software.

15. Select "One header only" under "Segment Headers."

Note: The header contains information like the date and time the data was measured. One header was chosen in this example. Otherwise, there would be a header for every data point if one header per segment was selected since this Express VI is executed every iteration.

16. Select "One column only" under "X Value (Time) Columns."

Note: The time the sensor data was measured relative to the first data point can also be included with the measured sensor data. One X (time) column was selected, which will show time in the first column followed by each analog input channel in subsequent columns in the order listed in the DAQ Assistant channel settings. "One column per channel" means there will be a time-variable pair of columns for every channel (variable measured).

17. Select "Tabulator" under "Delimiter" and click on OK. Tabs are used so that commas do not appear in a word processor.

Tip: You can double-click on the "Write to Measurement File" icon to edit the configurations at a later time, if needed.

18. Place the cursor over the "filename" input terminal (it's the bottom terminal on the left side of the unexpanded node-see view number 1 of Fig. 1.4.6), right-click the mouse, and create a control. The control will appear in the front panel and the corresponding terminal will appear on the block diagram.

Tip: If you are having difficulty locating the "filename" input terminal, there are two ways to easily find it if the node is not expanded. The first way is to place the "Connect Wire" (solder spool) cursor over the terminals to locate the filename input terminal. As the "Connect Wire" cursor passes over a terminal, the terminal name pops up. The second way is to use the "Context Help" window. Select "Show Context Help" from the "Help" pull-down menu to show labeled terminals. If you are using the "Connect Wire" cursor, the terminal will blink in the "Context Help" window and light up on the icon with the terminal name displayed in the block diagram.

Note: The filename control will allow a user to enter a filename without having to open the "Write to Measurement File" configuration window every time a different filename is desired.

19. Click on the filename input terminal with the "Position" (arrow) cursor and drag the terminal near the left border of the Case Structure, as shown in Fig. 1.4.1, so that it will be outside of the inner loop.

1.4.4   Timing VIs for Control of VI Execution

Overview of Timing VIs

Timing VIs are useful to control the execution of the program. In the development of the current analog input VI, a While Loop will be placed around the DAQ Assistant VI, as shown in Fig. 1.4.1. Without any timing VIs, the program will execute as fast as the computer can process the code. This is undesirable if you want to measure data at a specified rate. The timing VIs provide a means to control VI execution. When applied to data acquisition, this is referred to as software timing, since the timing VI is controlled by the computer's CPU clock.

The timing VIs provide only an approximate means to establish a sampling rate to acquire data. The time delay is added to the time it takes to execute all of the other code in the VI before the next measurement is taken. However, for moderate to slow sampling rates (approximately 1 second/sample or greater), the time for VI execution is typically not significant compared to the time delay. For fast sampling rates (on the order of milliseconds/sample), the time spacing between measurements is generally irregular anyway since the CPU must balance requests from LabVIEW for VI execution with other priorities. Once again, the additional time to execute the VI is not critical. Hardware timing should be employed if the time spacing between samples must be precise. Hardware timing is based on functions that transfer control of the data acquisition to a clock on an external device, like the DAQ board, and is discussed in Section 2.2.

There are both Express and traditional timing VIs in the Functions palette. The Express VIs are located in the **Express>>Execution Control** subpalette and the traditional VIs are located in the **Programming>>Timing** subpalette. The Express VI used in the current example, "Time Delay", inserts a specified time delay each time it is called. The "Time Delay" VI is shown as both an unexpanded and expanded node in the first two views in Fig. 1.4.7 and, in the third view, the configuration window that appears when the VI is placed in the block diagram.

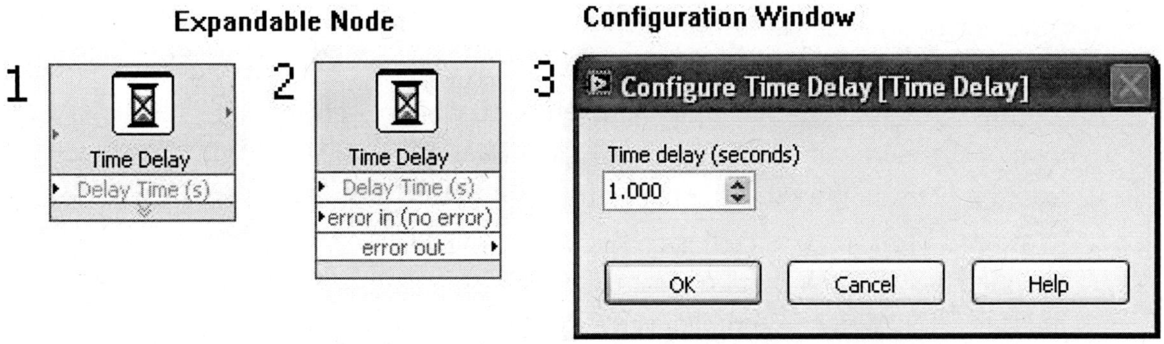

Figure 1.4.7   Time Delay Express VI

Steps 20-22: Time Delay VI

In the following steps, the VI is modified to provide a sampling rate for the measurement of the data. This will be accomplished by adding the Time Delay Express VI after data is recorded in the measurement file.

20. Select **Express>>Execution Control>>Time Delay** and drag the VI inside the Case Structure to the right of the "Write to Measurement File" VI in the block diagram.

21. Press OK for the default value of 1 second since it can be changed at a later time by double-clicking on the "Time Delay" icon.

Note: A more convenient means of changing the time delay when executing the VI is through a control in the front panel, which will be employed in the current example VI.

22. Place the cursor over the "Delay Time" input terminal, right click on the mouse, and select **Create>>Control**. Select the "Delay Time (s)" terminal (later renamed "Sample Interval") and drag it near the left border of the Case Structure as shown in Fig. 1.4.1.

1.4.5 While Loop

Overview of While Loops

The While Loop, shown in Fig. 1.4.8, is a structure that executes the sub diagram enclosed within its borders until a condition is met. The condition is checked at the end of the iteration. The "Iteration" and "Conditional" terminals appear within the While Loop when it is first placed in the block diagram. The "Iteration" terminal outputs the number of times the loop has iterated beginning with a value of zero for the first iteration. The "Conditional" terminal executes until a condition is met. The default terminal condition is to stop if the input to the terminal is true. However, the condition can be changed to continue if true by using the shortcut menu that appears when you right-click on the conditional terminal as shown in Fig. 1.4.8.

The "Conditional" terminal is an input terminal, which can be satisfied by one or more inputs. The most common input to the "Conditional" terminal is a Boolean control in the front panel that allows the user to control execution of the VI by selecting true or false. However, when the While Loop is used for data acquisition for example, it is also common to stop the While Loop when an error occurs in one of the data acquisition VIs. Since the "Conditional" terminal can accept only one wire, multiple inputs can be combined with a logical OR function such that the While Loop will stop execution if any of the inputs is true. A Boolean input is provided automatically if the While Loop is selected from the "Express" palette (**Functions>>Express>>Execution Control**) but not if selected from the "Programming" palette (**Functions>>Programming>>Structures**).

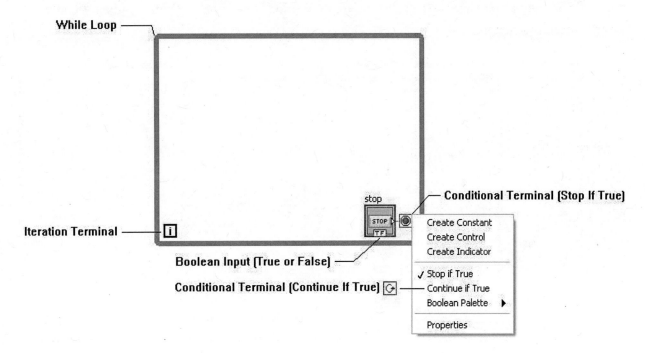

Figure 1.4.8   The While Loop

Step 23: Creating a While Loop

In this step, your program will be modified so that data measurements will be taken continuously, one sample per channel per iteration, until you stop execution. For this to be completed, a While Loop will be placed around the three Express VIs that create a measurement task, write the data to a file, and insert a time delay in the execution of the program.

23. Select **Express>>Execution Control>>While Loop**, place the cursor to the upper left of the three Express VIs, left-click the mouse and hold it down, drag the icon to the lower right to enclose the three Express VIs (but not the controls to the inputs of these Express VIs) as shown in Fig 1.4.9, and release the mouse key to create the While Loop.

Note: You do not have to depress the mouse key when dragging the border of the While Loop. However, you will have to left click the mouse key a second time to set the border if the mouse key does not remain depressed.

Tip: If you make a mistake dragging the While Loop, you can undo the creation of the While Loop using the "Undo" command from the "Edit" pull down menu and start over.

Tip: You may also resize the Case Structure or While Loop using the blue handles if you need more room.

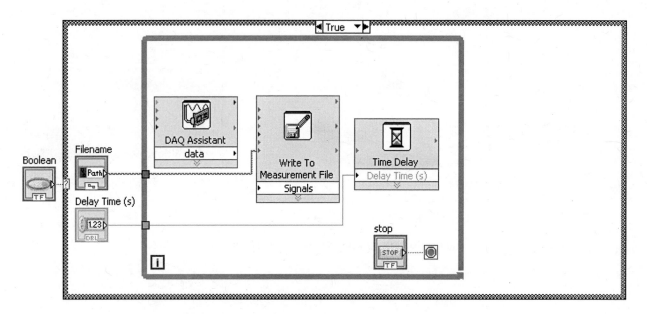

Figure 1.4.9   Intermediate view of the block diagram after the While Loop is created

Note: Two tunnels should appear on the left border of the While Loop showing that the "Filename" and "Time Delay" terminals become inputs. The conditional terminal is connected with a Boolean control and an iteration terminal also appears. You may also need to left-click the mouse on the Boolean control using the "Position" (arrow) cursor to drag it to expose the wire that connects to the conditional terminal.

Additional Information about While Loops

The input to the "Conditional" terminal must be placed inside the While Loop to prevent the possibility of an infinite loop, a condition that occurs when there is no way to stop execution of a repeated section of code. Values of variables that pass through the boundary of the While Loop remain constant during the execution of the While Loop until the loop stops. For example, consider that the value of a Boolean control in the front panel is set to false. If the corresponding Boolean terminal wired to the "Conditional" terminal in the block diagram is outside of the While Loop, then an infinite loop will be established. In this example, the false value is read once when the loop first executes and will not change, even if the user changes the value outside the loop at a later time as the loop is executing. If an infinite loop is established accidently, the VI can be aborted using the "Abort Execution" button on the block diagram toolbar.

The While Loop and "Conditional" terminal are preferred methods to control program execution over the "Run Continuously" and "Abort Execution" buttons on the block diagram toolbar. Additional data analyses or plotting of data may be desirable after a set of data have been measured, which would not be possible with the toolbar buttons.

While Loops pass data through tunnels at the loop border. Fig. 1.4.10 shows a simple example with data on the right border that can pass out of the loop. Tunnels also appear for data passing into the loop. Since data arrays are indexed by rows and columns, tunnels can have indexing enabled or disabled. If indexing is enabled, an array of data is *input* one element at a time every iteration starting with the first element. When indexing is disabled, the entire array is passed through the tunnel on the first iteration. When indexing is enabled for *output*, a variable's value is stored at each iteration as an element of a row array that is then passed out of the loop when execution is completed. The first element of the array is the value from the first iteration. With indexing disabled (Tunnel Mode>>Last Value), only the value from the last iteration is passed out of the loop.

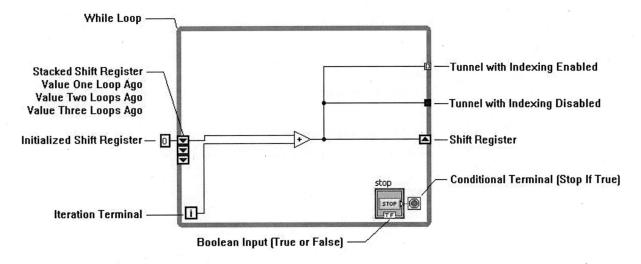

Figure 1.4.10 The While Loop with a simple example to show components

Shift registers pass variable values from previous iterations to the next iteration. A pair of terminals appears when a shift register is added. A shift register may be added by right clicking the mouse on the border and selecting "Add Shift Register." The terminal on the right border marked by the upward arrow stores a value at the end of the most recent iteration. This value then becomes available at the beginning of the next iteration from the corresponding shift register on the left border with a downward arrow. On the first iteration of the While Loop, the initial value may be specified by using a constant or control wired to the shift register. If the While Loop has never executed and nothing is wired to the shift register, a default value for the data type will be used, such as zero for the integer type used in the example in Fig. 1.4.10. If the loop executed previously, stopped, and is to execute again, the initial value is the last value written to the shift register when the loop last executed, if nothing is wired to the shift register. You may also stack shift registers on the left border by right clicking on the register and selecting "Add Element." Each additional element stores values from each previous loop, respectively.

The example in Fig. 1.4.10 will be used with three iterations to illustrate shift registers and tunnels. This simple VI adds the values of the iteration terminal and the shift register and provides output values at the right border of the loop. On the first iteration, both the iteration terminal and the shift register have values of zero so that the shift register on the right border will have a value of zero. On the second iteration, the iteration terminal will have a value of one and the shift register on the left border will have a value of zero (the value at the end of the previous iteration) so that the shift register on the right border will have a value of one. On the third iteration, the iteration terminal will have a value of two and the shift register on the left border will have a value of one (previous iteration value) so that the shift register on the right border will have a value of three. The tunnels on the right border contain values that may pass to another node outside of the While Loop. If the While Loop stops after three iterations, the tunnel with indexing disabled contains the value three, which is the value at the last iteration. The tunnel with indexing enabled will be a one-dimensional array of values from all iterations in row format (0, 1, and 3).

1.4.6   Waveform Chart

Overview of Waveform Charts

The waveform chart is a numeric indicator that can display and continuously update one or more plots. When the chart is filled with data, the plot scrolls from right to left with new data appended from the right. Since the chart is an indicator, it must be selected from the "Controls" palette. The chart is a great way to display the data in real time but the data is not saved after the VI execution ends. Saving data is covered in Section 1.4.3, Writing to a Measurement File.

Often it is convenient to see your data displayed while the experiment is being performed to verify the validity of the data. That way, if something goes wrong with the data measurement, you can perform the experiment again while everything is set up. Charts are most suitable for slow to moderate sampling rates and with single point sampling.

Steps 24-26: Plotting Data in a Chart

In the following steps, the program will be modified to plot data continuously as it is acquired. For this to be accomplished, a Waveform Chart will be added within the While Loop. One data point is acquired per channel every iteration and will be appended to the chart.

24. Place the cursor in the front panel, select **Express>>Graph Indicators>>Waveform Chart** and drag the icon to the front panel. You may also select the waveform chart in the "Modern" subpalette under **Modern>>Graph>>Waveform Chart**.

Note: Two data lines will eventually be displayed on the chart in the current example since we have two channels of analog input data yet a legend for only one line, Plot 0, is displayed at the upper right corner. Perform step 25 to add another plot legend.

25. Place the "Position" (arrow) cursor over the top middle blue handle of the plot legend and drag the boundary up one more plot legend to add Plot 1.

Tip: Locate the chart terminal in the block diagram by double-clicking on the chart in the front panel. A black border will temporarily appear around the chart terminal. The method of double-clicking on any of the controls and indicators in the front panel may be used to locate the corresponding terminals in the block diagram. Likewise, double-clicking on terminals in the block diagram may be used to locate corresponding controls and indicators in the front panel.

26. Using the "Position" (arrow) cursor, drag the chart terminal in the block diagram within the While Loop border and above the "Write to Measurement File" subVI, as shown in Fig. 1.4.1.

Additional Information on Waveform Charts

There are three modes to update the data displayed on the waveform chart: strip chart, scope chart, and sweep chart. The strip chart mode (default mode) continuously appends data to the right end of a curve. The chart area displays an array of data stored in the chart history. When all of the data points that are held in the chart history are plotted, the curve moves to the left as new data points are added. In the scope chart mode, the data are displayed in the plot area until the all of the points in the chart history are plotted and then clears the plot and starts over. The sweep chart mode is similar to the scope chart mode except new data overwrites the oldest data displayed instead of clearing the entire plot. The update mode can be changed by right-clicking on the plot and selecting **Advanced>>Update Mode** from the shortcut menu as shown in Fig. 1.4.11.

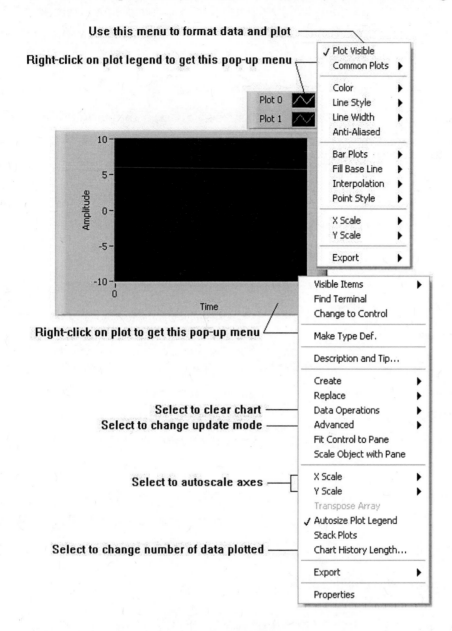

Figure 1.4.11 Waveform chart options

The chart can be modified in a number of ways to improve the viewing of the data as shown by the shortcut menus in Fig. 1.4.11. If you right-click the mouse over the plot legend (top right area of the plot containing the line), the line color, style, and width can be changed among other options on the shortcut menu. Furthermore, a number of options to modify the chart are available by right clicking on the panel in the chart where the data will be displayed. Common modifications include auto-scaling the x- and y-axes, clearing the chart, and changing the number of data points plotted through the chart history length.

These options are identified in Fig. 1.4.11. If the chart is not an appropriate size for your application, you can use the "Position" (arrow) cursor to resize the chart with the blue handles. Use the "Tools" palette "Edit Text" (letter A) cursor if you want to rename the chart to an appropriate name for your data.

1.4.7 Waveform Graph

Overview of Waveform Graphs

It's a good idea to plot the entire set of data at the end of an experiment to see if anything needs to be repeated. The waveform graph plots one or more arrays of data all at once, unlike the waveform chart, which continually updates the plot. The graph is a great way to display the data after a test but the data is not saved after the VI execution ends. Saving data is covered in Section 1.4.3, Writing to a Measurement File.

A single plot consists of an array of data in row format. Multiple plots require a 2-D array of data as input, where each plot is a row in the 2-D array. If the graph input consists only of a row of data (Y values), it is assumed that the initial X value, X_0, is zero and the spacing between X values, ΔX, is 1. Other values for the initial value of X and the spacing between X values may also be specified by building a waveform. However, for the purposes of this example VI, only the Y data will be plotted.

Steps 27-28: Graphing Data

In the following steps, the program will be modified to plot the entire set of data at the end of the experiment. This will be accomplished by adding a Waveform Graph outside of the While Loop.

27. Place the cursor in the front panel, select **Express>>Graph Indicators>>Waveform Graph** and drag the icon to the right of the chart. You may also select the waveform graph in the "Modern" subpalette under **Modern>>Graph>>Waveform Graph**.

Tip: The graph may be resized by selecting one of the blue handles using the "Position" (arrow) cursor and dragging the graph to the desired size.

28. Place the graph terminal in the block diagram to the right of the While Loop border but within the Case Structure as shown in Fig. 1.4.1.

Additional Information on Waveform Graphs

The waveform graph has options that are similar to the waveform chart. Right click on the graph to see the available options as shown in Fig. 1.4.12. For example, select "Data Operations" to clear the graph and select "X Scale" and "Y Scale" to auto-scale the axes.

The waveform graph has a useful palette to examine the data in more detail after the experiment. Right click on the graph and select **Visible Items>>Graph Palette** in the shortcut menu. The "Graph Palette" is identified at the bottom left of the graph in Fig. 1.4.12. The first of the three buttons is the "Cursor Movement Tool". This tool permits the cursor to move through the data on the plot, which can be used in conjunction with the "Cursor Legend" to obtain data values. The last button is the "Panning Tool", which grabs the plot and allows it to be moved. The middle button, "Zoom", can be used to magnify the data, zoom in or out, and isolate a small band of data to view.

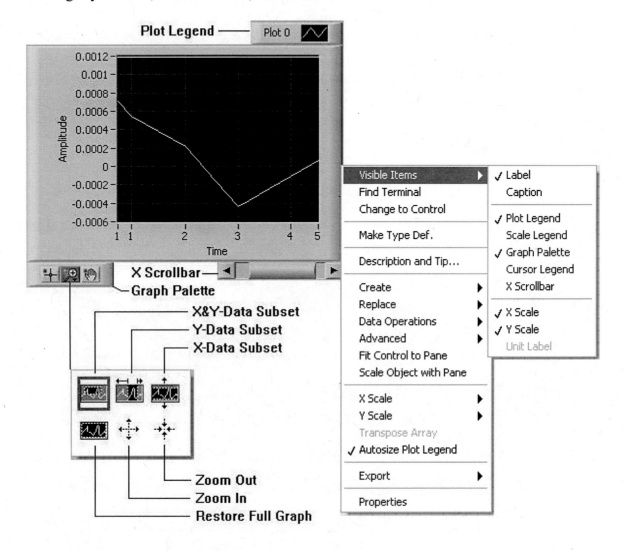

Figure 1.4.12   Waveform graph options

The subpalette at the bottom of Fig. 1.4.12 is displayed when the "Zoom" button is selected using the "Operate Value" (pointing hand) cursor. The top three options on the subpalette show that portions of the data can be enlarged by selecting one of the zoom buttons to expand the data and then dragging the cursor over the data of interest in your graph. You may also zoom in or out about a point with the lower right buttons. Finally, the lower left button auto-scales the x- and y-axes, which restores the plot to the original size.

The "X Scrollbar" is a convenient feature when you zoom in on the plot data. The "X Scrollbar" allows you to scroll through detailed (zoomed in) portions of data that are too magnified to fit on a single graph panel. Add the "X Scrollbar" by selecting **Visible Items>>X Scrollbar** from the shortcut menu.

1.4.8   Data Types

Overview of Data Types

LabVIEW operates under the principle of data flow. This means that a function executes only after it has received all required inputs regardless of its position in the block diagram.

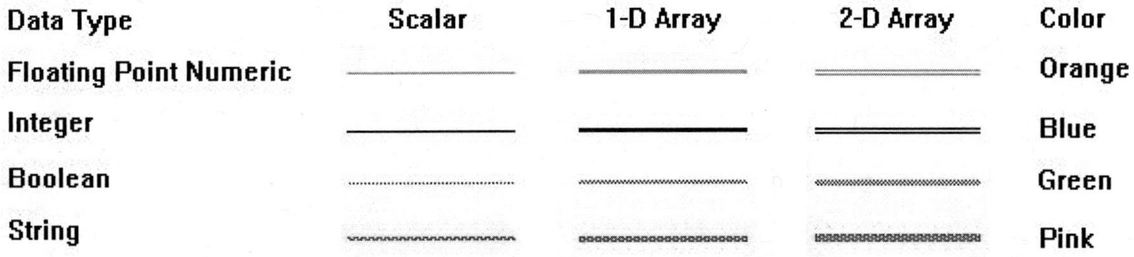

Data Type	Scalar	1-D Array	2-D Array	Color
Floating Point Numeric				Orange
Integer				Blue
Boolean				Green
String				Pink

Figure 1.4.13   Wire styles and colors for different LabVIEW data types

Dataflow is accomplished by LabVIEW via data paths, called wires, which connect nodes and terminals in the block diagram. A wire can emanate from one source terminal to one or more sink terminals. The wire's style, thickness, and color indicate the data type it carries. Examples of common wire types are shown in Fig. 1.4.13. A thin wire is displayed if the wire carries a single element, or scalar. A thicker wire will be displayed if the wire carries a 1-D array, for example, a row of data elements. This is typical of a number of data points taken over time on a single measurement channel. Depending on the data type, either an even thicker line or pair of lines will be displayed if the wire carries a 2-D array. An example of a 2-D array would be a number of data points taken over time on multiple measurement channels forming an array with each row representing a different channel. In Fig. 1.4.13, the floating point numeric and the integer data types have a pair of lines and the Boolean and string data types have thick lines.

Steps 29-30: Wiring Block Diagram Objects

In the following steps, you will learn wiring techniques and then wire nodes and terminals within the block diagram.

Note: Fig. 1.4.14 shows the block diagram objects that should appear in the VI you are creating. The exact size and position of the objects are not critical but the type of objects and general placement is. Likewise, your VI should have a "Run" button with an unbroken arrow, that is, the VI is ready to run. If your VI does not generally appear as shown in Fig. 1.4.14, repeat any appropriate step from Steps 1-28 to correct the error.

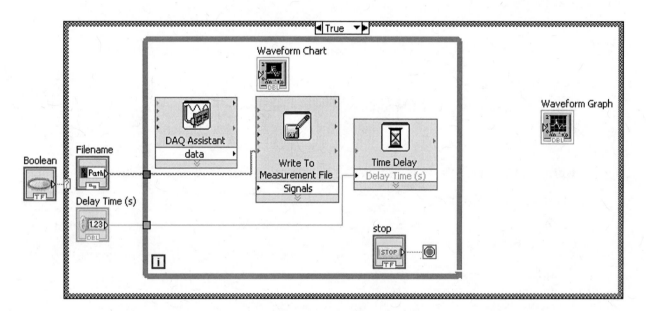

Figure 1.4.14   Intermediate stage of the example VI to continuously measure analog input data based on steps 1-28

Tip: An important aspect of wiring is to connect the correct terminals and there are a number of aids to help. Wiring is performed using the "Connect Wire" (solder spool) cursor. If this cursor is placed over a terminal, the terminal will highlight the data type color. A tip strip, which is the terminal identifier, also appears. You may also show the object's terminals by opening the "Context Help" window. If you haven't already done so, open this window using the "Help" pull-down menu and selecting **Help>>Show Context Help** or pressing <Ctrl H> on the keyboard. The "Control Help" window shows all of the object's terminals and, when the "Connect Wire" (solder spool) cursor is placed over a terminal in the block diagram, the corresponding terminal in the "Context Help" window blinks.

Tip: There are a number of tips to wiring two terminals together. Wiring may begin from the source terminal to the sink terminal or vice versa. Place the "Connect Wire" cursor over the desired terminal, left click the mouse to tack the wire to the terminal, move the mouse to the second terminal, and left click once again on the blinking receiving terminal. You do not need to hold down the left mouse button as you wire although you can tack down the wire at any point by left clicking on the mouse. As you proceed through this example, you may also notice that LabVIEW will automatically wire objects that have just been placed in the block diagram if the terminal of a close object has a similar name and data type as the one placed next to it. The automatic wiring feature may be disabled by pressing the space bar.

29. Wire terminals together as shown in Fig. 1.4.15. Wire the data output terminal from the DAQ Assistant to the waveform chart and the signals input terminal of the "Write to Measurement File" Express VI. Notice that the waveform chart changes to the dynamic data type when the wire is connected. You can start wiring from a wire that already connects two terminals.

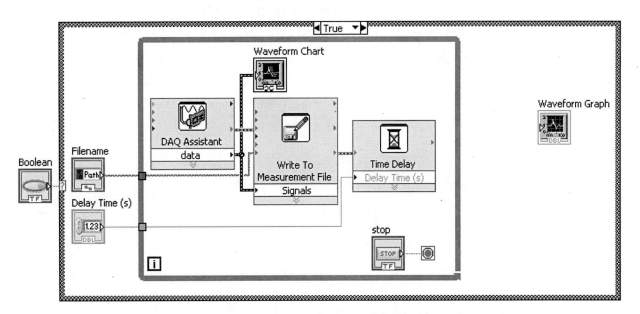

Figure 1.4.15   Example VI to continuously measure analog input data showing wiring

Note: The Express VIs also contain terminals that pass along information about errors that may have occurred before or during the execution of the VI. If an error occurs during the execution of the Express VI, an error message will be generated and pass through the "error out" terminal. Any error that occurs before the execution of the Express VI is passed along from the "error in" terminal to the "error out" terminal. The error message can be displayed with a dialog function, usually at the end of the execution of the VI. Connecting the error terminals between the Express VIs also forces the flow of data and controls the order of execution within the VI.

30. Wire the error input and output terminals between the Express VIs as shown in Fig. 1.4.15.

Additional Information on Data Types

There are a number of different data types. LabVIEW differentiates data types by color in the block diagram. A sample of common data types used by LabVIEW is shown in Table 1.4.1. Each data type will be briefly described.

- A floating point numeric contains a decimal point and may be a real or complex, positive or negative value. It may have a single precision (32 bit), double precision (default precision, 64 bit), or extended precision (128 bit) representation.
- Integers are whole numbers and may be positive only (unsigned) or both positive and negative (signed). Integers may be represented as a byte (8 bit), word (16 bit), long (32 bit), or quad (64 bit) integer.
- The Boolean data type contains two values: logical TRUE and FALSE.
- A string is a sequence of ASCII characters, most commonly alphanumeric characters. For example, a data measurement stored in binary format must be converted to a string of human-recognizable numbers to store in a text or spreadsheet file.
- A cluster is a group of data elements of mixed type. An important cluster is the error cluster, which groups the error status (Boolean, that is, there is an error-TRUE or no error-FALSE), the error code (integer), and the source of the error (string).
- The path data type contains the location of a file or directory.
- Most Express VIs use the dynamic data type, which includes the data and its attributes, such as the signal name or time the data was taken. Other functions and subVIs do not accept this data type.
- The waveform data type contains not only data but the start time and uniform time spacing of the data. A common example of the waveform data type is when you use it as an input to a graph.

Data Type	Color	Representation	Default Value
Floating Point Numeric	Orange	SGL-Single Precision DBL-Double Precision EXT-Extended Precision CSG-Complex Single CDB-Complex Double CXT-Complex Extended	0.0 0.0+0.0i
Integer	Blue	8-bit, 16-bit, 32-bit, or 64-bit Signed or Unsigned	0
Boolean	Green		False
String	Pink		Empty String
Cluster	Brown-Numeric Pink-Non-numeric Yellow-Error code		
Path	Teal Green		Empty Path
Dynamic	Dark Blue		
Waveform	Brown		

Table 1.4.1   Common LabVIEW Data Types

LabVIEW allows different data types to be used in many functions by coercing one of the data types. For example, it can add an integer to a floating point numeric. Data that is coerced will have a small coercion dot placed at the function's input terminal.

If an attempt is made to wire a source and sink terminal that are not compatible, a dashed line will appear with an X, which is called a broken wire. Examples include attempting to wire two controls or indicators together, wiring a terminal of one data type to a terminal of a different data type, or wiring a scalar to an array. The Run button on the block diagram toolbar will appear as a broken arrow (see Fig. 1.3.4) if there are any broken wires. The error associated with the broken wire can be displayed by left clicking on the "Run" button. You may also use the keyboard shortcut <Ctrl B> to remove broken wires.

1.4.9 Converting Dynamic Data

Overview of Dynamic Data

Since Express VIs generally use the dynamic data type but other functions and subVIs don't, a means to convert from the dynamic data type to other data types and vice versa is provided by LabVIEW. The "Convert from Dynamic Data" Express VI converts dynamic data to various forms of numeric or Boolean data types. Likewise, the "Convert to Dynamic Data" Express VI converts various forms of numeric or Boolean data types to the dynamic data type. Both Express VIs are found in the **Express>>Signal Manipulation** subpalette.

When the Express VI is placed in the block diagram, a configuration window appears with conversion options as shown in Fig. 1.4.16. You may retrieve this window to make changes at a later time by double-clicking on the Express VI. The conversion will depend on the type of inputted data. For example, if the DAQ Assistant has been configured to take one sample (on demand) from one channel, then "Single scalar" would be selected as the converted data type. You may also retrieve data from a specified channel with some of the available options. "Scalar Data Type" options format values of dynamic data to either floating point numbers or Boolean values.

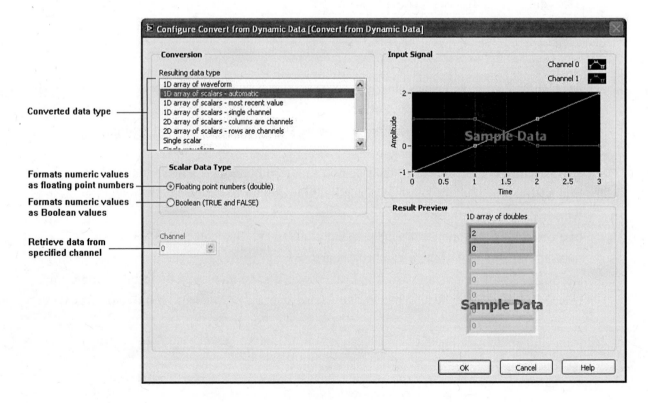

Figure 1.4.16 Convert from Dynamic Data Express VI

Steps 31-35: Converting Dynamic Data

In the following steps, the program will be modified so that the entire set of data from both channels can be graphed at the end of the measurement task. Express VIs that convert dynamic data to numeric data and back to dynamic data are required to store the data properly for graphing.

31. Select **Express>>Signal Manipulation>>Convert from Dynamic Data** and place the Express VI inside the While Loop and near the right border opposite the Graph terminal.

32. Configure the Convert from Dynamic Data Express VI as follows. Keep the default option "1-D array of scalars-automatic" as the resulting data type in the conversion. Keep the default option "Floating point numbers (double)" since the data samples are numerical values. Your configuration window should appear as shown in Fig. 1.4.16.

Note: The option "1-D array of scalars-automatic" was selected because the single samples taken from the two measurement channels are arranged in a row, in other words, a 1-D array. The first value in the row is from channel 0 and the second value is from channel 1.

33. Select **Express>>Signal Manipulation>>Convert to Dynamic Data** and place the Express VI outside of the While Loop opposite the other Convert from Dynamic Data Express VI.

34. Configure the Convert to Dynamic Data Express VI as follows. Select "2-D array of scalars-columns are channels" as the data type in the conversion. Keep the default option "Floating point numbers (double)" since the data samples are numerical values. The "Start Time" can start at zero.

Note: The option "2-D array of scalars-columns are channels" was selected because the rows of data will be indexed at the tunnel. Each time the While Loop iterates, another row of a pair of channel 0 and channel 1 values is added below the previous rows. When the While Loop is done, a 2-D array exists: all values in the first column are from channel 0 starting with the first value sampled in the first row to the most recent sample in the last row. Likewise, the second column contains values from channel 1.

35. Using the "Connect Wire" (solder spool) cursor, wire the Express VIs as shown in Fig. 1.4.17 (third option). A broken wire will appear until indexing is enabled. Right click on the tunnel and select **Tunnel Mode>>Indexing**.

Additional Information on Converting Dynamic Data

You might wonder why the output of the DAQ Assistant is not directly wired to the waveform graph as was done with the waveform chart. There are two problems with this approach as shown in Fig. 1.4.17. The problem with the first approach to display data in a graph (option 1 in Fig. 1.4.17) is that the tunnel at the border of the While Loop has indexing disabled, as shown by the solid tunnel. The graph will display only the last measurement of each channel. For most data types, this problem can be corrected by enabling indexing so that the values at every iteration are stored in an array. However, the problem with this approach (option 2 in Fig. 1.4.17) is that the waveform graph cannot accept an array of dynamic data as shown by the broken wire. A solution is shown in the third approach using the Express VIs to convert dynamic data.

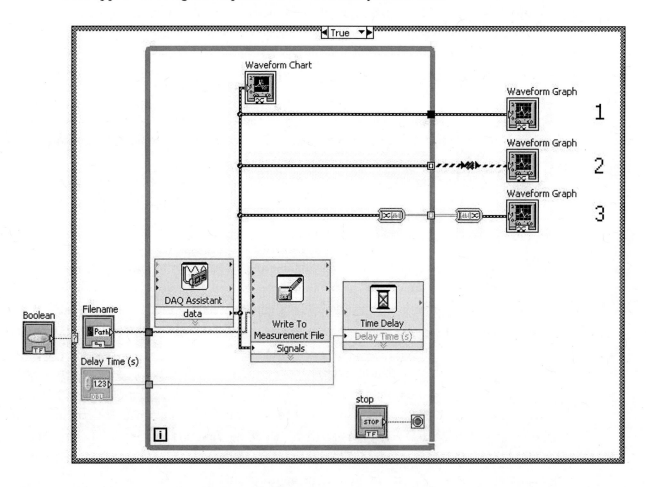

Figure 1.4.17 Intermediate stage of the example VI to continuously measure analog input data: three attempts to display data in a graph

In the third approach (option 3 in Fig. 1.4.17), indexing occurs with the numeric data type. Two analog input measurements are made every iteration of the While Loop. The "Convert from Dynamic Data" Express VI converts the two values of dynamic data into a

1-D array of numeric data in row format, as seen by the thick line. The 1-D arrays are indexed at the tunnel forming a 2-D array where each channel of data is a column. The 2-D array of numeric data is then converted back into the dynamic data type using the "Convert to Dynamic Data" Express VI.

1.4.10 Controlling While Loop Execution

Overview of Controlling While Loop Execution with Multiple Inputs

A While Loop will continue to execute until a condition is met at the conditional terminal. The default condition is "Stop if True", although this can be changed to "Continue if True" by right-clicking the mouse on the conditional terminal. If you select the While Loop from the "Express" subpalette (**Express>>Execution Control>>While Loop**), a Boolean control will be wired automatically to the conditional terminal. The control allows the user to stop the VI when desired. It is also desirable to stop the VI if an error has occurred within the While Loop. In this case, the While Loop should stop if either an error occurs or the user stops it. Boolean functions are available to perform logical operations, such as AND and OR, on Boolean values. The Boolean functions can be found in the "Express" subpalette (**Express>>Arithmetic & Comparison>>Express Boolean**) or the "Programming" subpalette (**Programming>>Boolean**). Use the "Context Help" window from the "Help" pull-down menu to get detailed information on each function.

Step 36-40:   Controlling While Loop Execution

In the following steps, the program will be modified to stop the While Loop if either an error occurs or if the user stops it. A Boolean OR function is required to combine multiple logical inputs since the conditional terminal can accept only one input.

Note: As discussed in Section 1.4.8, the error is a cluster data type containing the error status (Boolean, that is, there is an error-TRUE or no error-FALSE), the numerical error code (integer), and text to describe the source of the error (string). Since clusters can have mixed data types, they must be unbundled to have access to the Boolean error status or any other element.

36. Select **Programming>>Cluster, Class & Variant>>Unbundle by Name** and place the function above the Boolean (stop) control wired to the conditional terminal.

37. Using the "Connect Wire" (solder spool) cursor, connect the "Unbundle by Name" function to the error wire between the "Write to Measurement File" and "Time Delay" Express VIs as shown in Fig. 1.4.18.

Note: The word "status" should appear in the "Unbundle by Name" function with a green color to indicate that a Boolean value is available as an output. Although the other values in the cluster are available by dragging down on the function's blue handles, they are not needed in the current example.

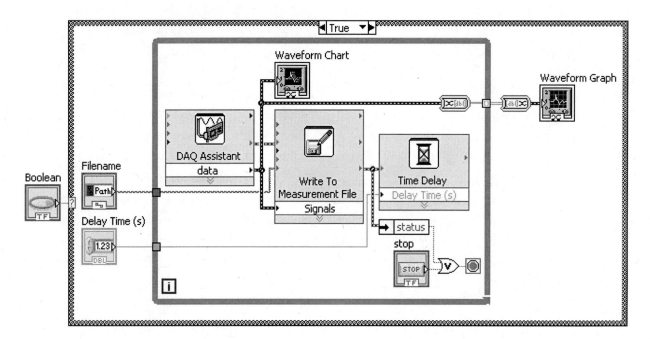

Figure 1.4.18 Completed portion of the example VI to take continuous analog input measurements

Note: The While Loop should stop if either an error occurs (error status is TRUE) or the user stops execution (Boolean control is TRUE). Since the conditional terminal can accept only one input, the output from the error cluster and the Boolean control must pass through a logical OR.

38. Select the wire between the Boolean control and the conditional terminal using the "Position" (arrow) cursor and delete it with the <Delete> key on the keyboard.

Tip: The wire may also be deleted by placing the "Position" (arrow) cursor over the wire, right-clicking the mouse, and selecting "Delete Wire Branch" from the shortcut menu.

39. Select **Express>>Arithmetic & Comparison>>Express Boolean>>Or** and place the function between the conditional terminal and the Unbundle by Name function and Boolean control as shown in Fig. 1.4.18. The "Or" function may be automatically wired to the conditional terminal. If not, wire the "Or" function to the conditional terminal.

40. Wire the Unbundle by Name function and Boolean control to the "Or" function as shown in Fig. 1.4.18.

You have just completed the portion of the VI to measure analog input data continuously. Your VI should look like Fig. 1.4.18 and the "Run" button on the toolbar should not be broken. If the arrow on the button is broken, left-click the mouse on the "Run" button to list the error(s) and repeat the appropriate step(s) to make corrections.

1.4.11 Good Housekeeping Tips: Cleaning up the Block Diagram

The following are tips to clean up the block diagram:

- Select "Clean up Diagram" from the "Edit" pull-down menu or click on the "Clean up Diagram" button on the block diagram toolbar to let LabVIEW automatically clean up the block diagram
- If you do not like the results from the automatic cleanup, you can select a node or a segment of a wire with the "Position" (arrow) cursor and drag the node or wire using the cursor or make fine changes in its location using the arrow keys on your keyboard
- You can also take the "Position" (arrow) cursor, drag a box around a group of functions and wires, and drag the entire group around with the mouse or make fine adjustments using the arrow keys on the keyboard
- Course adjustments can be made holding down the <Shift> key while using the arrow keys
- Drag a box around a group of nodes or select a group of nodes using the keyboard <Shift> key in conjunction with the left mouse key and align the group using the "Align Objects" button in the toolbar
- Distribute a group of nodes with uniform spacing using the "Distribute Objects" button on the toolbar

1.4.12 Starting the Finite Measurements Case of the Example VI

Overview of the Finite Measurements Case

The "False" case of the Case Structure will be programmed to take a finite set of analog input measurements. The VI will be structured so that one sample per channel will be taken for a fixed number of iterations. The sampling rate will employ software timing. That is, the timing between iterations will be controlled by a software timing function based on the computer's CPU clock.

The DAQ Assistant Express VI will be used to configure and create a measurement task to take one sample each from two analog input channels. The samples will then be written to a permanent file using the Write to Measurement File Express VI. The DAQ Assistant and Write to Measurement File Express VIs will be contained within a For Loop, which is a structure that executes the enclosed code a finite number of times. The Time Delay Express VI will also be contained within the For Loop to add a time delay between iterations. Without the Time Delay Express VI, the samples would be taken as fast as the computer could execute the VI. Data will be plotted during the measurement of the samples using a Waveform Chart and the entire set of data will be plotted in a Waveform Graph after the VI has completed execution.

Steps 41-47: Express VIs for the Finite Measurements Case

The following steps will configure and create an analog input measurement task, write data to a permanent file, and add a time delay to control the rate at which the samples are taken. This will be accomplished using the DAQ Assistant, Write to Measurement File, and Time Delay Express VIs

41. Before a new DAQ Assistant is placed in the block diagram, use the "Position" (arrow) cursor to select the "False" case in the "Selector Label" at the top of the Case Structure. Select **Express>>Input>>DAQ Assistant** from the "Functions" palette in the block diagram and drag it inside the Case Structure.

42. To create an analog input measurement task to sample voltages on two channels, select "Acquire Signals", "Analog Input", and "Voltage."

43. Click on the hardware device to show the channels that are available to measure analog input signals on your DAQ board. Select analog input channel 0 ("ai0") and channel 1 ("ai1") by depressing the control key <Ctrl> on the keyboard while selecting the channels with the left mouse key. After you select "Finish", the DAQ Assistant window appears.

44. Since this VI uses software timing, select "1Sample (On Demand)" from the "Acquisition Mode" pull-down menu and then OK at the bottom right corner of the window.

Note: The sample mode "1 Sample (On Demand)" is selected since software timing has been selected for this example VI to control the time spacing between each sample. Software timing is achieved using a time delay function, which is based on the CPU clock, to control timing between iterations. The acquisition mode "N Samples" is an intuitive choice for a finite set of measurements. This option was not selected since it uses hardware timing, which is based on a clock on the data acquisition board. An example VI that uses hardware timing is developed in Section 2.2.4.

Note: All other default settings in the DAQ Assistant configuration window are acceptable.

- A differential terminal configuration is selected, which means that the voltage difference between the positive and negative leads of the signal is measured. The other options include measuring the signal's voltage on the positive lead relative to the DAQ hardware system ground (referenced single-ended, RSE) or to a common reference that is not the system ground (non-referenced single-ended, NRSE).

- No custom scaling is selected since we are only interested in the signal's voltage. Custom scaling would be selected if we were using a calibration curve to convert the voltage into some physically meaningful unit, like temperature.

- Since no custom scale is used, the scaled unit is voltage. However, if custom scaling has been used, the scaled unit could have been a unit of temperature, like degree Celsius (°C), which would have been defined in the custom scaling.

- The signal input range was selected as ±10 V, the maximum range permitted by the DAQ board. Within the safe operating range of the hardware, any voltage range could have been selected.

- The signal input range corresponds to the scaled unit. For example, if custom scaling was used to convert voltage to a temperature, entering ±10 in the "Signal Input Range" would correspond to ±10 °C, if °C was used for "Scaled Units."

45. Select **Express>>Output>>Write to Measurement File** from the "Function" palette in the block diagram and drag the icon inside of the Case Structure and to the right of the DAQ Assistant.

46. Select the options shown in Table 1.4.2 and choose an alternate filename if the default is not acceptable.

47. Select **Express>>Execution Control>>Time Delay** from the "Functions" palette in the block diagram and drag the VI inside the Case Structure to the right of the "Write to Measurement File" VI in the block diagram. Press OK for the default value of 1 second as this will be modified in a later step through a control in the front panel.

Note: The VI should appear like the one shown in Fig. 1.4.19.

Option	Description
Save to one file	This option is selected because you don't want to write to a new file every iteration. You don't want to ask the user to choose a file either because it may interfere with data collection, especially at fast sampling rates.
Append to file	After the first iteration, a file will already exist. The option to append to the existing file is selected because the sample measured every iteration is part of the overall test.
Text (LVM)	The **L**abVIEW **M**easurement (LVM) file format allows human readable text in a file to be opened in a word processing or spreadsheet application at a later time. The binary file format is not human readable and is used to transfer data between NI software.
One header only	This option is selected to place a header that contains information, such as the date and time the test was conducted, at the beginning of the file. Otherwise, there would be one header every time data was appended to the file with the "One header per segment" option.
One column only	This option writes the time that data is sampled in the first column only. The "One column per channel" option writes time-data pairs for every channel.
Tabulator	Data within a row are separated by either a comma or tab spacing.

Table 1.4.2   Write to Measurement File Express VI options for the finite measurement case of the analog input example VI

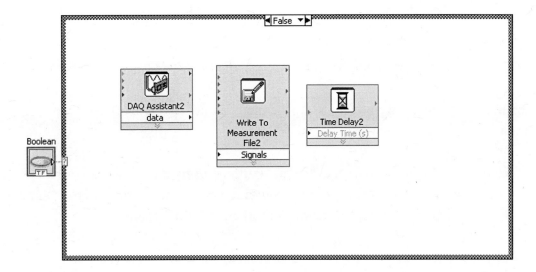

Figure 1.4.19 Intermediate stage of the example VI to measure a finite set of analog input data

1.4.13 For Loop

Overview of the For Loop

The For Loop is a structure that executes the sub diagram enclosed within its borders a specified number of times. The components that appear within the For Loop when it is first placed in the block diagram include the "Count" and "Iteration" terminals. The "Count" terminal is an explicit means to determine the number of times, N, the sub diagram within the borders of the For Loop executes by wiring a control or constant to it. The "Count" terminal may also be used as an input to a function within the For Loop. The "Iteration" terminal contains the number of times the loop has iterated beginning with a value of zero for the first iteration and ending with the N-1 iteration. The value of the "Iteration" terminal is available as an input to other functions within the For Loop. The For Loop will be used in the example VI to take a finite set of analog input measurements.

Steps 48-49: For Loop

In the following steps, the program will be modified to take samples a finite number of times as specified by the user. This is accomplished by placing a For Loop around the Express VIs added in Steps 41-47.

48. Select **Programming>>Structures>>For Loop** from the "Functions" palette in the block diagram and drag the structure above and to the left of the DAQ Assistant. Left click the mouse, drag the border around the three Express VIs, and release the mouse to create the For Loop.

Tip: If you make a mistake dragging the For Loop, you can undo the creation of the For Loop and start over using the "Undo" command from the "Edit" pull-down menu.

Tip: You may also resize the structure using the blue handles if you need more room at a later time.

49. Right-click the mouse over the "Count" terminal using the "Position" (arrow) cursor and select "Create Control" from the shortcut menu. Rename the control "Number of Samples (Finite Mode Only)" using the "Operate Value" (hand) cursor.

Note: The "Count" terminal and the "Iteration" terminal are the only terminals that appear. The number of loop iterations will be determined explicitly by the user using a control wired to the "Count" terminal.

Additional Information on For Loops

A "Conditional" terminal may also be added to terminate execution of the For Loop if a condition is met, even before the "Count" terminal condition is reached. This may be used, for example, to stop execution when an error occurs or when specified by a user through a Boolean control. The conditional terminal can be added by right clicking the mouse on the border and selecting "Conditional Terminal" from the shortcut menu. The default terminal condition is to stop if the input to the terminal is true. However, the condition can be changed to continue if true by using the shortcut menu that appears when you right-click on the conditional terminal as shown in Fig. 1.4.20.

A shift register can store one or more values from one iteration to the next. A shift register may be added to a For Loop by right clicking the mouse on the border and selecting "Add Shift Register" from the shortcut menu as shown in Fig. 1.4.20. The value stored in the shift register at the right border at the end of one iteration will be available in the shift register at the left border at the beginning of the next iteration. Values from previous iterations may be made available by using stacked shift registers. Stacked shift registers are created by right clicking the mouse on the left shift register and selecting "Add Element" from the shortcut menu. The left shift register is initialized by wiring a constant or control to the register. Otherwise, the initial value used in the shift register will be the default value of the data type the first time the For Loop is executed or the value stored in the shift register from the last time the For Loop was executed.

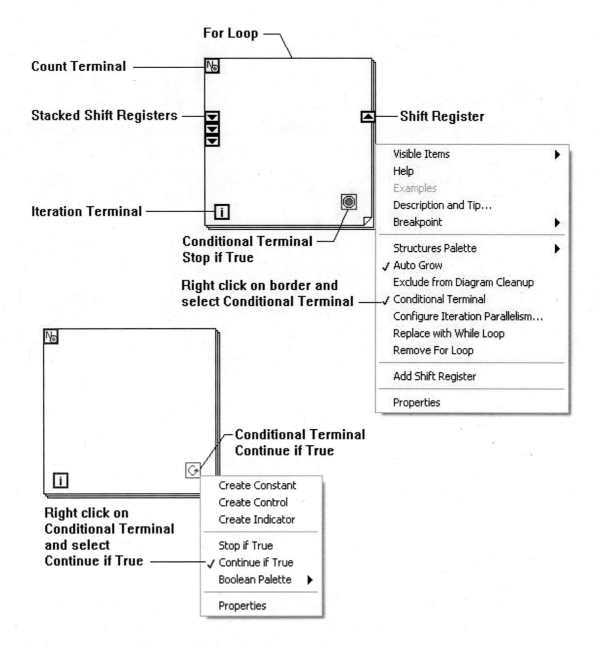

Figure 1.4.20 For Loop with terminals and shift registers

For Loops pass data through tunnels (represented as squares on the border) in the same manner as While Loops, as discussed in Section 1.4.5. Specifically, for an array that passes into a For Loop, the entire array passes through the tunnel on the first iteration if indexing is disabled. This is seen by the thick line to the right of the tunnel in the top For Loop of Fig. 1.4.21. If indexing is enabled, the array will pass one of its elements through the tunnel every iteration as seen by the thin line to the right of the tunnel in the bottom For Loop of Fig 1.4.21.

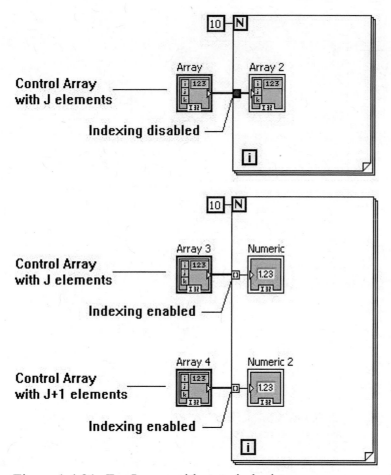

Figure 1.4.21 For Loops with auto-indexing

The number of times the For Loop executes can be set implicitly using auto-indexing. This contrasts to an explicit specification of the loop count when a constant or control is wired to the "Count" terminal. When the "Count" terminal has no input, the loop count will equal the number of elements in the array, if indexing is enabled.

If the "Count" terminal has an input value and/or if there are two are more arrays passing into the For Loop, the loop count is determined by the minimum value. Using the bottom For Loop in Fig. 1.4.21 as an example, if J < 10, the For Loop will execute J times. If J > 10, the For Loop will execute 10 times, which is the input to the "Count" terminal.

1.4.14 Local Variables

Overview of Local Variables

It would be nice to use the same inputs, graph, and chart from the continuous measurement case of the VI but the terminals are not available in the finite measurement case. Local variables can solve this problem.

Local variables are structures that pass data between a front panel object and more than one location in the block diagram. Front panel objects have one corresponding terminal in the block diagram. A local variable allows data in a terminal to be used in a different location on the same block diagram.

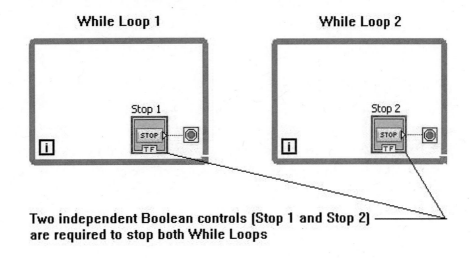

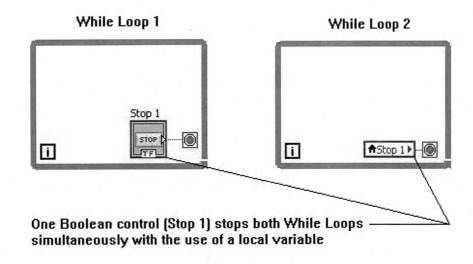

Figure 1.4.22   Example to show the use of a local variable of a Boolean control to stop two While Loops simultaneously

An example when a local variable is beneficial occurs when two While Loops are running in parallel in a VI. Without the use of a local variable, two While Loops running in parallel in the same VI require two independent Boolean controls as shown in the top of Fig. 1.4.22. Furthermore, the While Loops could not be stopped simultaneously since the two Boolean controls would have to be selected sequentially in the front panel. The bottom of Fig. 1.4.22 shows how both While Loops can be stopped simultaneously when a single Boolean control is used with a local variable associated with it. Data passed to the Boolean control through the front panel is also available to the local variable.

Local variables can be created using the "Functions" palette by selecting "Local Variable" in the "Structures" subpalette. You must then associate it with a control or indicator in the front panel. You may also create a local variable by right clicking on the desired front panel object or block diagram terminal.

Steps 50-63: Creating Local Variables

In the following steps, local variables will be created for two controls, the chart, and the graph. This will allow, for example, the same chart to be used for either mode of data acquisition (finite or continuous) and avoid the use of two charts.

50. Select **Programming>>Structures>>Local Variable** from the "Function" palette in the block diagram and place it to the left of the DAQ Assistant and the For Loop border but within the Case Structure as shown in Fig. 1.4.23. The color will first be black.

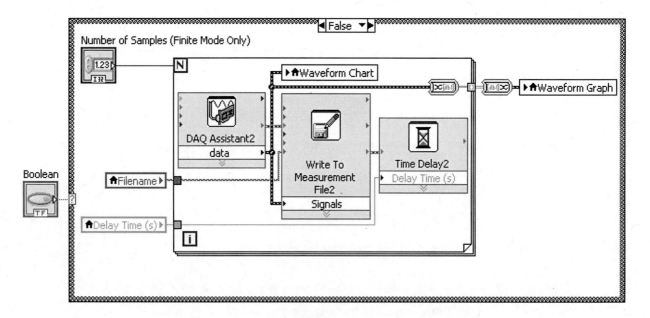

Figure 1.4.23   Completed portion of the example VI to take a finite set of analog input measurements

51. Left click on the local variable with the "Operate Value" (hand) cursor and associate the "Filename" control with the node.

Note: By default, a new local variable receives data and behaves as an indicator. However, the node can also be configured to behave as a control. In this case, the local variable will read data from the associated front panel control and then provide that data as a control would.

52. Right click on the node and select "Change to Read" from the shortcut menu to configure this node as a control.

53. Wire the local variable to the appropriate terminal on the "Write to Measurement File" Express VI.

54. Select **Programming>>Structures>>Local Variable** from the "Function" palette. Perform similar operations for the "Time Delay (s)" terminal and wire it to the appropriate terminal on the "Time Delay" Express VI as shown in Fig. 1.4.23.

55. Select **Programming>>Structures>>Local Variable** from the "Function" palette and place it above the "Write to Measurement File" Express VI as shown in Fig. 1.4.23.

56. Left click on the local variable with the "Operate Value" (hand) cursor and associate the "Waveform Chart" indicator with the node.

Note: By default, the local variable will behave as an indicator, which is desired for a chart, so there is no need to change the read or write mode.

57. Wire the "data" output terminal of the DAQ Assistant to the waveform chart local variable.

58. Wire the "data" output terminal on the DAQ Assistant Express VI to the "Signals" input terminal on the "Write to Measurement File" Express VI as shown in Fig. 1.4.23. Likewise, wire the error terminals between the three Express VIs.

Note: The final addition to the VI is to plot the data in a graph after the measurements are completed. The data are collected in the tunnel at the border of the For Loop, that is, indexing is enabled by default. Therefore, the data must be converted from the dynamic data type to the numeric data type so that a data array is created. The data can then be converted back to the dynamic data type as input to the graph. This is the same process that was used at the border of the While Loop for the continuous data measurement portion of the VI as discussed in Section 1.4.9.

59. Select **Programming>>Structures>>Local Variable** from the "Function" palette in the block diagram and place it to the right of the For Loop border but within the Case Structure as shown in Fig. 1.4.23.

60. Left click on the local variable with the "Operate Value" (hand) cursor and associate the "Waveform Graph" indicator with the node.

61. Select **Express>>Signal Manipulation>>Convert from Dynamic Data** and place the Express VI inside the For Loop near the right border and across from the waveform graph local variable. The default options are suitable as described in Step 32 and the note following it so click OK.

62. Select **Express>>Signal Manipulation>>Convert to Dynamic Data** and place the Express VI between the right border of the For Loop and the waveform graph local variable.

63. Select "2-D array of scalars-columns are channels" and click OK since the other default options are suitable. The selection of these options is described in Step 34 and the note following it. Using the "Connect Wire" (solder spool) cursor, wire the Express VIs as shown in Fig. 1.4.23.

You have just completed the portion of the VI to measure a finite set of analog input data. Your VI should look like Fig. 1.4.23 and the "Run" button on the toolbar should not be broken. If the arrow on the button is broken, left-click the mouse on the "Run" button to list the error(s) and repeat the appropriate step(s) to make corrections.

Congratulations! Your VI is complete. Be sure to save your program using one of the save options on the "File" pull-down menu.

1.4.15 Documenting VIs

Overview of Documenting VIs

It is beneficial to document a VI for both the developer and other users. Comments in the VI document information that you, as the developer of the VI, may forget over time and also document information that other users may need to understand the program if you are not available. Documentation may include, among other information, a title, name of the developer, date the VI was developed, purpose of the VI, how it functions, and comments on input requirements.

Labels may be used to identify front panel and block diagram objects. When using the automatic tool selection feature, add labels by double clicking in an open area of the front panel or block diagram and begin typing. Otherwise, you may use the "Edit Text" (cursor with the letter "A") to create the label. The label can be moved at a later time using the "Position" (arrow) cursor.

Descriptive information about a VI or subVI can be documented through the "VI Property" dialog as shown in Fig. 1.4.24. The documentation can be viewed at a later time through the "Context Help" window (retrieved through the "Help" pull-down menu) by placing the cursor over the VI's icon as shown in Fig. 1.4.25.

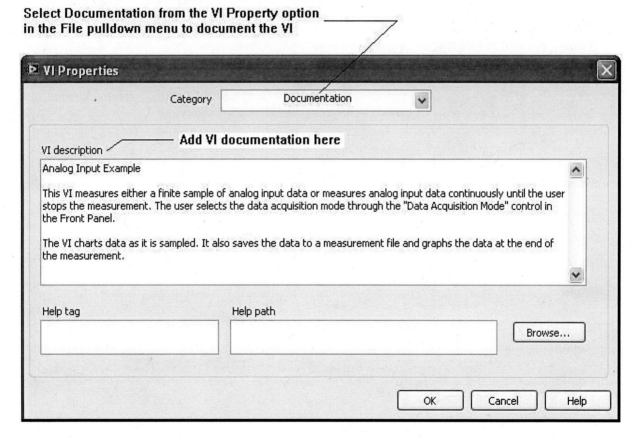

Figure 1.4.24   Example to illustrate the method to document a VI through the VI Properties window

Step 64: Documenting the VI

The following step shows how to document the VI using the VI Properties window.

64. Select "VI Properties" from the "File" pull-down menu and then select "Documentation" from the "Category" options as shown in Fig. 1.4.24. Add documentation in the "VI description" pane.

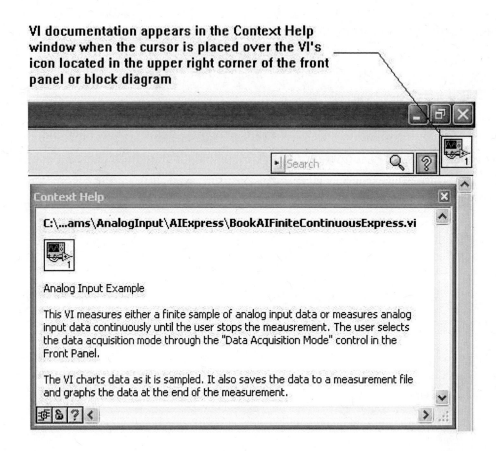

VI documentation appears in the Context Help window when the cursor is placed over the VI's icon located in the upper right corner of the front panel or block diagram

Figure 1.4.25   Example to show VI documentation in the VI Context Help window

1.4.16 Good Housekeeping Tips: Organizing the Front Panel

Until now, the focus has been on the block diagram although an ordered and labeled front panel will make the VI easier to use. A simple example is shown in Fig. 1.4.26, which orders the user inputs sequentially followed by the chart and graph. The following steps were done to modify the front panel.

Steps 65-67: Organizing the Front Panel

65. The Boolean push button control to the Case Structure was replaced with a vertical toggle switch. Right click on the Boolean control in the front panel and select **Replace>>Modern>>Boolean>>Vertical Toggle Switch** from the shortcut menu. Double click on the label or use the "Edit Text" (letter A) cursor to change the label name from "Boolean" to "Data Acquisition Mode".

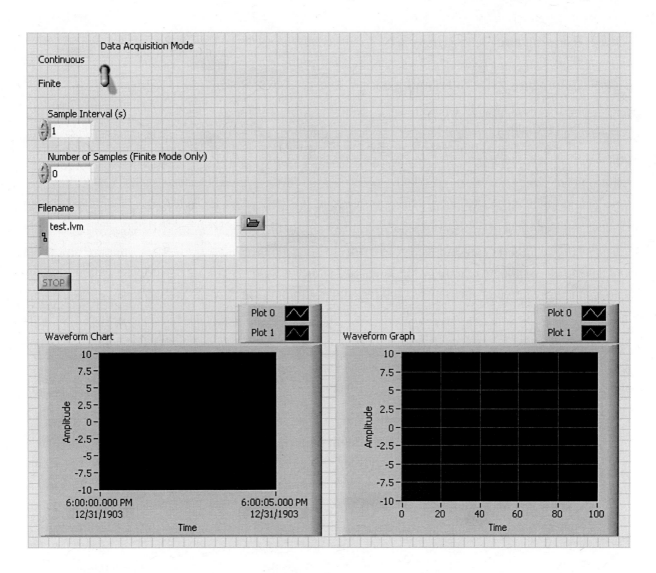

Figure 1.4.26 Sample front panel for the example VI to take analog input data

66. Add labels to clarify the function of the data acquisition mode toggle switch. Double click on a blank area next to the control to create the "Continuous" and "Finite" labels.

67. Align and/or distribute objects using the "Align Objects" and "Distribute Objects" buttons on the front panel toolbar.

Tip: Controls and indicators that are to be aligned or distributed can be selected in one of two ways. Using the "Position" (arrow) cursor, you can drag a box around a group. Alternatively, you can use the "Position" (arrow) cursor to select a group with the keyboard shift key, <Shift>, in conjunction with the left mouse key.

1.4.17 Running and Debugging a VI

Debugging Prior to Running a VI

You will spend less time in the long run if you are very deliberate when developing your VI with the goal that it works right the first time. Putting the VI together hastily and then depending on your debugging skills can quickly lead to frustration.

LabVIEW will not allow your program to execute if there are any broken wires. If there are broken wires, then the Run Arrow button on the block diagram toolbar will be "broken." You can remove broken wires using the "Remove Bad Wires" feature on the "Edit" pull-down menu or the keyboard shortcut <Ctrl B>. This feature is particularly useful when a broken wire is hidden under another object.

LabVIEW will provide useful diagnostics if the "Run Arrow" is broken and you are unable to determine the cause of the broken arrow. If you click on the "Broken Run" button, then LabVIEW will list the errors that prevent the program from executing. The problem that is causing the highlighted error can be identified using the "Show Error" button in the "Error List" window. You may also access the same window by selecting "Error List" under the "View" pull-down menu.

One common source of error is to switch an indicator for a control and vice versa. If the error states that a function "contains unwired or bad terminal," it's possible, for example, that an object that is intended to be a control (user supplied information) is an indicator. Check the objects connected to bad wires and determine if any should be a control (or indicator, depending on the case). Right click on the object and select the "Change to Control" option (or "Change to Indicator" option, depending on the case).

Steps 68-75: Running the Example VI

The last set of steps shows how to run the VI with analog voltage sources attached to the DAQ board via the terminal connector block. You will run the VI in both finite and continuous data acquisition modes.

68. For each channel selected, attach a voltage source, such as a sensor, function generator, a power supply, or even a battery if other equipment is not available, to the terminal connector block. The voltage difference between the two leads, the positive and negative leads, will be measured.

Tip: Use the "Connection Diagram" in the DAQ Assistant to determine the terminals assigned to the designated analog input channels. An example for the first analog input channel, "ai0" (identified as "Voltage_0"), is shown in Fig 1.4.27 for a National Instruments NI 6221 (68-pin) DAQ board. Double click on the DAQ Assistant in the block diagram and select the "Connection Diagram" tab to see the terminal connections for your DAQ hardware. Click on each channel in the "Channels in Task" pane to see all of the connections.

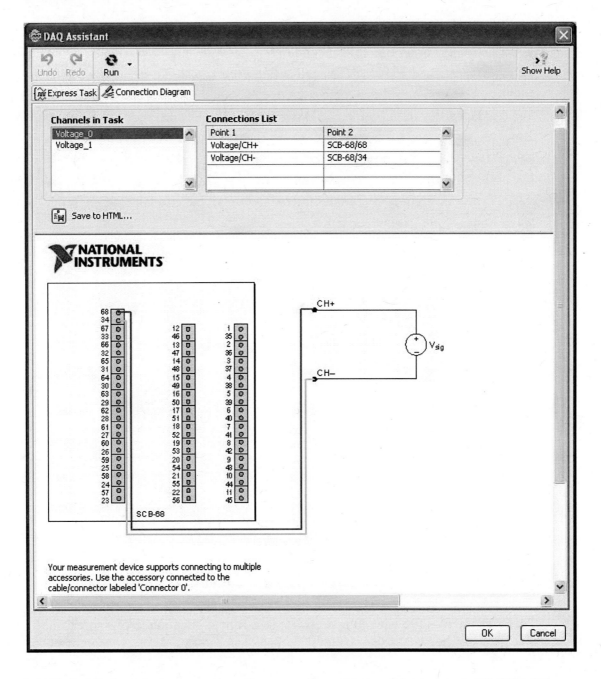

Figure 1.4.27 DAQ Assistant connection diagram using a National Instruments NI 6221 (68-pin) DAQ board as an example to show the terminal block connections for analog input channel ai0 for the positive and negative leads of an attached voltage source

Note: The VI's inputs in the front panel will first be configured for continuous analog input measurements.

69. Use the "Operating Value" (hand) cursor to flip up the vertical toggle switch for the continuous data acquisition mode.

Note: The sample interval can be set as desired with only a few restrictions. Very small sample intervals (on the order of a millisecond or smaller) may not be attainable with software timing because the CPU clock has competing priorities. Also, if you are using a frequency generator as the voltage source, your sampling rate must be sufficiently high to avoid a data acquisition problem called aliasing, which is discussed in Section 2.1.3. However, at this point it is sufficient to say that the signal's frequency content can be adequately captured if the sampling rate is at least twice the signal frequency or greater. For now, adjust the signal frequency to ensure that you measure at least 2 samples per cycle. Since the input is the sample interval, you will have to take the reciprocal of the wave frequency to get the wave period.

70. Set the "Sample Interval" equal to or less than half of the wave period of the input signal.

71. Specify an appropriate filename or use the default.

Note: Data will be stored in "My Documents\LabVIEW Data\test.lvm" by default. Click on the open folder to the right of the "Filename" dialog box to specify a different file that currently exists or type in a new file path in the dialog box.

72. Press the "Run" button on the block diagram toolbar and observe the data on the chart.

Note: Data will not be displayed on the graph until the While Loop is stopped and the data collected at the tunnel is passed to the graph.

73. Stop the VI by left clicking on the "Stop" Boolean control in the front panel.

74. Open the data file with an appropriate software application, like a spreadsheet, to view the data.

75. Reconfigure the front panel to run the VI in finite data acquisition mode. Toggle the "Data Acquisition Mode" control to "Finite" using the "Operate Value" (hand) cursor. Select a number of samples that will give a reasonable data acquisition period when the sample interval is considered. If you do not want the data appended to the previous file, specify a different filename.

Debugging While the VI is Running

If the program runs but the values appear to be incorrect, one useful debugging feature is the "Highlight Execution" (light bulb) button on the tool bar of the block diagram window as shown in Fig. 1.4.28. It animates the data flow in the block diagram and lists the values at every function. Click on the "Highlight Execution" button to animate dataflow or click again to return to normal run mode while the VI is running. If you use this feature as the VI is running, values may flash up too quickly to process. However, you can use the "Step Into," "Step Over," and "Step Out" buttons next to the "Highlight Execution" button to proceed step-by-step through the VI's execution. Click on the "Pause/Continue" button to return to the normal run mode.

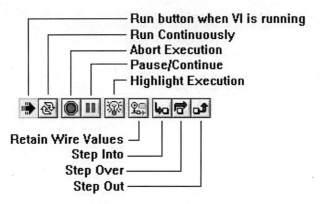

Figure 1.4.28 Block diagram toolbar when a VI is executing

You can also use the "Probe Data" feature to observe values at selected locations as opposed to all values from the use of the "Highlight Execution" button. To use this feature, select the "Probe Data" cursor (letter P inside yellow circle) from the "Tools" palette and place it over the wire where you want to view the values in the VI. If you click on the area of the block diagram that is blinking, a "Probe Watch" window will appear that will display the values during the execution of the program. You may select multiple probe locations that will appear in the "Probe Watch" window. Click on any of the listed probe locations to observe the latest values.

An example of the use of probes is shown in Fig. 1.4.29. Three probes were placed on the block diagram of the example VI to measure analog input data by left clicking the mouse over the wires using the "Probe Data" cursor. The "Probe Watch" window appears upon the placement of the first probe and subsequent probes appear as entries in the pane. The "Probe Watch" window shows "Not Executed" under the "Value" column until executions begins, at which point the latest value is displayed. Select any of the probes in the "Probe Watch" window during or after execution to get that probe's latest value.

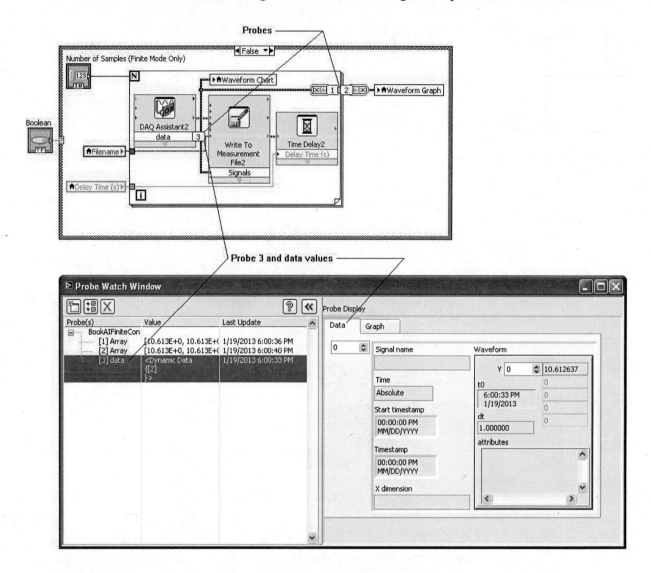

Figure 1.4.29   Example to show the Probe Watch Window and the use of probes

Congratulations! You have developed and tested a VI that can be configured to measure either a finite set of analog input data or measure the data continuously using software timing. See Chapter 2 to develop analogous VIs using hardware timing.

1.5 LabVIEW Example VIs

Part 2 covers the use of LabVIEW for data acquisition applications using the configuration approach with Express VIs. Data acquisition concepts are first covered for each of the main data acquisition areas: analog input and output, digital input and output, and counters. Tutorials with step-by-step instructions are provided for the development of basic data acquisition programs to learn LabVIEW through hands-on experience. The tutorials are provided for what are termed skill-development problems since they typically are single function (single data acquisition mode) VIs that reinforce the basic data acquisition concepts. Additional problems, which may involve multi-function data acquisition, are also provided to develop your proficiency acquiring data using LabVIEW.

LabVIEW also provides example VIs. Examples using the configuration approach with Express VIs can be found in the following directory, which assumes default installation of the National Instruments software:

C:\Program Files\National Instruments\LabVIEW 2012\examples\express

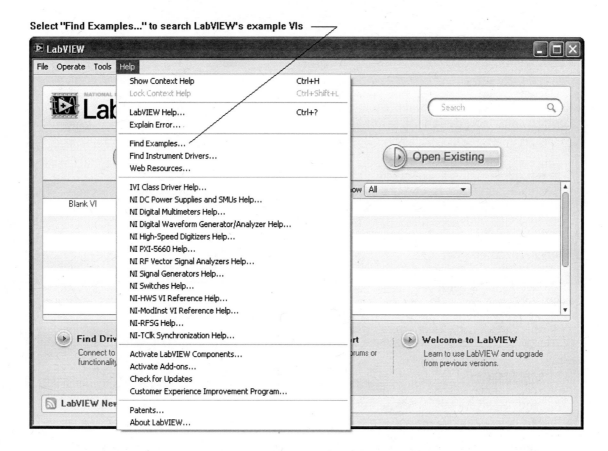

Figure 1.5.1   Procedure to launch the NI Example Finder

The example Express VIs can be easily accessed using the NI Example Finder. Select "Find Examples…" from the "Help" pull-down menu in the LabVIEW startup window, as shown in Fig. 1.5.1, which launches the NI Example Finder. Select "Directory Structure" under the Browse tab, as shown in Fig. 1.5.2, and then double-click on the "express" folder to expose the example VIs. Double-click on any of the example VIs to launch the program. Chapter 1 focuses on the Express VIs so you will be limited to any examples in the "express" folder shown in Fig. 1.5.2 for data acquisition. Data acquisition examples in the other folders were developed with DAQmx, an alternate approach to developing LabVIEW VIs.

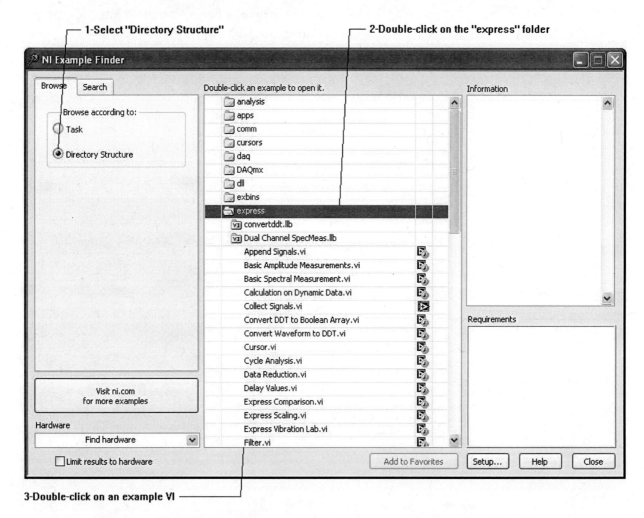

Figure 1.5.2   Procedure to access LabVIEW example VIs using NI Example Finder

The NI Example Finder is also an easy way to search for LabVIEW example VIs. Under the "Search" tab, enter the topic of interest, as shown in Fig. 1.5.3, and select an example VI. Some example VIs will run on only selected DAQ hardware. You can see if your hardware will run the example VI by checking under the "Requirements" area.

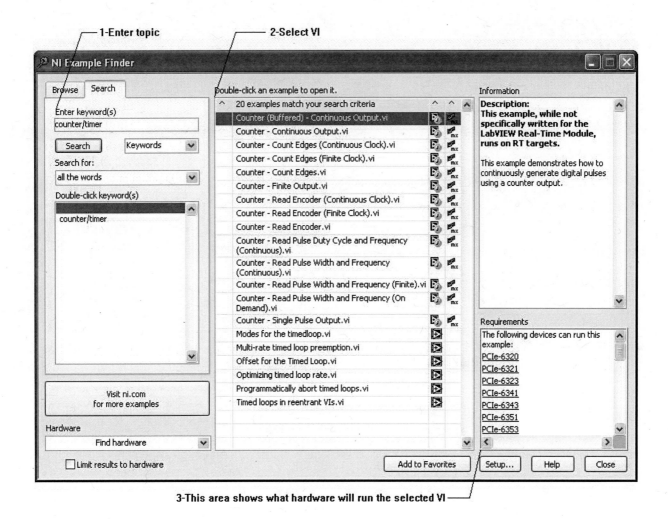

Figure 1.5.3   Procedure to search for LabVIEW example VIs using NI Example Finder

Notes:

Part 2   Data Acquisition: LabVIEW Configuration Approach

The purpose of Part 2 is to show you how to perform data acquisition using LabVIEW's configuration approach. LabVIEW provides Express VIs that simplify the configuration of measurement and generation tasks, writing to measurement files, and other operations. The Express VIs provide dialog windows that guide the user through the selection of required inputs, which reduces programming errors. The Express VIs are straightforward and relatively simple to learn thus making them suitable for the new LabVIEW user.

Part 2 covers the main areas of data acquisition: analog input/output, digital input/output, and counters/timers. Because of the modular nature of this primer, you may read your topic of interest without regard to the order in which it is presented in Part 2.

- Read Chapter 2 if your interest is in the measurement or generation of analog signals. This chapter covers analog measurement and generation at slow and fast sampling or update rates, finite or continuous data acquisition, and triggered data acquisition.

- Read Chapter 3 if your interest is in the measurement or generation of digital signals. The digital signals discussed in this chapter are low voltage (0 V or 5 V) transistor-transistor-logic (TTL) signals where the interest is on the state of the signal. Typical applications of material covered in this chapter include reading the state of switches, relays, or LEDs or controlling these same devices.

- Read Chapter 4 if your interest is in the measurement or generation of digital pulse trains. The focus of this chapter is on measuring the period or frequency of a digital pulse or pulse train. It also focuses on generating a digital pulse or pulse train.

Part 2 emphasizes an experiential approach to learning LabVIEW for data acquisition through skill-development and proficiency-development problems. Skill-development problems are provided in each section to learn data acquisition concepts through the experience of hands-on activities. Main data acquisition concepts are discussed and a guide is provided to develop each skill-development problem. The skill-development problems are typically single-mode data acquisition problems. Single mode means that the skill-development problem will focus on one data acquisition mode, like analog input or output, to emphasize the main data acquisition concept. Steps to develop the VI are provided in the guide. However, the steps in Part 2 are not as detailed as the steps given in Part 1 since the VI in Chapter 1 was used to introduce LabVIEW concepts instead of data acquisition concepts. If you are a new LabVIEW user, complete the example in Chapter 1 if you have not already done so. Proficiency-development problems are provided at the end of each chapter. These problems typically focus on practical applications of data acquisition concepts and may involve multi-mode data acquisition. The front panel and block diagram of the VI are provided for each proficiency-development problem but the development steps are left to the reader. It is hoped that the progression from the highly structured guidance provided in the development of the example problem in Chapter 1 through the progressively less structured development of the skill-development and proficiency-development problems will provide the experience and confidence to develop your own data acquisition VIs.

Chapter 2   Analog Signal Measurement and Generation

2.1. Analog Signal Basics

An analog signal is an electrical (voltage or current) input or output that can vary continuously in amplitude and time. Analog input signals would typically originate from sensors and transducers, such as a thermocouple or strain gage. Analog output signals would typically be used to control an output device, like a motor. To accurately measure an analog signal requires attention to at least the following three areas: (1) the nature of the signal source and the signal measurement system that is, how the signal is connected to the DAQ hardware, (2) the resolution of the signal, and (3) the rate at which the measured signal is sampled.

2.1.1 Signal Measurement System

The connection between a signal source and the data measurement system depends on whether the signal source is grounded or floating. Grounded (also called referenced) signal sources are referenced to an earth or building ground. A signal source from a device, such as a signal generator or a power supply, with a three-pronged plug connected to a grounded building outlet produces a grounded signal. Grounded signal sources and the measurement system, for example the DAQ board installed in the computer, share the same building ground although the grounds are not necessarily at the same voltage due to contact resistances. A floating (also called non-referenced) signal source is not referenced to any earth or building ground. Examples of floating signal sources would be battery-powered devices or devices that generate their own potential difference, like a photovoltaic cell or a thermocouple. If you are unsure if the signal is grounded or floating, a floating signal source will show an open circuit when using a multimeter to measure the resistance across the signal ground (or negative lead) and the measurement system ground, even when the multimeter leads are switched. There are three methods to connect the signal source to the measurement system: referenced single-ended, non-referenced single ended, and differential. The nature of the connection depends if the signal source is grounded or floating.

In a referenced single-ended measurement system, all of the signal sources are referenced to the same building ground, therefore requiring only one analog input connection to the DAQ board to measure the signal's voltage. For a floating or grounded signal source, one lead (typically the positive lead) is connected to an analog input channel on the DAQ board while the other lead is connected to the measurement system ground, AI GND, on the DAQ board. While it is physically possible to construct a referenced, single-ended measurement system, it is not recommended for a grounded signal source because of the potential voltage differences between the signal source and measurement system grounds that form ground loop losses. Because of contact resistances within the input device and within the building outlets and connections, a voltage difference can exist between grounds, called a common-mode voltage. The DAQ board measures the voltage difference between the signal source's positive lead and the measurement system's ground; a voltage difference that includes the common-mode voltage. This can lead to erroneous measurements and possibly damage the measurement system for large common-mode voltages. There is no similar problem connecting a floating signal source in a referenced single-ended measurement system since it is not referenced to any building ground.

A non-referenced single-ended measurement system is a variation of the referenced single-ended measurement system with the only difference being that the signal sources share a common reference, like the same power supply and ground. For a grounded signal source, one lead (typically the positive lead) is connected to an analog input channel on the DAQ board while the other lead is connected to a common reference, AI SENSE, on the DAQ board. A floating signal source is connected in the same way as a grounded signal source except that a bias resistor is recommended to be placed between the AI SENSE and AI GND connections on the DAQ board to keep the signal reference tied to the measurement system ground. Bias resisters are typically between 10 kΩ and 100 kΩ.

In a differential measurement system, the positive and negative leads of either a floating or grounded signal source are each connected to an analog input channel of the DAQ board and only the voltage difference between the signal leads is measured. For a floating signal source, it is recommended that a separate bias resister is placed between each of the signal leads and the measurement system ground, AI GND, on the DAQ board.

There are both advantages and disadvantages with each measurement system. The differential measurement system is generally recommended as the common-mode voltage does not influence this form of measurement, which results in a more accurate measurement of the signal. It is also recommended for low-voltage signals, signals passing through long cables or cables passing through electrically noisy environments, and signals sources that share different references. Otherwise, single-ended measurements may be made, especially if more channels are needed than are available on the DAQ board if a differential measurement system was used.

2.1.2   Signal Resolution

Computers function in the digital realm and must make conversions between analog and digital signals. An analog to digital conversion (ADC) is required for analog measurement and, likewise, a digital to analog conversion (DAC) is required for analog generation.

The ability of the computer to represent an analog voltage is determined by the resolution and range of the DAQ device and the signal input range. The device range is the span of voltages that the DAQ board can handle, for example, -10 V to 10 V. Voltages beyond the device range cannot be measured and may damage the DAQ board beyond a device-specific safety range. DAQ boards permit the user to select the span of voltages accepted for the incoming signal based on software selectable programmed gain. For example, the National Instruments DAQ board NI 622x M-Series device family has input ranges of ± 10 V, ± 5 V, ± 1 V, and ± 200 mV. The NI 622x M-Series devices permit only bipolar signal ranges (a negative voltage to the same numerically valued positive voltage) although other DAQ boards permit unipolar ranges (0 V to a positive voltage value). The ADC or DAC provides a digital number representation of the analog signal's voltage. The accuracy of the conversion depends on the number of bits used to characterize the analog voltage.

The input range is divided into a number of levels, called codes, where the number of possible levels is determined by the number of bits in the digital conversion. For example, if a digital number has 2 bits, the analog voltage can be represented by one of four levels, or codes, (00, 01, 10, 11). Since each bit can have two states (0 and 1), there are $2^2 = 4$ possible states for a two-bit digital number. A DAQ board would typically have 12-bit or 16-bit digital representation. This means that the signal input range can be divided into $2^{12} = 4096$ or $2^{16} = 65536$ possible digital levels, or codes. The code width is the ratio of the input range and the number of digital codes. For example, the code width for a 12-bit DAQ board with a 10 V bipolar signal input range is 4.8 mV.

$$V_{cw} = \frac{Range}{2^{resolution}} = \frac{20\ V}{2^{12}} = 4.8\ mV$$

Under the same conditions, a 16-bit DAQ board has a code width of 0.3 mV.

$$V_{cw} = \frac{Range}{2^{resolution}} = \frac{20\ V}{2^{16}} = 0.3\ mV$$

The signal resolution depends on matching the input range on the DAQ board to the anticipated limits of the analog signal. A type-K thermocouple connected directly to a 16-

bit NI 6221 DAQ board will be used as an example. Let's say that the thermocouple will be used to measure a temperature change of 1000°C in an oven. The type-K thermocouple outputs about 40 μV/°C change in temperature so the thermocouple will generate a total voltage difference of approximately 40 mV with the total change in oven temperature. If a signal input range of ±10 V is selected, the smallest detectable change is 0.3 mV (300 μV) as shown in the above equation. This means that the temperature in the oven would have to change 7.5 °C,

$$(300 \ \mu V)/(40 \ \mu V/°C){=}7.5°C$$

before the DAQ board would be able to detect any change in temperature. However, if the smallest input range of ±200 mV of the NI 6221 DAQ board is selected, the code width is 6.1 μV.

$$V_{cw} = \frac{Range}{2^{resolution}} = \frac{400 \ mV}{2^{16}} = 6.1 \ \mu V$$

The DAQ board could detect a significantly smaller temperature change of only 0.15 °C,

$$(6.1 \ \mu V)/(40 \ \mu V/°C){=}0.15°C,$$

a great improvement in signal resolution over the previous example. Typically, a thermocouple is not connected directly to a DAQ board but this example was used to illustrate the need to match the anticipated limits of the analog signal to the DAQ board's input range. If the anticipated limits of the analog signal are uncertain, selecting an appropriate input range is not as simple as the previous example. Analog input voltages that exceed the input range cannot be measured and the measured value will remain at the maximum or minimum of the input range.

2.1.3   Signal Sampling Rate

In order to accurately represent the frequency content of an incoming time-varying analog signal, the sampling rate must be sufficiently high to prevent a problem called aliasing. The sampling rate is the rate at which the DAQ device performs a digital conversion of the analog signal. Aliasing occurs when the sampling rate is too slow, which can yield an apparent waveform with a lower frequency than the incoming analog signal. An example of aliasing is shown in Fig. 2.1.1. In the top plot, the incoming time-varying analog signal is sampled at a sufficiently high rate such that the frequency content of the original signal is reproduced when the digitized waveform is displayed. The sampling rate is not high enough in the bottom plot and the digitized data would display a waveform with a lower frequency than the incoming time-varying analog signal. It is important to note that aliasing does not imply errors in the sampled data but rather the time dependence of the wave inferred from the sampled data.

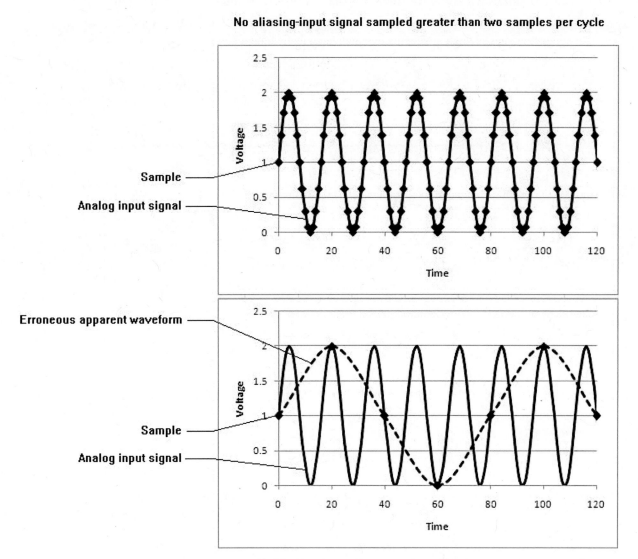

Figure 2.1.1   Illustration to show the effect of aliasing resulting from improper sampling rate

To avoid aliasing errors, the analog signal should be sampled at a frequency at least twice as large as the highest frequency component of the incoming signal. In other words, you should take at least two samples every "cycle." From a practical viewpoint, the sampling rate would likely have to be an order of magnitude higher to adequately capture the time history, as compared to just the frequency content, of the signal.

There is a challenge to selecting an appropriate sampling rate for an incoming analog signal with unknown frequency content. One option to avoid aliasing of an unknown incoming signal is to choose an arbitrary sampling rate and then use an analog low-pass filter to attenuate any incoming signal frequencies at or above the Nyquist frequency, which is one-half of the pre-determined sampling rate. Of course, a low-pass filter may remove unknown signal frequencies that would be of interest. A conservative option is to select a sampling rate well beyond what would be expected from the phenomenon, even up to the maximum supported by the DAQ hardware. After the first test is recorded and the frequency content of the physical phenomenon is now known, the sampling rate may adjusted relative to the newly determined signal frequency if the size of the data file is unmanageable.

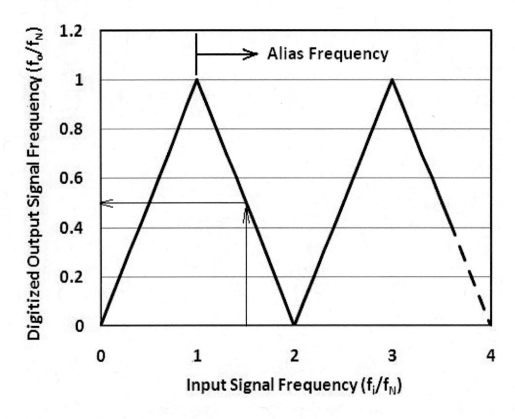

Figure 2.1.2   Relationship between the input signal frequency and the digitized output signal frequency

A phenomenon known as folding occurs when the sampling rate is fixed and the frequency of the input signal exceeds the Nyquist frequency, which is defined as one-half of the sampling rate. Input signal frequencies greater than the Nyquist frequency will appear as alias frequencies in the digitized signal. The alias frequencies will always be lower than the Nyquist frequency but will follow the folding pattern shown in Fig. 2.1.2. For input frequencies just above the Nyquist frequency, the alias frequency decreases until the input signal frequency equals twice the Nyquist frequency, which is also the sampling rate. Because the sampling rate is the same as the frequency of the input signal, only one sample is taken per cycle and at the same time in the cycle. Since the digitized data all have the same value, the digitized signal appears to be steady (0 Hz). The alias frequency of the digitized signal can be determined from the folding diagram as shown by the arrows in Fig. 2.1.2 for an example input frequency of 1.5 times the Nyquist frequency. Of course, the frequency of the input signal is correctly represented by the frequency of the digitized signal below the Nyquist frequency.

2.2. Finite Analog Input Using Buffers, Hardware Timing, and Triggering

This section will be useful if your data measurement needs require precise timing of the measurement, high-speed data measurement, or the need to synchronize the data measurement with an external event. For example, suppose you were interested in measuring the pressure in a combustion event, such as a deflagration or a detonation. Depending on the mode of combustion, the speed of the flame front can vary from an order of magnitude of meters per second to kilometers per second. High-speed data measurement is required to accurately capture the pressure history. Furthermore, since the sampling rate will be very large, copious quantities of data must be taken unless the data measurement is synchronized with the combustion event. In this case, a digital signal that activates a relay to energize an igniter can also be used to trigger the data measurement.

2.2.1 Hardware Timing

The analog input VI developed in Chapter 1 employs software timing and can be used to emphasize the differences between hardware and software timing. In this example VI, a single analog to digital conversion is initiated when the LabVIEW DAQ Assistant Express VI is executed. Of course, the Express VI may be called repeatedly using a For Loop or a While Loop to generate a finite set of data or a continuous stream of data as illustrated in the Chapter 1 analog input VI. Software timing relies on the use of LabVIEW timing functions, like the "Time Delay" Express VI embedded in a For Loop or While Loop. LabVIEW timing functions rely on the computer's internal clock and, therefore, to the accuracy of the clock. An advantage of software-timed data measurement is that you have point-by-point access to the data, such as analyzing or plotting, as the data is acquired. This allows you to make corrections if the measurement is not proceeding correctly. A disadvantage of software-timed data measurement is that the timing is controlled by the computer's CPU, which must also balance requests from LabVIEW with other priorities. This limits how fast samples can be taken and may lead to unequal time intervals between samples. This is typically not a problem for slow sample rates but is a problem for high-speed data measurement. Hardware-timed data measurement can overcome this problem. This section will describe how to perform buffered analog input with hardware timing and hardware (digital and analog) triggering for data acquisition.

Hardware-timed data measurement uses a digital hardware signal to control the measurement rate. The digital hardware signal can be generated by a clock on the DAQ board or through an external device. When hardware timing is employed, control of the data measurement is transferred from the computer to the DAQ board. This permits fast sampling rates and uniform time intervals between samples. The sampling rate is limited only by the maximum sampling rate the DAQ board permits. This is manufacturer and board model dependent so you will have to check your hardware specifications for your particular board's maximum sampling rate. For example, National Instrument's PCI 6221 board has a maximum sampling rate of 250,000 samples per second. Hardware timing permits precise intervals of time between data samples. The resolution of hardware timing is based on the DAQ board timer. For example, NI's PCI 6221 DAQ board contains an 80 MHz timer and this level of resolution is not an issue at the board's maximum sampling rate of 250 kS/sec.

2.2.2 Buffers

Prior to hardware-timed buffered data measurement of a finite number of samples, a buffer large enough to handle the finite set of data is set up in computer memory during channel configuration. A buffer is a fixed amount of computer memory set aside to temporarily store data during the measurement. During measurement, samples are obtained at time intervals determined by the digital hardware signal from the DAQ board. Samples are temporarily stored in the DAQ device's on-board FIFO (First In First Out) memory while blocks of data are transferred periodically from the FIFO memory to the buffer in computer memory. When the buffer in computer memory is full, control passes back to the LabVIEW software so that the data can be analyzed, plotted, or stored in permanent memory, like a hard drive or a flash drive. One potential disadvantage of buffered data measurement is that the data cannot be analyzed or plotted until all of the data is measured. This is generally not a problem for high-speed sampling rates when the total measurement time is small. However, it may be problematic for slow sampling rates with data measurement extending over long time periods.

Hardware-timed data measurement can also be non-buffered. Hardware-timed non-buffered data measurement occurs when a single sample is obtained with a digital hardware signal. A software-timed single sample is also a non-buffered measurement.

2.2.3 Triggers

Triggering allows the data acquisition to be synchronized with an external event as opposed to the analog input VI developed in Chapter 1 where data measurement begins when the DAQ Assistant Express VI is executed. Triggering is useful when you want precise control over starting or stopping data acquisition, synchronizing data acquisition with another event, or you want to retrieve acquired data that meets specified conditions.

Hardware triggering can be either digital or analog. Digital triggering occurs when a transistor-transistor-logic (TTL) signal switches from low to high or vice versa. Most DAQ boards support digital triggering. Analog triggering occurs when an analog signal level or slope has met user specified conditions. Fewer DAQ boards support analog triggering capability. For example, the NI PCI 6221 DAQ board supports digital triggering but not analog triggering. You must consult the hardware specifications of your DAQ board to see what capabilities it supports.

Hardware triggering can be external or internal. External triggering occurs when an external hardware device sends the triggering signal to the DAQ board. Internal triggering occurs when LabVIEW is programmed to output a signal, typically a digital pulse, to initiate acquisition after conditions for an analog input channel have been met. This is a viable method if the DAQ board does not support analog hardware triggering.

External devices connected to your DAQ board generate digital signals that initiate analog data acquisition. The connection is DAQ board specific but usually the external device is connected to the RSTI or PFI pins. For example, any of the PFI pins on NI's 68-pin PCI-6221 DAQ board can be used as a digital trigger. The external device creates a digital TTL signal and the data acquisition is triggered on a rising or falling edge of the signal. A rising (falling) edge occurs when the digital signal switches from a low (high) to a high (low) state. Older model DAQ boards may use the STARTTRIG*, EXTTRIG*, DTRIG, TRIG 1, and TRIG 2 pins. The pins that have an asterisk behind their name, STARTTRIG* and EXTTRIG*, accept only a falling edge signal as a trigger. You must consult your DAQ board manual to see what type of triggering is supported and the pin connections for triggering.

A DAQ board may support one or more of three different types of triggering: start, reference, and pause triggers. When the start trigger is used, the only data that is recorded is that which occurs after the trigger. The reference trigger is similar except that a fixed number of pre-trigger samples are also recorded in addition to the post-trigger samples. The reference trigger works by placing data in a buffer and looking for the trigger conditions. A trigger is ignored if the number of requested pre-trigger samples has not yet been obtained. If the buffer becomes full before the trigger condition has been met, the DAQ board overwrites the oldest data with the newest data until the trigger conditions are met. The pause trigger allows data measurement to pause while the external trigger is active and resume when it is inactive.

2.2.4 Skill-Development Problem: Finite Analog Input Example VI using Hardware Timing, Buffering, and Triggering

This section describes how to write a relatively simple analog input VI to introduce basic data acquisition concepts and develop your skills. The VI can be used to record a finite set of analog measurements from multiple channels. This section is structured so that you can develop the VI as you read the material. The idea is that it will be easier to learn and retain key data acquisition concepts by applying the concepts as you learn them. This VI is most appropriate when you acquire data at relatively high sampling rates and the length of time to record data is reasonably known. For example, this VI would be appropriate to measure strain sensed by strain gages affixed to structural members in an automotive test crash.

This VI employs buffered data measurements with hardware timing and triggering. Read Sections 2.2.1-2.2.3 to learn about these data acquisition concepts. The material discussed in this section assumes that LabVIEW Professional Version or Student Version software, NI-DAQ software, and a data acquisition board have been installed on your computer.

Equipment

1. Analog input sources comprising a sensor, function generator, power supply, or even a battery if other equipment is unavailable.
2. Digital trigger source (optional).

Goals

1. Become acquainted with some basic analog input data acquisition concepts on hardware timing, buffering, and triggering using LabVIEW's configuration approach.
2. Develop the multi-channel buffered hardware-timed analog input VI shown in Figs. 2.2.1 and 2.2.2, which can acquire a finite set of measurements using a digital trigger.

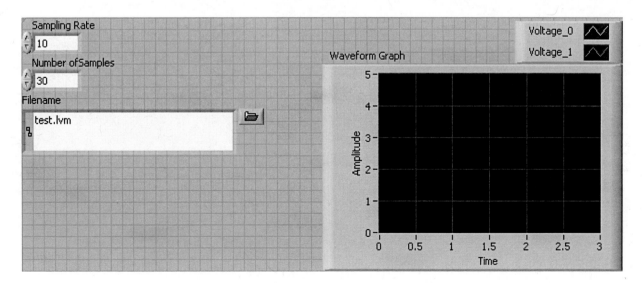

Figure 2.2.1   Front panel of the example finite analog input VI with hardware timing, buffering, and triggering

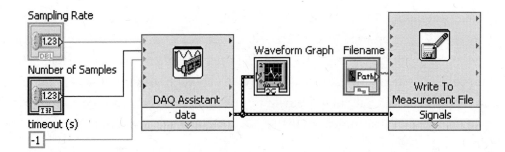

Figure 2.2.2   Block diagram of the example finite analog input VI with hardware
timing, buffering, and triggering

Developing the VI

1. Beginning at the Start Menu, select **All Programs>>National
    Instruments>>LabVIEW 2012>>LabVIEW 2012**

Note: Read Section 1.3 if you need background on the LabVIEW environment.

2. Select "Blank VI" to open a new file

Tip: Use the keyboard shortcut <Ctrl T> to tile the windows with the front panel on top and the
block diagram beneath it.

3. From the Functions palette, select **Express>>Input>>DAQ Assistant** and drag it in
    the block diagram.

4. Click on "Acquire Signals", "Analog Input", and "Voltage" in the "Create New …"
    window as shown in Fig. 2.2.3.

5. Click on the hardware device to show the channels that are available to measure
    analog input signals on your DAQ board.

6. Select analog input channel 0 ("ai0") and channel 1 ("ai1"), or two other appropriate
    channels, as shown in Fig. 2.2.3 by depressing the control key, <Ctrl>, on the
    keyboard while selecting the channels with the left mouse key.

7. Select "Finish" and the DAQ Assistant window appears.

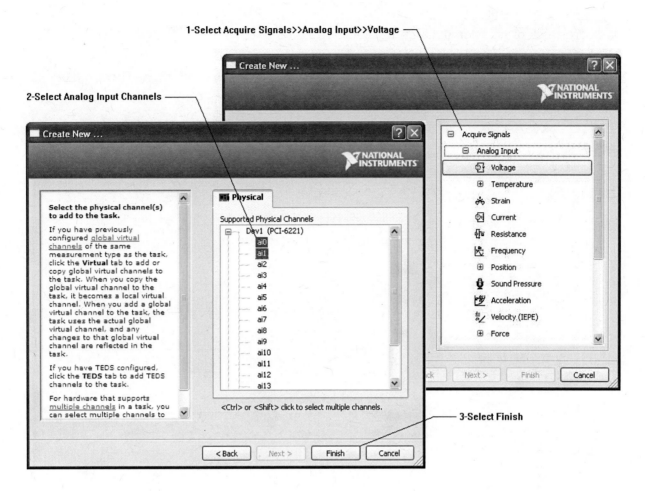

Figure 2.2.3   Steps to use the DAQ Assistant to select the channels for the finite analog input
VI

8. Select values of 30 samples to read at a rate of 10 samples per second (3 seconds of
data measurement time) as shown in Fig. 2.2.4.

Note: The default settings that appear in the DAQ Assistant window are generally acceptable
except that you must ensure that the frequency of the analog input signal will be sufficiently low
to avoid aliasing or else you must change the sampling rate. Read Section 2.1.3 regarding
aliasing. Also note that a differential measurement system has been selected. Read Section 2.1.1
regarding a discussion of different measurement systems.

9. Select "N Samples" for the acquisition mode, if not already selected.

Note: Software timing is employed when "1 Sample (On Demand)" is selected as the
acquisition mode. A sample is taken when the DAQ Assistant Express VI is executed and the
timing between samples is controlled by a LabVIEW timing function and the clock controlling
the computer's CPU. The other three acquisition modes rely on hardware timing using the DAQ

on-board clock or an external hardware clock. The acquisition mode "1 Sample (HW timed)" is non-buffered since it only acquires one sample. The acquisition mode "N Samples" is used in the current VI because it temporarily stores a finite set of samples in a buffer. The acquisition mode "Continuous Samples" continuously reads old samples from buffer while it is storing new samples.

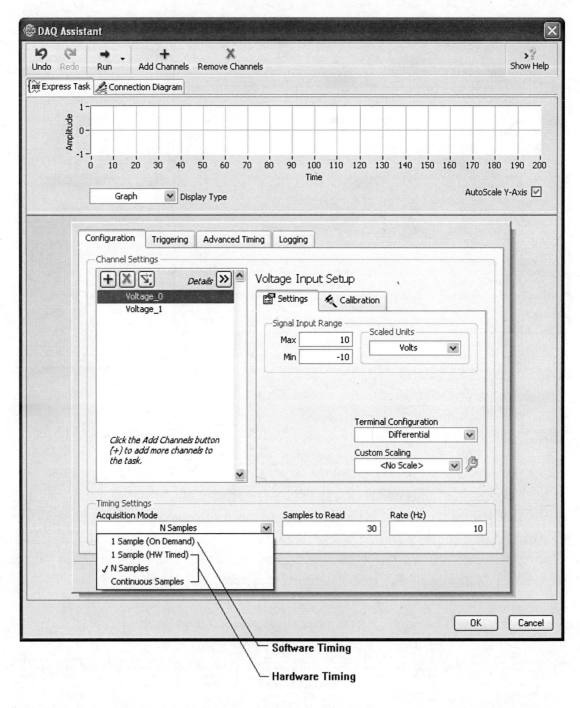

Figure 2.2.4   Configuration for both channels for the finite analog input VI using the DAQ Assistant

10. Select the "Triggering" tab and the triggering values shown in Fig. 2.2.5.

Note: The example VI may be developed without the use of a trigger. If you do not want to use the optional trigger, select "<None>" under the trigger options and skip Steps 10 and 11.

11. Select a channel for the trigger source that is available for your DAQ board if Programmable Function Interface (PFI) channels are not available.

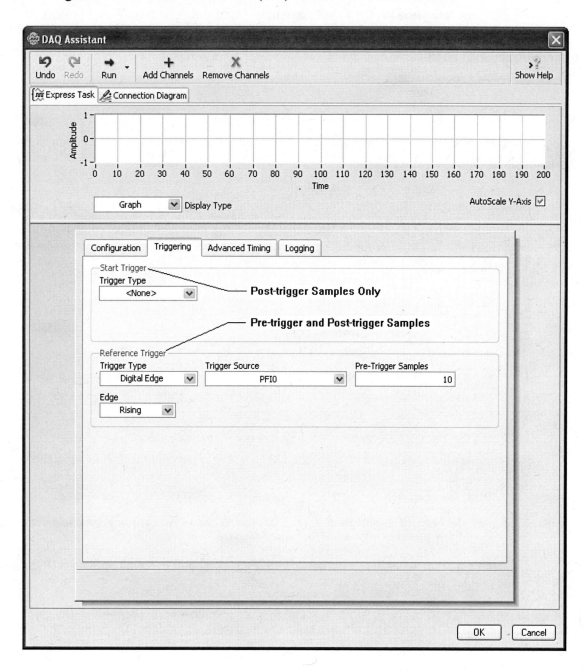

Figure 2.2.5   Trigger settings for the finite analog input VI using the DAQ Assistant

12. Select OK and the DAQ Assistant will generate the appropriate code.

13. Create controls for the "rate" and "number of samples" input terminals and a constant for the "timeout (s)" input terminal to the DAQ Assistant as shown in Fig. 2.2.2. See the tip below for help creating controls.

Tip: To identify the terminals on the DAQ Assistant, place the "Connect Wire" (solder spool) cursor over the terminal, right-click on the terminal of interest, and Create>>Control. The terminals may also be identified in the "Content Help" window that can be retrieved from the "Help" pull-down menu.

Note: Creating controls for the "rate" and "number of samples" inputs allows the user the convenience of changing these values through the front panel without having to open the DAQ Assistant each time the values change.

Note: Data measurements must begin before the default timeout limit of 10 seconds elapses. Otherwise an error will occur. If the trigger will not occur before the default timeout limit, increase the timeout limit value or enter a value of -1, which means the data measurement VI will wait indefinitely.

14. From the Controls palette, select **Express>>Graph Indicators>>Waveform Graph** and drag the icon to the front panel.

15. In the block diagram, place the graph to the right of the DAQ Assistant and wire the graph to the "data" output terminal of the DAQ Assistant as shown in Fig. 2.2.2.

16. From the Functions palette, select **Express>>Output>>Write to Measurement File** and drag the icon to the right of the DAQ Assistant and graph terminal in the block diagram.

17. Select the options as shown in Fig. 2.2.6 in the configuration window and press OK.

18. Create a control for the "Filename" input terminal and enter an appropriate filename, if the default is not acceptable.

Note: The "Filename" control will allow a user to enter a filename from the front panel without having to open the "Write to Measurement File" configuration window every time a different filename is desired.

19. Wire the "data" output of the DAQ Assistant to the "Signals" input of the Write to Measurement File Express VI.

Congratulations! You have completed a VI to measure a finite set of multi-channel data using hardware timing and triggering. Be sure to save your program using one of the save options on the "File" pull-down menu.

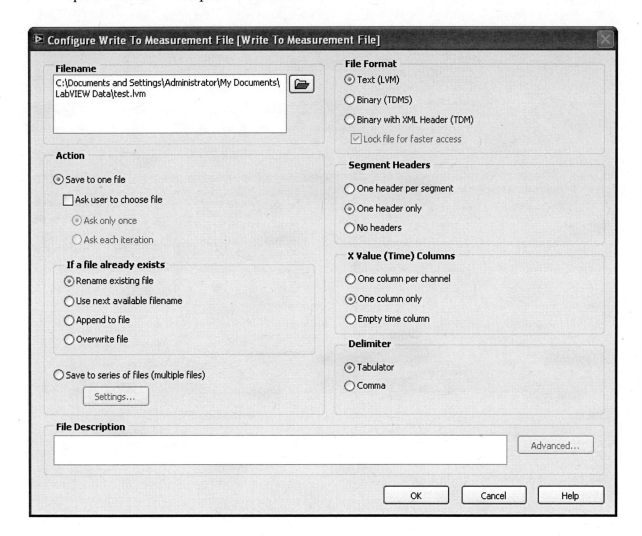

Figure 2.2.6   Write to Measurement File Express VI settings for the finite analog input VI

Testing the VI

Attach voltage sources for the two channels, such as a sensor, function generator, a power supply, or even a battery if other equipment is not available, to the terminal connector block. The voltage difference between the two leads, the positive and negative leads, will be measured since the channels were configured for a differential measurement system.

Use the "Connection Diagram" in the DAQ Assistant to determine the terminals assigned to the designated analog input channels. For a DAQ board with 16 analog input channels configured for a differential measurement system, the positive leads connect with the first eight channels, <ai0...ai7>, and the negative leads with the next eight channels, <ai8...ai15>, respectively. More specifically, if you selected "ai0" as one of your input channels in the DAQ Assistant, the positive lead connects to "ai0" and the negative lead connects to "ai8." You do not explicitly specify "ai8" as one of the input channels during channel configuration as LabVIEW automatically expects that "ai8" is paired with "ai0" for differential measurement.

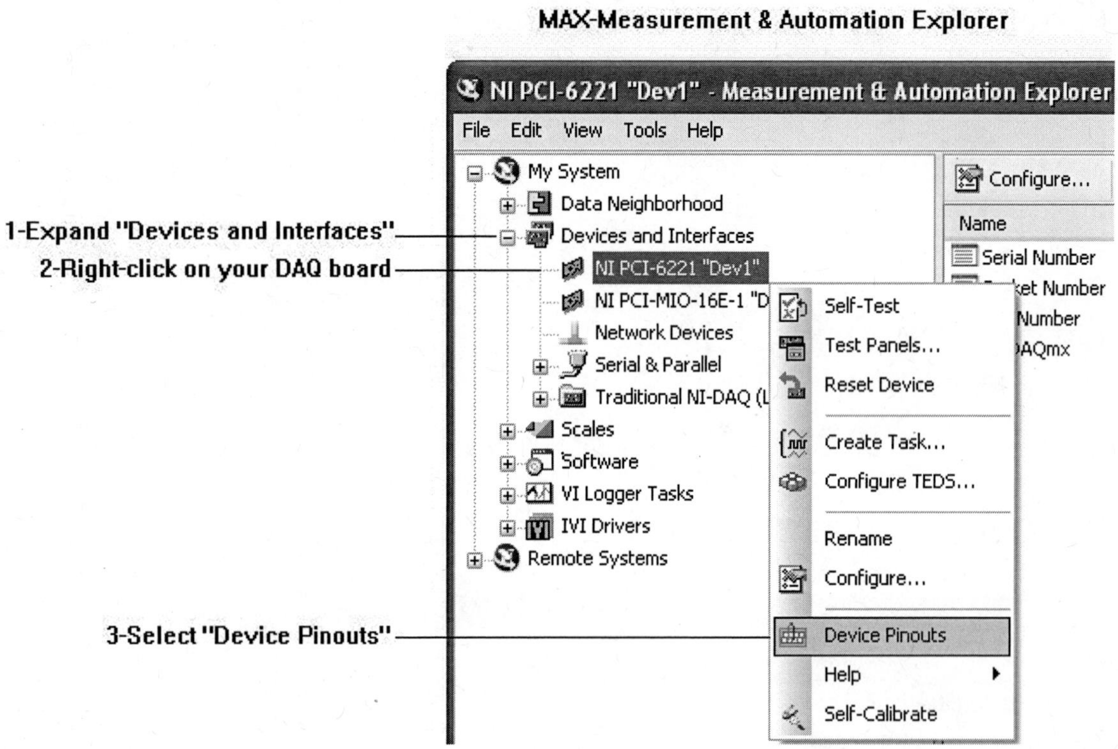

Figure 2.2.7   Using the Measurement &Automation utility to identify pin connections for the input channels and the trigger channel

If you are using the optional trigger, attach a digital trigger to the channel specified as the trigger source. If you do not have a digital trigger, you may use a lead from a 5 V pin on the terminal connector block and manually apply the 5 V lead wire to the trigger pin, PFI 0, to trigger data measurement. Unfortunately, the "Connection Diagram" tab does not show the trigger source connection. However, a device pinout diagram for your DAQ board can be found using the Measurement & Automation Explorer (MAX) software program, a National Instruments utility to manage hardware. For the purposes of determining the pin connection for the trigger, select "Measurement & Automation

Explorer…" from the "Tools" pull-down menu. A window will appear like the one that is partially shown in Figure 2.2.7. Expand "Devices and Interfaces", right click on the DAQ board that was selected when you configured your channels using the DAQ Assistant, and select "Device Pinouts." Device Pinouts may also be selected in the toolbar at the top of the MAX window. The pinout sheet appears in a new window and the pin number for PFI 0 (or the channel you selected for the trigger source) can be identified. For example, PFI 0 is pin 11 on the NI PCI/PXI 6221 DAQ board. After the leads for the analog input signals and the trigger have been connected, the VI is ready to run.

Click on the Run button in the toolbar to begin execution of the VI and apply the trigger before the timeout limit for the data measurement VI. An error message, like the one shown in Fig. 2.2.8, will be displayed if the trigger is not activated before the timeout limit.

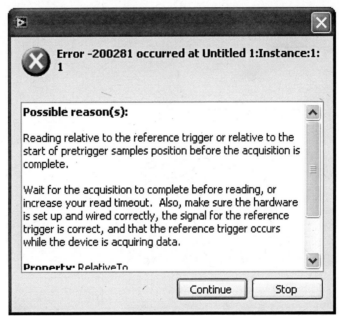

Figure 2.2.8   Error message that is displayed if the trigger is not activated within the timeout limit

Once the samples have been taken, a graph of the data will be displayed and the data will be written to the default file, "My Documents\LabVIEW Data\test.lvm," or other file name that you specified. The measurement file may be opened with a spreadsheet or other suitable application software.

Discussion

It is interesting to make a comparison between two VIs that perform the same function but employ hardware timing versus software timing. The block diagrams of the VIs shown in Fig. 2.2.9 both measure a finite set of analog input data. The VI in Fig. 2.2.9(a) is the VI developed in this section and employs hardware timing while the VI in Fig. 2.2.9(b) was developed as part of Section 1.4 and employs software timing. They share the same Express VIs to measure and record data (albeit with different configurations) and graph the data after the set is complete. The main difference occurs due to the mode of timing.

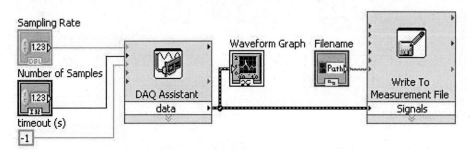

(A) Finite analog input with hardware timing

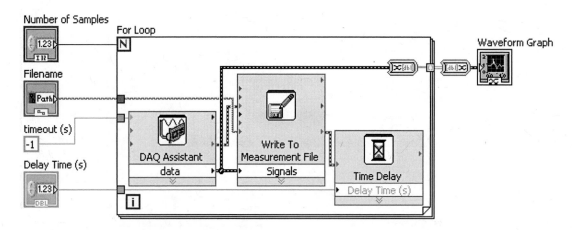

(B) Finite analog input with software timing

Figure 2.2.9   Comparison between hardware and software timing used in two VIs that perform the same function of measuring a finite set of analog data

The initiation of a measurement and the time interval between measurements is controlled by software commands with software timing. Since only a single measurement is taken when the DAQ Assistant Express VI is executed with software timing, the DAQ Assistant must be placed inside a For Loop to measure a finite set of samples. Hardware timing permits a finite set of samples to be measured when the DAQ Assistant is executed with one call so a For Loop is not required. With software timing, the time interval between samples is also determined by the execution of software commands, which are controlled by the CPU clock as it runs the LabVIEW VI. The Time Delay

Express VI is necessary to sample at a desired rate and to keep the sub diagram within the For Loop from executing as fast as the CPU would permit. On the other hand, hardware timing is controlled by the clock on the DAQ board and additional software commands, like the Time Delay Express VI, are not necessary to control the time interval between samples. In both cases, measurement is initiated when the DAQ Assistant is executed, unless triggering is employed with hardware timing.

The differences between hardware and software timing manifest themselves in the time intervals between samples. A test measurement of 30 samples with a specified time interval of 0.1 s was taken using both VIs shown in Fig. 2.2.9. The VI with hardware timing measured 30 samples in 2.90000 s (the first sample begins at 0.0 s) with 0.10000 s between samples. The VI with software timing measured 30 samples in 3.140625 s with the time interval between samples ranging from 0.09375 s to 0.15625 s. Results will vary between computers and with different computer usage during measurement, such as graphic-intensive tasks like moving a window.

2.3 Continuous Analog Input using Hardware Timing, Circular Buffers, and Triggers

This section will be useful if buffered data acquisition is required for precise timing between sample intervals but the total time of the event is uncertain so that you cannot confidently estimate the number of samples to measure using the finite analog input technique described in Section 2.2. For example, suppose you are interested in measuring the pressure at which a tank ruptures using a pressure gauge. You are also interested in measuring the strain in different locations of the tank using strain gages to look at the tank failure mode and to provide data to assess a finite element code. The process leading to failure will be slow as the tank is pressurized but the failure event will be rapid, requiring precise and small time intervals between samples. The use of circular buffers with continuous analog input is a potential data measurement solution since you manually stop the data measurement after the event is completed.

Continuous analog input using a circular buffer may also be a data measurement solution if you need precise time intervals between samples but also need access to the data before the measurement would be complete using the simple buffer described in Section 2.2. For example, if you needed to take meteorological data over a 24 hour period with precise time intervals, you would not have access to the data before the 24 hour period was complete using the finite analog input technique described in Section 2.2. Continuous analog input using a circular buffer allows you to access blocks of data as it is taken so that you can analyze it or view it as it is measured. Of course, if you do not need precise control over the sample intervals, you may use the continuous analog input technique using software timing described in Section 1.4. This may be an acceptable data measurement solution, especially for low-speed sampling rates.

A trigger may also be used to synchronize the data measurement with an event. However, unlike finite analog input using simple buffers, which can use triggers for both pre-trigger and post-trigger data, continuous analog input using circular buffers can only use triggers for post-trigger data. More information on triggering, as well as hardware timing, can be found in Section 2.2.

2.3.1 Circular Buffer

A circular buffer is a fixed amount of computer memory set aside to temporarily have data written to it and blocks of data read from it, which permits continuous analog measurement. A circular buffer is similar to the simple buffer described in Section 2.2.2, except for how data is written to it and read from it.

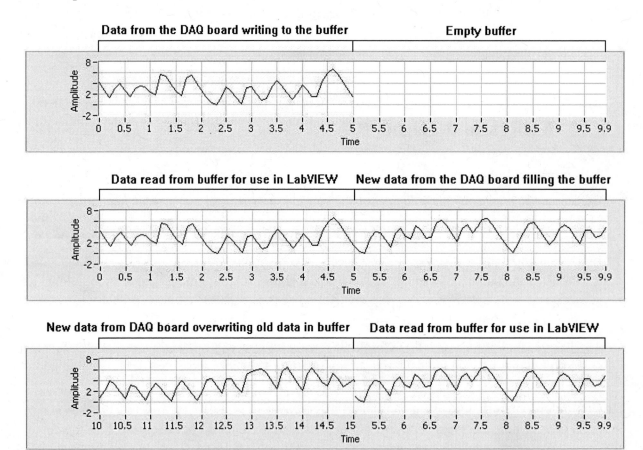

Figure 2.3.1   Example to show how a circular buffer works with continuous buffered analog input

Fig. 2.3.1 shows how a circular buffer works. The size of the buffer is fixed when the data channel is configured. Data from the DAQ board is written to the buffer just like the simple buffer. When the buffer is full, new data from the DAQ board overwrites the oldest data in the buffer. As data is written to the buffer, blocks of data are read from it, always reading the oldest data. Ideally, data would be written into the buffer as fast as data is read from it.

There are two situations that may occur when the rates of writing data into the buffer and reading data from the buffer do not match. An error may occur when data is written into the buffer faster than it can be read from it. Unread data in the buffer may be overwritten by new data from the DAQ board and the data is lost. This problem may be resolved by increasing the buffer size, which allows more time to write data, or by decreasing the sampling rate. The other situation occurs when data is read from the buffer faster than it is written into it. Blocks of data are retrieved from the buffer and LabVIEW may have to wait for enough data from the DAQ board to be written to fill a block of data. No error will occur in this situation but LabVIEW will be unavailable to perform other LabVIEW tasks until enough data has been written.

2.3.2   Skill-Development Problem: Continuous Analog Input Example VI using Hardware Timing, Circular Buffering, and Triggering

This section describes how to write a relatively simple analog input VI to introduce basic data acquisition concepts and develop your skills. The VI can be used to record analog measurements continuously from multiple channels until the user stops the acquisition. This section is structured so that you can develop the VI as you read the material. The idea is that it will be easier to learn and retain key data acquisition concepts by applying the concepts as you learn them. This VI is most appropriate when you acquire data at relatively high sampling rates and the length of time to record data is unknown. For example, this VI would be appropriate to measure strain sensed by strain gages affixed to a structural member in fatigue test.

This VI employs data measurements with hardware timing, circular buffering, and triggering. Read Sections 2.2.1, 2.2.3, and 2.3.1 to learn about these data acquisition concepts. The material discussed in this section assumes that LabVIEW Professional Version or Student Version software, NI-DAQ software, and a data acquisition board have been installed on your computer.

Equipment

1. Analog input sources comprising a sensor, function generator, power supply, or even a battery if other equipment is unavailable.
2. Digital trigger source (optional).

Goals

1. Become acquainted with some basic analog input data acquisition concepts on hardware timing, circular buffering, and triggering using LabVIEW's configuration approach.

2. Develop the multi-channel hardware-timed analog input VI shown in Figs. 2.3.2 and 2.3.3, which can initiate acquisition by a digital trigger and acquire measurements continuously using a circular buffer until stopped by the user.

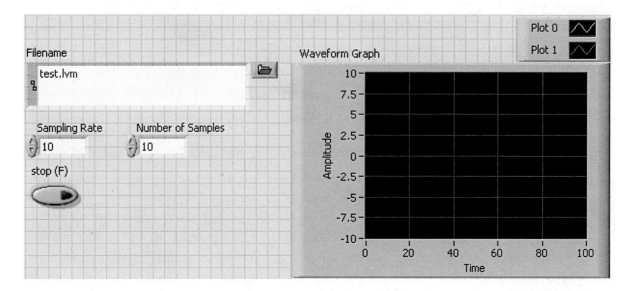

Figure 2.3.2   Front panel of the continuous analog input example VI with hardware timing, circular buffering, and triggering

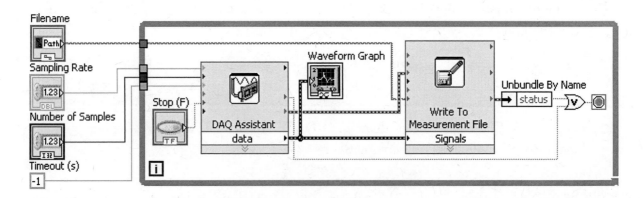

Figure 2.3.3   Block diagram of the continuous analog input example VI with hardware timing, circular buffering, and triggering

Developing the VI

1. Beginning at the Start Menu, select **All Programs>>National Instruments>>LabVIEW 2012>>LabVIEW 2012**

Note: Read Section 1.3 if you need background on the LabVIEW environment.

2. Select "Blank VI" to open a new file

Tip: Use the keyboard shortcut <Ctrl T> to tile the windows with the front panel on top and the block diagram beneath it.

3. From the Functions palette, select **Express>>Input>>DAQ Assistant** and drag it in the block diagram.

4. Click on "Acquire Signals", "Analog Input", and "Voltage" in the "Create New…" window as shown in Fig. 2.3.4.

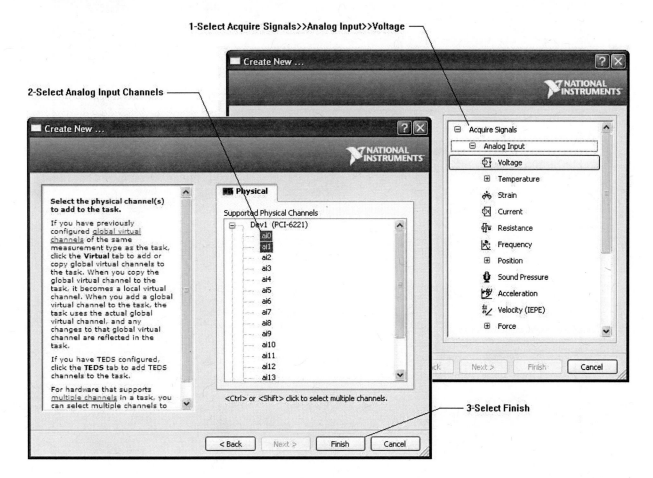

Figure 2.3.4   Steps to use the DAQ Assistant to select the channels for the continuous analog input VI

5. Click on the hardware device to show the channels that are available to measure analog input signals on your DAQ board.

6. Select analog input channel 0 ("ai0") and channel 1 ("ai1"), or two other appropriate channels, as shown in Fig. 2.3.4 by depressing the control key, <Ctrl>, on the keyboard while selecting the channels with the left mouse key.

7. Select "Finish" and the DAQ Assistant window appears.

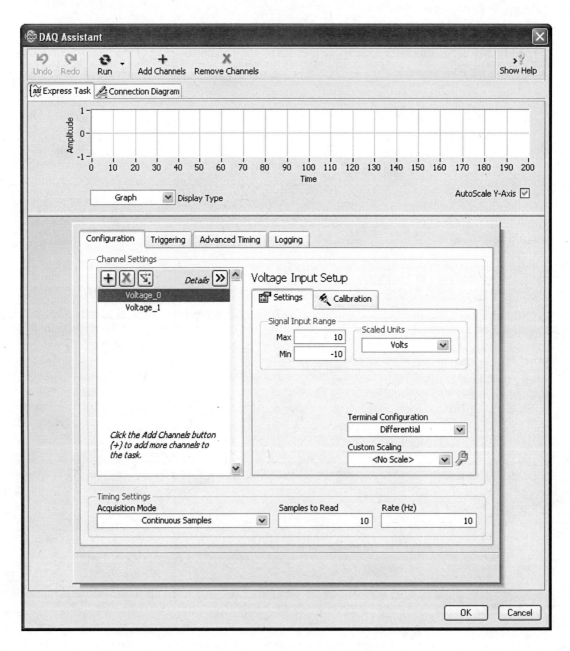

Figure 2.3.5   Configuration for both channels for the continuous analog input VI using
the DAQ Assistant

8. Select values of 10 samples to read at a rate of 10 samples per second (1 second of
data measurement time) as shown in Fig. 2.3.5.

Note: The default settings that appear in the DAQ Assistant window are generally acceptable
except that you must ensure that the frequency of the analog input signal will be sufficiently low
to avoid aliasing or else you must change the sampling rate. Read Section 2.1.3 regarding
aliasing. Also note that a differential measurement system has been selected. Read Section 2.1.1
regarding a discussion of different measurement systems.

9. Select "Continuous Samples" for the acquisition mode.

Note: The acquisition mode "Continuous Samples" continuously reads and writes samples from
a circular buffer. See Section 2.3.1 for information on circular buffers.

10. Select the "Triggering" tab and the triggering values shown in Fig. 2.3.6

Note: The example VI may be developed without the use of a trigger. If you do not want to use
the optional trigger, select "<None>" under the trigger options and skip Steps 10 and 11.

11. Select a channel for the trigger source that is available for your DAQ board if
Programmable Function Interface (PFI) channels are not available.

12. Select OK and the DAQ Assistant will generate the appropriate code. Select "No" in
the "Confirm Auto Loop Creation" window when asked to place the DAQ Assistant
in a loop. This will be done at a later time.

13. Create controls for the "rate," "number of samples," and "Stop (F)" input terminals
and a constant for the "timeout (s)" input terminal to the DAQ Assistant as shown in
Fig. 2.3.3.

Note: Creating controls for the "rate" and "number of samples" inputs allows the user the
convenience of changing these values through the front panel without having to open the DAQ
Assistant each time the values change.

Note: Data measurements must begin before the default timeout limit of 10 seconds elapses.
Otherwise an error will occur. If the trigger will not occur before the default timeout limit,

increase the timeout limit value or enter a value of -1, which means the data measurement VI will wait indefinitely.

14. Move the "rate" and "number of samples" controls and the "timeout (s)" constant sufficiently to the left of the DAQ Assistant to lie outside of a While Loop that will be added later, as shown in Fig 2.3.3.

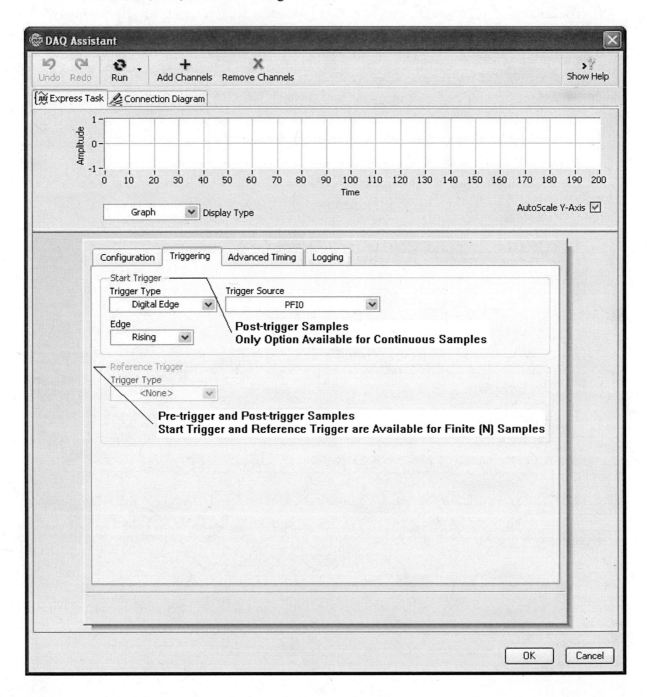

Figure 2.3.6   Trigger settings for the continuous analog input VI using the DAQ Assistant

15. From the Controls palette, select **Express>>Graph Indicators>>Waveform Graph** and drag the icon to the front panel.

16. In the block diagram, place the graph terminal to the right of the DAQ Assistant and wire it to the "data" output terminal of the DAQ Assistant as shown in Fig. 2.3.3.

17. From the Functions palette, select **Express>>Output>>Write to Measurement File** and drag the icon to the right of the DAQ Assistant and graph icon in the block diagram.

18. Select the options as shown in Fig. 2.3.7 in the configuration window and press OK.

19. Create a control for the "Filename" input terminal and enter an appropriate filename, if the default is not acceptable.

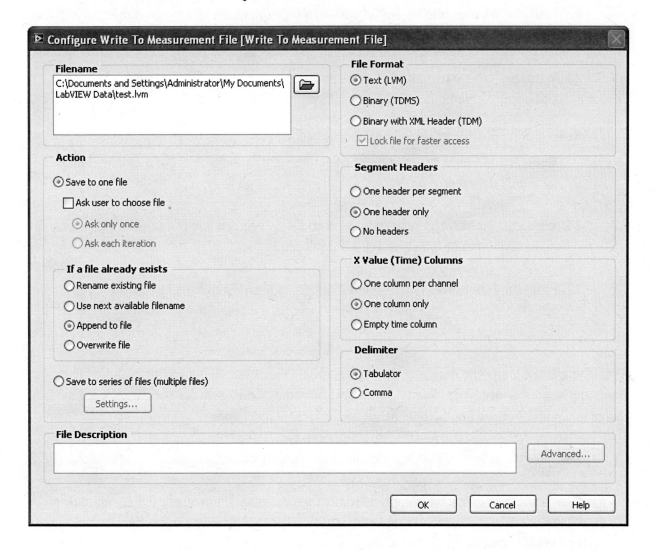

Figure 2.3.7   Write to Measurement File Express VI settings for the continuous analog input VI

Note: The "Filename" control will allow a user to enter a filename from the front panel without having to open the "Write to Measurement File" configuration window every time a different filename is desired.

20. Move the "Filename" control sufficiently to the left of the DAQ Assistant to lie outside of a While Loop that will be added later as shown in Fig 2.3.3.

21. Wire the "data" output of the DAQ Assistant to the "Signals" input of the Write to Measurement File Express VI

22. Wire the "error out" output of the DAQ Assistant to the "error in (no error)" input of the Write to Measurement File Express VI.

23. From the Functions palette, select **Programming>>Cluster, Class, & Variant>>Unbundle by Name** and drag the icon in the block diagram to the right of the Write to Measurement File Express VI.

24. Wire the "error out" output of the Write to Measurement File Express VI to the Unbundle by Name function and observe that "status" appears.

25. From the Functions palette, select **Express>>Arithmetic & Comparison>>Express Boolean>>Or** and drag the function to the right of the Unbundle by Name function in the block diagram.

26. Wire the Unbundle by Name function and the "stopped" output of the DAQ Assistant to the two input terminals of the Or function.

27. From the Functions palette, select **Programming>>Structures>>While Loop** and drag the While Loop around all objects except the controls and constant at the left of the diagram.

Tip: If you make a mistake dragging the While Loop, you can undo the creation of the While Loop and start over using the "Undo" command from the "Edit" pull-down menu. You may also resize the While Loop using the blue handles if you need more room.

28. Wire the output of the Or function to the conditional terminal.

Congratulations! You have completed a VI to continuously measure data from multiple channels using hardware timing and triggering. Be sure to save your program using one of the save options on the "File" pull-down menu.

Testing the VI

Attach voltage sources for the two channels, such as a sensor, function generator, a power supply, or even a battery if other equipment is not available, to the terminal connector block. The voltage difference between the two leads, the positive and negative leads, will be measured since the channels were configured for a differential measurement system. Use the "Connection Diagram" in the DAQ Assistant to determine the terminals assigned to the designated analog input channels. For a DAQ board with 16 analog input channels configured for a differential measurement system, the positive leads connect with the first eight channels, <ai0…ai7>, and the negative leads with the next eight channels, <ai8…ai15>, respectively. More specifically, if you selected "ai0" as one of your input channels in the DAQ Assistant, the positive lead connects to "ai0" and the negative lead connects to "ai8."

If you are using the optional trigger, attach a digital trigger to the channel specified as the trigger source. If you do not have a digital trigger, you may use a lead from a 5 V pin on the terminal connector block and manually apply the 5 V lead wire to the trigger pin, PFI 0, to trigger data measurement. Unfortunately, the "Connection Diagram" tab does not show the trigger source connection. However, a device pinout diagram for your DAQ board can be found using the Measurement & Automation Explorer (MAX) software program, a National Instruments utility to manage hardware. For the purposes of determining the pin connection for the trigger, select "Measurement & Automation Explorer…" from the "Tools" pull-down menu. A window will appear like the one that is partially shown in Figure 2.3.8. Expand "Devices and Interfaces", right click on the DAQ board that was selected when you configured your channels using the DAQ Assistant, and select "Device Pinouts." Device Pinouts may also be selected in the toolbar at the top of the MAX window. The pinout sheet appears in a new window and the pin number for PFI 0 (or the channel you selected for the trigger source) can be identified. For example, PFI 0 is pin 11 on the NI PCI/PXI 6221 DAQ board. After the leads for the analog input signals and the trigger have been connected, the VI is ready to run.

Click on the Run button in the toolbar to begin execution of the VI and apply the trigger before the timeout limit for the data measurement VI. An error message, like the one shown in Fig. 2.3.9, will be displayed if the trigger is not activated before the timeout limit.

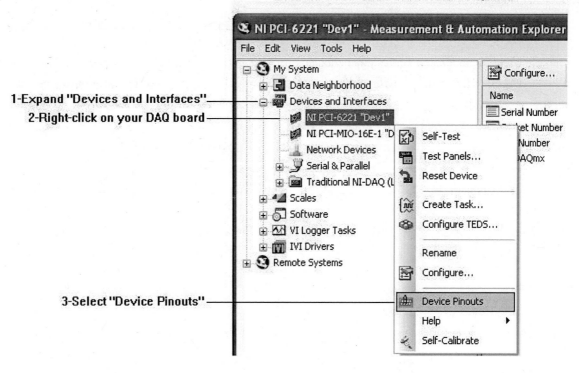

Figure 2.3.8   Using the Measurement &Automation utility to identify pin connections for the input channels and the trigger channel

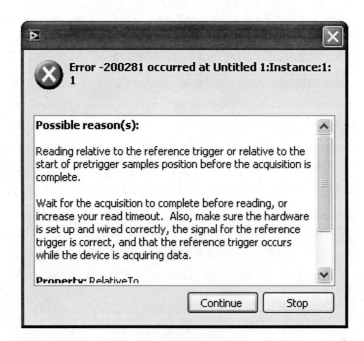

Figure 2.3.9   Error message that is displayed if the trigger is not activated within the timeout limit

Within each iteration of the While Loop, the VI measures a block of data equal to the number of "Samples to Read" specified in the DAQ Assistant, overwrites the old data in the graph and displays the new samples, and appends the samples to the default measurement file, "My Documents\LabVIEW Data\test.lvm," or other file name that you specified. The measurement file may be opened with a spreadsheet or other suitable application software. The VI will measure data continuously until the user selects the stop control in the front panel.

Your application may dictate a higher sampling rate. However, caution must be exercised to avoid overwriting unread samples in the circular buffer. If you increase the sampling rate and the VI will not run, increasing the number of samples can help avoid overwriting data in the circular buffer.

Discussion

It is interesting to make a comparison between two VIs that perform the same function but employ hardware timing versus software timing. The block diagrams of the VIs shown in Fig. 2.3.10 both continuously measure analog input data. The VI in Fig. 2.3.10(a) is the VI developed in this section and employs hardware timing while the VI in Fig. 2.3.10(b) was developed as part of Section 1.4 and employs software timing.

Both VIs contain the same Express VIs to measure and record data within a While Loop to allow for continuous data measurement and display the data as it is measured but have different Express VI configurations to accommodate different modes of timing. With hardware timing, the DAQ Assistant is configured to measure a finite set of samples, which requires a graph to display the blocks of data during each iteration of the While Loop. A new block of data is displayed in the graph every iteration. Likewise, a new block of data is appended to the measurement file every iteration after the data is recorded in the first iteration of the While Loop. No LabVIEW timing functions are required since the time interval between samples is controlled by the clock on the DAQ board. When the DAQ Assistant is configured for software-timed data measurement, a single sample is measured, which requires a chart, as opposed to a graph, to display and update the data in strip chart mode. The oldest sample is removed as the newest sample is added to the chart and displayed. One sample is appended to the measurement file each iteration of the While Loop. With software timing, the time interval between samples is determined by the execution of software commands, which are controlled by the CPU clock as it runs the LabVIEW VI. The Time Delay Express VI is necessary to sample at a desired rate and to keep the sub diagram within the While Loop from executing as fast as the CPU would permit.

The differences between hardware and software timing manifest themselves in the time intervals between samples. A test measurement with a specified time interval of 0.1 s was taken using both VIs shown in Fig. 2.3.10. The VI with hardware timing measured samples with 0.10000 s between samples. The VI with software timing measured samples with the time interval between samples ranging from 0.09375 s to 0.15625 s. Results will vary between computers and with different computer usage during measurement, such as graphic-intensive tasks like moving a window.

Both VIs in Fig. 2.3.10 demonstrate the use of the principle of data flow to control VI execution. With data flow, an executable element will not execute until it has received all required input. For example in Fig. 2.3.10 (b), the DAQ Assistant, Write to Measurement File Express VI, Time Delay Express VI, and the Unbundle By Name function must execute sequentially because of the error cluster wiring.

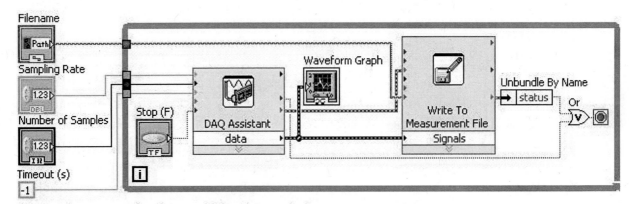

(A) Continuous analog input with hardware timing

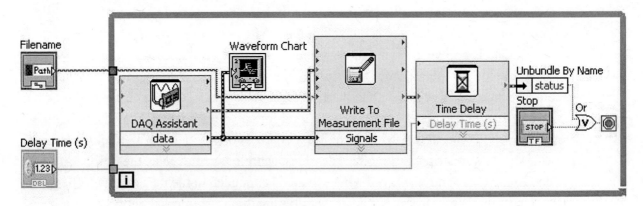

(B) Continuous analog input with software timing

Figure 2.3.10   Comparison between hardware and software timing used in two VIs that perform the same function of continuously measuring analog data

2.4 Continuous Analog Output using Software Timing

2.4.1 Introduction to Analog Output

Analog output involves digital-to-analog conversion, the process of converting a digital value specified by the computer to an analog signal at the DAQ board's terminal connector block. Analog output signal generation can be software timed (non-buffered) or hardware timed (buffered or non-buffered). Non-buffered data generates one update at a time as opposed to buffered generation in which a finite number of digital values are stored temporarily in buffered memory on the computer before updates are generated at the DAQ board. Software-timed intervals are controlled by LabVIEW software timing functions, which depend on the computer's CPU clock. Software timing can produce irregular intervals, especially if the requested time intervals are small or the CPU has large demands for resources, such as a graphics-intensive task like moving a window on the screen, while data is updated. Hardware timing means that the time interval between updates is controlled by the clock on the DAQ board. Hardware timing permits generation of data at regular intervals with precise time steps.

For example, if a waveform is desired as a buffered analog output signal, LabVIEW would first create an array of digital values to represent the waveform, perhaps with a For Loop, in the VI. The array is then written to a buffer in computer memory. One by one, according to the update rate specified by the user, each element of the array undergoes a digital-to-analog conversion in the DAQ board, which yields an analog signal at the terminal connector block that may be wired to an output device. Likewise, for non-buffered analog output, a user-supplied or LabVIEW-created digital value would then undergo a digital-to-analog conversion in the DAQ board. Once the analog signal is output on the terminal connector block, it remains at a constant value until the next update. The analog signal can be voltage and/or current, whatever is supported by the DAQ hardware.

Analog input and output concepts are analogous. The concepts discussed in Section 2.1 on signal measurement system, resolution, and sampling (update) rate apply. Likewise, the concepts of hardware timing, buffers, and triggers discussed in Section 2.2 also apply to analog output signal generation.

2.4.2 Skill-Development Problem: Non-Buffered, Software-Timed, Continuous Analog Output Example VI

This section describes how to write a relatively simple analog output VI to introduce basic data acquisition concepts and develop your skills. The example VI in this section employs non-buffered data generation and software timing and can be used to continuously generate an analog output signal from a single channel until the user stops the updates. This section is structured so that you can develop the VI as you read the material. The idea is that it will be easier to learn and retain key data acquisition concepts by applying the concepts as you learn them. This VI is most appropriate when you update at relatively low generation rates and the length of time to update is unknown. For example, this VI could be used as a low-frequency function generator. Software-timed non-buffered analog output is not recommended for high frequency waveform generation because the potential irregular time spacing between updates may not faithfully reproduce the desired waveform. A more effective way to generate a waveform, like that done with function generator hardware, is to use buffered generation described in Sections 2.5 or 2.6. However, a function generator example has been selected for the non-buffered software-timed example to make comparisons with similar example VIs using buffers and hardware timing.

Non-buffered software timed analog generation is more applicable when the output level is more important than the frequency content of the signal. An example of this would be a VI that controls an output device. The control may require input from an environmental variable, like fluid level, which is used to calculate an analog output level to a device, like a valve, that modifies the environment.

The material discussed in this section assumes that LabVIEW Professional Version or Student Version software, NI-DAQ software, and a data acquisition board have been installed on your computer.

Equipment

1. An oscilloscope to display the analog output signal or, if an oscilloscope is not available, a multimeter may be used for low frequency signals.

Goals

1. Become acquainted with some basic analog output data acquisition concepts on software timing using LabVIEW's configuration approach.

2. Develop the single channel, non-buffered, software-timed analog output VI shown in Figs. 2.4.1 and 2.4.2, which can generate updates continuously until stopped by the user.

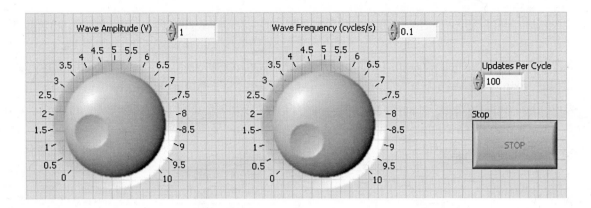

Figure 2.4.1   Front panel of the non-buffered continuous analog output example VI with software timing

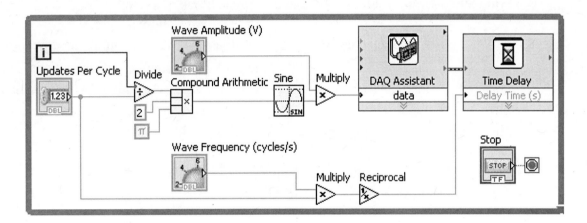

Figure 2.4.2   Block diagram of the non-buffered continuous analog output example VI with software timing

Developing the VI

1. Beginning at the Start Menu, select **All Programs>>National Instruments>>LabVIEW 2012>>LabVIEW 2012**

Note: Read Section 1.3 if you need background on the LabVIEW environment.

2. Select "Blank VI" to open a new file

Tip: Use the keyboard shortcut <Ctrl T> to tile the windows with the front panel on top and the block diagram beneath it.

Note: Sine values are created in Steps 3-14 to represent a function generator's voltage sine waves at the terminal connector block. The sine wave is divided into a number of points, called updates, which will later serve as the locations where the DAQ board generates (updates) a voltage at the terminal connector block. The more points (updates) on the sine wave, the better the resolution to enable the analog voltage signal to represent the intended sine wave. A cycle of the sine wave will be created within a While Loop one point at a time as the number of iterations goes from zero to the total number of updates per cycle. A new wave cycle is completed every time the number of iterations equals the number of updates per cycle. The sine wave is created as shown in the following expression.

$$\text{Wave Amplitude} * \sin\left(2\pi \frac{\text{Iteration Number}}{\text{Number of Updates per Cycle}}\right)$$

3. From the Functions palette, select **Express>>Arithmetic & Comparison>>Express Numeric>>Divide** and drag the function to the block diagram.

4. Create a control on the bottom input terminal of the Divide function, label it "Updates Per Cycle", and enter a value of 100 in the front panel control. The label name can be changed automatically when the label background is black, which occurs immediately after the control is created. Otherwise, you must use the "Edit Text" cursor or double-click on the label to change the label text.

5. From the Functions palette, select **Express>>Arithmetic & Comparison>>Express Numeric>>Compound Arithmetic** and drag the function to the right of the Divide function in the block diagram.

6. Resize the Compound Arithmetic function by selecting the function and dragging down on the bottom blue handle to add one more input terminal as shown in Fig. 2.4.3 or right-click over an input terminal and select "Add Input" to do the same thing.

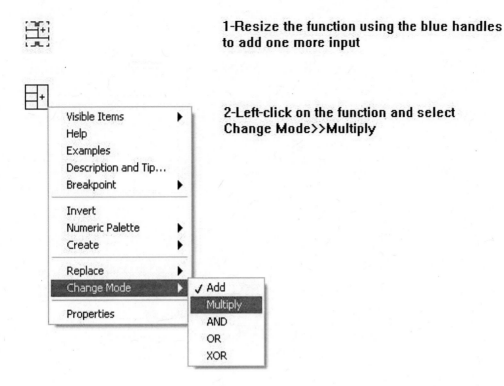

1-Resize the function using the blue handles to add one more input

2-Left-click on the function and select Change Mode>>Multiply

Figure 2.4.3   Resizing and modifying the Compound Arithmetic function for the continuous analog output example VI

7. Right-click on the function and select **Change Mode>>Multiply** as shown in Fig. 2.4.3.

8. Create a constant for the middle input terminal of the Compound Arithmetic function and assign the constant a value of two as shown in Fig. 2.4.4.

9. From the Functions palette, select **Express>>Arithmetic & Comparison>>Express Numeric>>Express Math & Scientific Constants>>Pi** and place the constant to the left of the bottom input terminal of the Compound Arithmetic function.

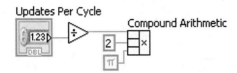

Figure 2.4.4   Wiring the Divide function and constants to the Compound Arithmetic function for the continuous analog output example VI

10. Wire the Divide function and constants as shown in Fig. 2.4.4, if the wiring did not occur automatically.

11. From the Functions palette, select **Express>>Arithmetic & Comparison>>Express Math>>Express Trigonometric Functions>>Sine** and drag the function to the right of the Compound Arithmetic function.

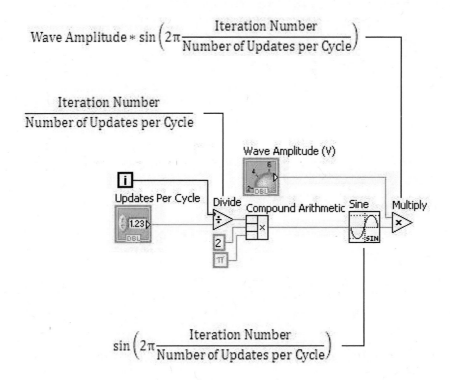

Figure 2.4.5   Wiring diagram of the functions to create the sine wave showing the state of the calculations throughout the sub diagram

12. From the Functions palette, select **Express>>Arithmetic & Comparison>>Express Numeric>>Multiply**, drag the function to the right of the Sine function in the block diagram, and wire the Sine function to the lower left input of the Multiply function.

13. Create a control from the top input of the Multiply function, name the control "Wave Amplitude (V)", and enter a value of 1 V in the front panel control.

14. Make sure to wire the sub diagram to create a sine wave as shown in Fig. 2.4.5 except for the iteration count terminal, which will be added later.

Tip: Labels can be added by right-clicking on an icon and selecting **Visible Items>>Labels** to document your VI.

15. From the Functions palette, select **Express>>Output>>DAQ Assistant** and drag the DAQ Assistant to the right of the sub diagram to create the sine wave.

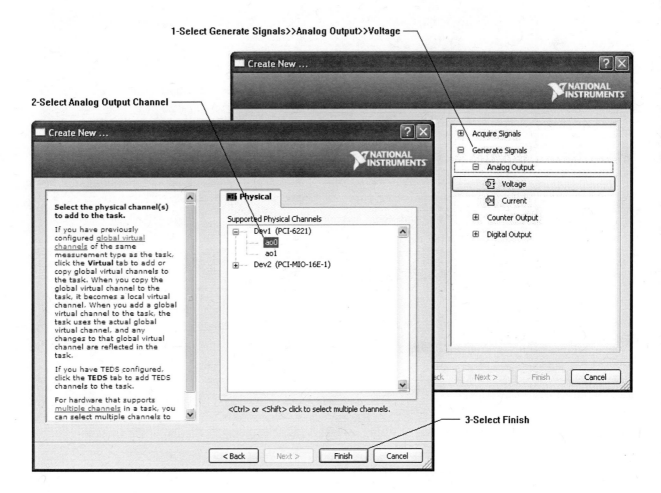

Figure 2.4.6   Steps to use the DAQ Assistant to select the channel for the continuous analog output VI

16. Click on "Generate Signals", "Analog Output", and "Voltage" in the "Create New…" window as shown in Fig. 2.4.6.

17. Click on the hardware device to show the channels that are available to generate analog output signals on your DAQ board.

18. Select analog output channel 0 ("ao0"), or another appropriate channel for your DAQ hardware, as shown in Fig. 2.4.6.

19. Select "Finish" and the DAQ Assistant window appears.

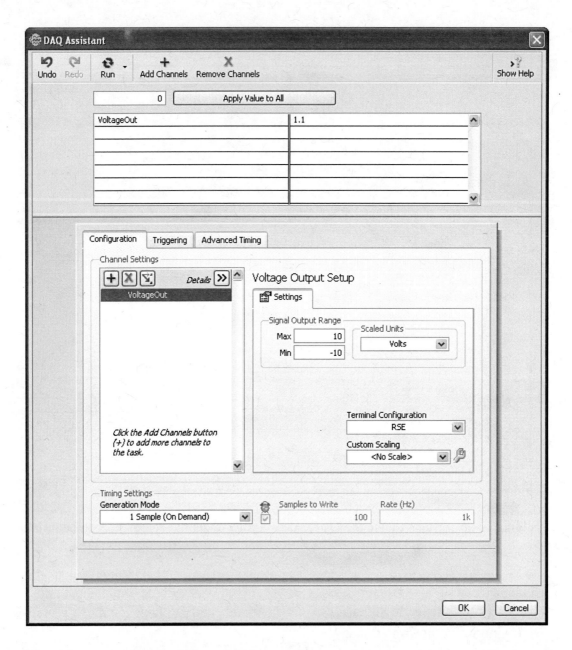

Figure 2.4.7   Output channel configuration for the continuous analog output VI using the DAQ Assistant

20. Select "1 Sample (On Demand)" for the acquisition mode (keep the other default settings as shown in Fig. 2.4.7) and click OK.

Note: Software timing is employed when "1 Sample (On Demand)" is selected as the generation mode. An update is generated when the DAQ Assistant Express VI is executed and the timing between updates is controlled by a LabVIEW timing function and the clock controlling the computer's CPU.

Note: The terminal configuration is referenced single ended (RSE) because the output voltage on channel "ao0" is referenced to the measurement system ground available on the analog output ground channel on the terminal connector block. Read Section 2.1.1 regarding a discussion of reference single-ended terminal configuration. The pin numbers for the analog output channel and the analog output ground channel can be found from the pinout sheet obtained through the Measurement and Automation Explorer (MAX).

21. Select **Express>>Execution Control>>Time Delay** and drag the Express VI to the right of the DAQ Assistant Express VI in the block diagram. Click OK for the default time setting of 1 second in the "Configure Time Delay" window as the time delay between updates will be determined automatically in a later step.

22. Wire the output of the Multiply function to the "data" input of the DAQ Assistant and the "error out" terminal of the DAQ Assistant to the "error in" terminal of the Time Delay Express VI as shown in Fig. 2.4.8.

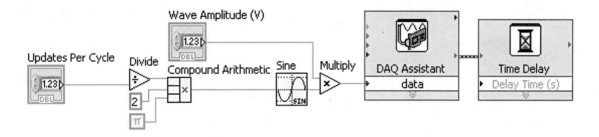

Figure 2.4.8   Intermediate wiring of the Express VIs for the continuous analog output example VI

Note: The time delay required between updates is a function of the wave frequency (cycles/second) and the update resolution (number of updates per wave cycle). The time interval between each update can be expressed as the reciprocal of the product of the wave frequency and the update resolution.

$$\text{time interval (s/update)} = \frac{1}{\text{wave frequency(cycles/s)} * \text{update resolution (updates/cycle)}}$$

It can be seen from the equation that the units of the time interval are in seconds per update, which will be used as an automatic input to the Time Delay Express VI in Steps 23-27.

23. Select **Express>>Arithmetic & Comparison>>Express Numeric>>Multiply** and place the Multiply function below the other Multiply function as shown in Fig. 2.4.9.

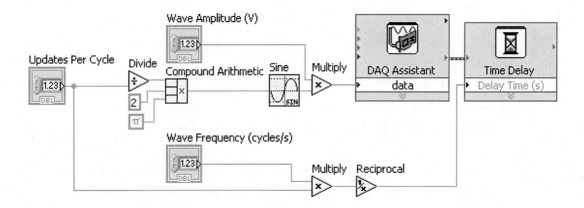

Figure 2.4.9   Intermediate block diagram showing the steps to create the automatic time interval between updates for the continuous analog output example VI

24. Create a control from the top left input terminal of the Multiply function, name it "Wave Frequency (cycles/s)", and enter a value of 0.1 cycles/second.

25. Wire the "Updates Per Cycle" terminal to the lower left input terminal of the Multiply function.

26. Select **Express>>Arithmetic & Comparison>>Express Numeric>>Reciprocal**, place it to the right of the Multiply function, and wire the two functions together.

27. Wire the output terminal of the Reciprocal function to the "Delay Time (s)" input terminal of the Time Delay Express VI.

28. Select **Express>>Execution Control>>While Loop** and drag the structure over the objects in the block diagram from the top left corner to the bottom right corner.

29. Wire the iteration terminal to the top left input terminal of the Divide function as shown in Fig. 2.4.10.

Note: The VI is complete and the Run arrow should not be broken. If the arrow is broken, click on the broken Run arrow to show the error(s).

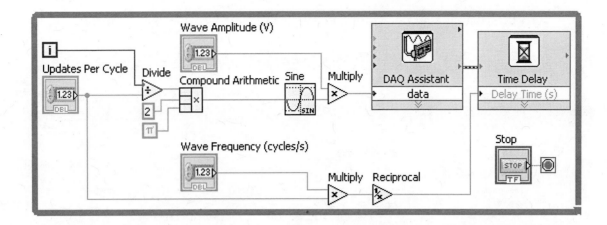

Figure 2.4.10 Completed block diagram of the continuous analog output example VI

Note: The front panel should look similar to that shown in Fig. 2.4.11. The front panel may be modified using knobs to give it more of the feel of a function generator. If you choose to include these optional modifications, follow Steps 30-33. Otherwise, you have completed the development of the VI and may proceed to the **Testing the VI** section.

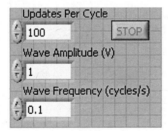

Figure 2.4.11 Default appearance of the front panel for the continuous analog output
example VI

30. Separate the controls to allow space between them. Place the cursor over the "Wave Amplitude (V)" control in the front panel, right click, select "Replace" from the pop-up menu, and select **Express>>Numeric Controls>>Knob** as shown in Fig. 2.4.12.

31. Enlarge the knob using the blue handles, reposition the label above the knob, and add a digital display by right-clicking the cursor over the knob and selecting **Visible Items>>Digital Display**. Reposition the digital display if desired.

Note: The digital display allows the user to enter precise values for voltages that would otherwise be difficult to enter via the knob.

Warning: The knob's upper limit should be within the range of voltages allowed on the DAQ board to prevent any damage to the hardware.

32. Perform the same steps for the "Wave Frequency (cycles/s)" control.

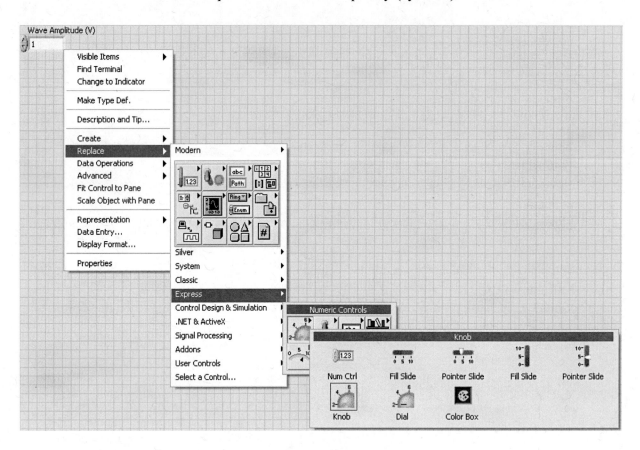

Figure 2.4.12   Sequence to replace a front panel control in the continuous analog output example VI

33. Enlarge the "stop" button using the blue handles, if desired, and ensure the values are as shown in Fig. 2.4.13.

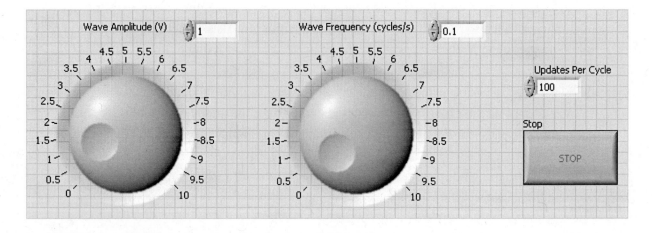

Figure 2.4.13   Modified front panel for the continuous analog output example VI

Congratulations! You have developed a single channel, non-buffered, software-timed analog output VI that can generate updates continuously until stopped by the user. The VI may be used to simulate a function generator continuously generating a sine wave. Be sure to save your program using one of the save options on the "File" pull-down menu.

Testing the VI

Determine the analog output and analog ground pin numbers on the terminal connector block so that a set of leads may be connected to an oscilloscope or multimeter. Unlike with analog input connections, the DAQ Assistant does not have a Connector Diagram tab to show the pin number for the analog output channel, "ao0", or the analog ground terminal, "ao GND". However, a device pinout diagram for your DAQ board can be found using the Measurement & Automation Explorer (MAX) software program, a National Instruments utility to manage hardware. Select "Measurement & Automation Explorer…" from the "Tools" pull-down menu. A window will appear like the one that is partially shown in Figure 2.4.14. Expand "Devices and Interfaces", right click on the DAQ board that was selected when you configured your channels using the DAQ Assistant, and select "Device Pinouts." Device Pinouts may also be selected in the toolbar at the top of the MAX window. The pinout sheet appears in a new window and the pin number for the analog output and analog ground terminals can be identified. For example, "ao0" is pin 22 and "ao GND" is pin 55 on the NI PCI/PXI 6221 DAQ board.

Attach leads from the terminal connector block to an oscilloscope or a multimeter, if an oscilloscope is not available. Attach the terminal connector block's analog output channel to the oscilloscope's positive terminal and the terminal connector block's analog output ground channel to the oscilloscope's negative terminal. Note that the analog output ground is used for the negative terminal since a referenced single-ended system configuration was specified in the DAQ Assistant as shown in Fig. 2.4.7, which requires that the output signal is referenced to the measurement system ground on AO GND.

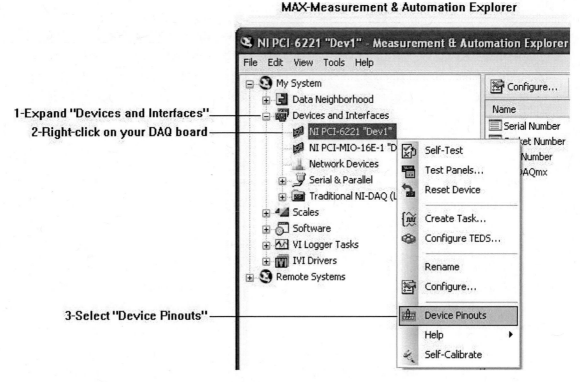

Figure 2.4.14   Using the Measurement &Automation Explorer utility to identify the pin
connection for the output and ground channels

After the leads have been connected, the VI is ready to run. If you are using a multimeter,
the wave frequency must be low to display the sine wave, like the value of 0.1 cycles per
second recommended in Step 24, because of the integrating effect of the multimeter.
Click on the Run button in the toolbar to begin execution of the VI and observe the signal
on the oscilloscope or multimeter. The VI will generate data continuously until the user
selects the stop control in the front panel.

As a general practice, you should always ensure that the output voltage on the analog
output channel is zero V when you are done with the VI. One easy way to do this is to
use the test feature of the DAQ Assistant.

Double click on the DAQ Assistant in the block diagram to bring up the DAQ Assistant
window as shown in Fig. 2.4.15. Enter an output voltage of 0 V for the analog output
channel and click on the "Apply Value to All" button. Click on the "Run" button and
observe on the oscilloscope or multimeter that 0 V is output on the analog output channel.

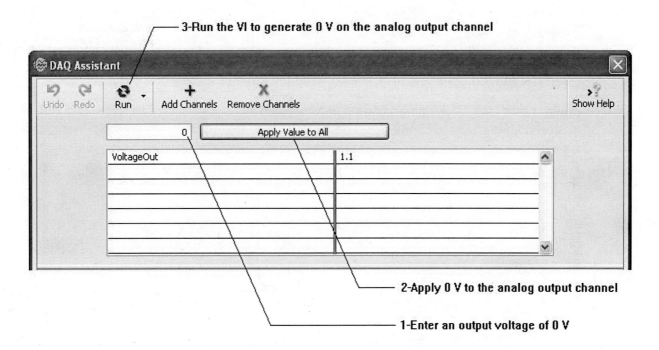

Figure 2.4.15   Partial view of the DAQ Assistant showing the process to generate a test voltage
using the continuous analog output example VI

Discussion

Fig. 2.4.16 shows the function of each sub diagram within the VI to generate a
continuous voltage on the output channel at the terminal connector block. For the
generation of analog output signals, values must first be created through the software and
temporarily stored in memory. These values are then used to generate a voltage at the
analog output channel of the terminal connector block via the DAQ Assistant Express VI.
Because the DAQ Assistant generates only one update, it must be placed inside a While
Loop for continuous generation of a voltage signal. The timing between the updates
generated through the DAQ Assistant is controlled by the computer's clock through a
LabVIEW timing Express VI. The time interval is calculated automatically based on the
wave frequency and the resolution of the generated wave, as defined by the number of
updates per wave cycle the user specifies.

Timing VI that allows software timing for data generation

Generates a voltage, point by point, at the terminal
connector block that represents the intended sine wave

Generates a sine wave, point by point, that
is stored temporarily in memory

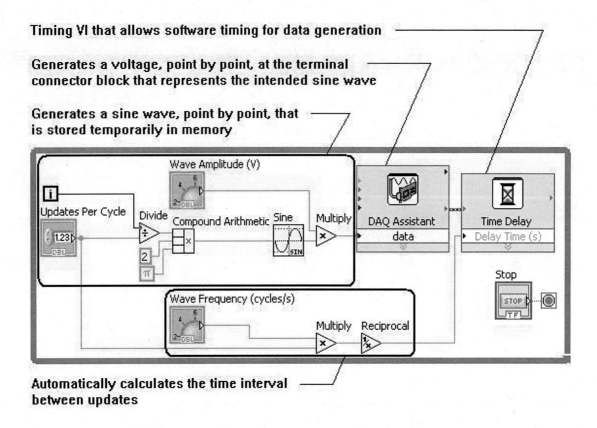

Automatically calculates the time interval
between updates

Figure 2.4.16   Functions of the various components of the example VI to continuously
generate voltages on an analog output channel

2.5   Finite Analog Output using Buffers and Hardware Timing

This section describes how to write a relatively simple analog output VI to introduce
basic data acquisition concepts and develop your skills. The example VI in this section
employs buffered data generation with hardware timing and triggering and can be used to
generate a finite analog output signal from a single channel. This section is structured so
that you can develop the VI as you read the material. The idea is that it will be easier to
learn and retain key data acquisition concepts by applying the concepts as you learn
them. This VI is most appropriate when you update at relatively fast generation rates and
the length of time to update is known. For example, this VI could be used as a high-
frequency function generator for a finite number of wave cycles. The example VI is used
to generate a sine wave although other types of waves, like a saw tooth wave, could also
be generated.

The material discussed in this section assumes that LabVIEW Professional Version or
Student Version software, NI-DAQ software, and a data acquisition board have been
installed on your computer.

Equipment

1. An oscilloscope to display the analog output signal or, if an oscilloscope is not available, a multimeter may be used for low frequency signals.

2. A digital trigger source (optional).

Goals

1. Become acquainted with some basic analog output data acquisition concepts on hardware timing using LabVIEW's configuration approach.

2. Develop the single channel, buffered, triggered, hardware-timed analog output VI shown in Figs. 2.5.1 and 2.5.2, which generates a finite number of updates.

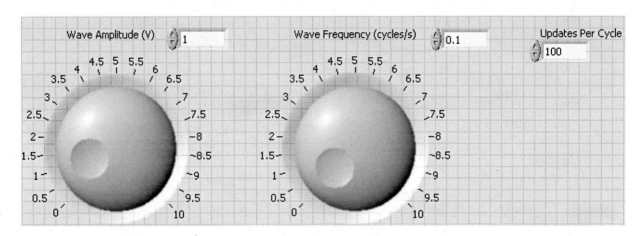

Figure 2.5.1   Front panel of the example finite analog output VI with hardware timing, buffering, and triggering

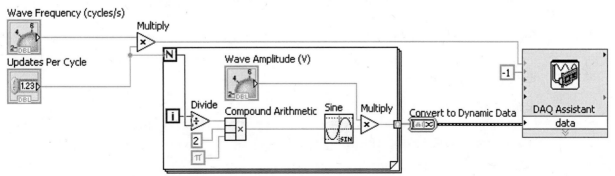

Figure 2.5.2   Block diagram of the example finite analog output VI with hardware timing, buffering, and triggering

Developing the VI

1. Beginning at the Start Menu, select **All Programs>>National Instruments>>LabVIEW 2012>>LabVIEW 2012**

Note: Read Section 1.3 if you need background on the LabVIEW environment.

2. Select "Blank VI" to open a new file

Note: Sine values are created in Steps 3-19 to represent a function generator's voltage sine wave at the terminal connector block. The sine wave is divided into a number of points, called updates, which will later serve as the locations where the DAQ board generates (updates) a voltage at the terminal connector block. The more points (updates) on the sine wave, the better the resolution to enable the analog voltage signal to represent the intended sine wave. An array consisting of values for one cycle of the sine wave will be created within a For Loop as the number of iterations goes from zero to the total number of updates per cycle. The sine wave is created as shown in the following expression.

$$\text{Wave Amplitude} * \sin\left(2\pi \frac{\text{Iteration Number}}{\text{Number of Updates per Cycle}}\right)$$

3. From the Functions palette, select **Programming>>Structures>>For Loop** and drag the For Loop in the block diagram to create an area large enough to contain the sub diagram shown in Fig. 2.5.2.

Tip: The For Loop can be resized, if needed, at a later time by using the blue handles.

4. From the Functions palette, select **Express>>Arithmetic & Comparison>>Express Numeric>>Divide** and drag the function inside the For Loop.

5. Wire the iteration terminal (box containing the letter "i") to the upper left input terminal of the Divide function and the loop count terminal (box containing the letter "N") to the lower left input terminal.

6. From the Functions palette, select **Express>>Arithmetic & Comparison>>Express Numeric>>Compound Arithmetic** and drag the function to the right of the Divide function in the block diagram.

7. Resize the Compound Arithmetic function by selecting the function and dragging down on the bottom blue handle to add one more input terminal as shown in Fig.

2.5.3 or right-click over an input terminal and select "Add Input" to do the same thing.

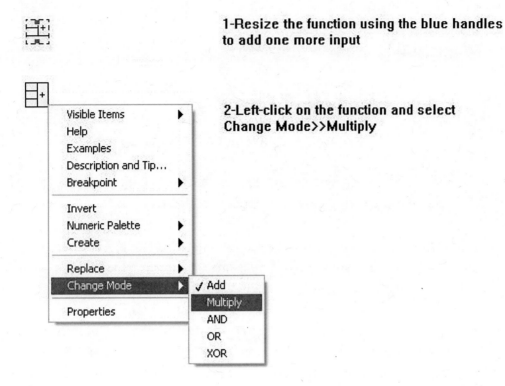

1-Resize the function using the blue handles to add one more input

2-Left-click on the function and select Change Mode>>Multiply

Figure 2.5.3   Resizing and modifying the Compound Arithmetic function for the finite analog output example VI

8. Right-click on the function and select **Change Mode>>Multiply** as shown in Fig. 2.5.3.

9. Create a constant for the middle input terminal of the Compound Arithmetic function and assign the constant a value of two as shown in Fig. 2.5.4. The value can be changed automatically when the background is black, which occurs immediately after the constant is created. Otherwise, you must use the "Edit Text" cursor or double-click on constant to change the value.

10. From the Functions palette, select **Express>>Arithmetic & Comparison>>Express Numeric>>Express Math & Scientific Constants>>Pi** and place the constant to the left of the bottom input terminal of the Compound Arithmetic function.

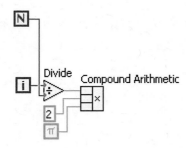

Figure 2.5.4   Wiring the Divide function and constants to the Compound Arithmetic function for the finite analog output example VI

11. Wire the Divide and Compound Arithmetic functions and constants as shown in Fig. 2.5.4, if any of the wiring did not occur automatically.

12. From the Functions palette, select **Express>>Arithmetic & Comparison>>Express Math>>Express Trigonometric Functions>>Sine**, drag the function to the right of the Compound Arithmetic function, and wire the two functions together.

13. From the Functions palette, select **Express>>Arithmetic & Comparison>>Express Numeric>>Multiply**, drag the function to the right of the Sine function in the block diagram, and wire the Sine function to the lower left input of the Multiply function.

14. Create a control from the top input of the Multiply function, name the control "Wave Amplitude (V)", and enter a value of 1 V in the front panel control.

15. Wire the output of the Multiply function to the border of the For Loop

Note: When the Multiply function is wired to the For Loop, the tunnel appears with indexing enabled, by default. This ensures that a one-dimensional array of sine values will be supplied to the DAQ Assistant.

16. Make sure to wire the sub diagram to create a sine wave as shown in Fig. 2.5.5.

Tip: Labels can be added by right-clicking on an icon and selecting **Visible Items>>Labels** to document your VI.

17. From the Functions palette, select **Express>>Arithmetic & Comparison>>Express Numeric>>Multiply** and drag the function to the left and above the For Loop ensuring that the function is sufficiently far from the For Loop to avoid automatic wiring.

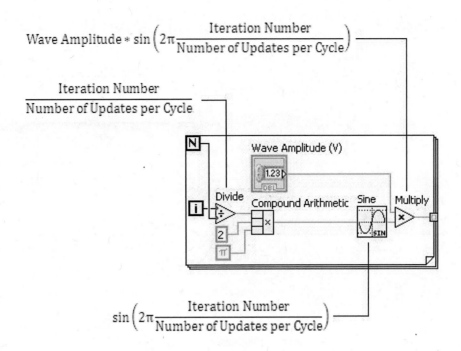

$$\text{Wave Amplitude} * \sin\left(2\pi\frac{\text{Iteration Number}}{\text{Number of Updates per Cycle}}\right)$$

$$\frac{\text{Iteration Number}}{\text{Number of Updates per Cycle}}$$

$$\sin\left(2\pi\frac{\text{Iteration Number}}{\text{Number of Updates per Cycle}}\right)$$

Figure 2.5.5   Wiring diagram of the functions to create the sine wave showing the state of the calculations throughout the sub diagram

18. Create a control for the upper left input of the Multiply function, name it "Wave Frequency (cycles/s)", and enter a value of 0.1 in the front panel as shown in Fig. 2.5.6.

19. Create a control for the lower left input of the Multiply function, name it "Updates Per Cycle", wire it to the loop count terminal (box containing the letter N) on the For Loop, and enter a value of 100 in the front panel. It is also beneficial to move both controls to the left to make room for future wiring.

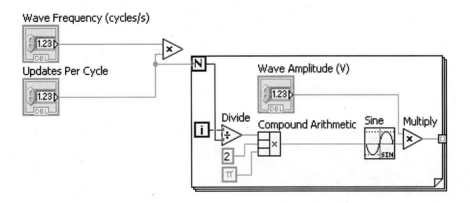

Figure 2.5.6   Intermediate block diagram for the finite analog output example VI

20. From the Functions palette, select **Express>>Output>>DAQ Assistant** and drag the DAQ Assistant to the right of the For Loop.

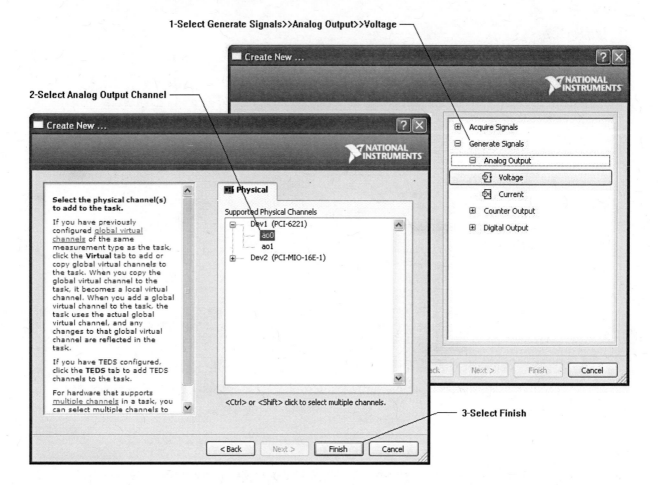

Figure 2.5.7   Steps to use the DAQ Assistant to select the channel for the finite analog output VI

21. Click on "Generate Signals", "Analog Output", and "Voltage" in the "Create New…" window as shown in Fig. 2.5.7.

22. Click on the hardware device to show the channels that are available to generate analog output signals on your DAQ board.

23. Select analog output channel 0 ("ao0"), or another appropriate channel for your DAQ hardware, as shown in Fig. 2.5.7.

24. Select "Finish" and the DAQ Assistant window appears.

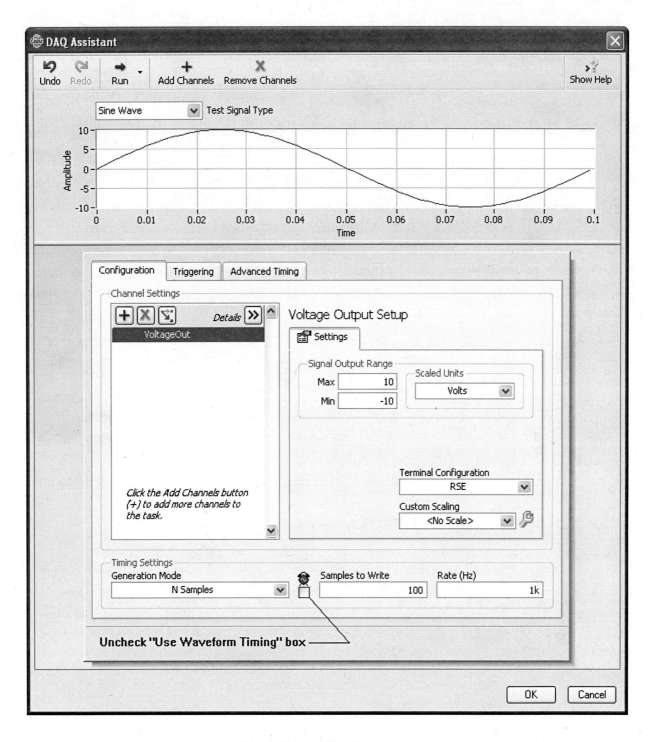

Figure 2.5.8   Output channel configuration for the finite analog output VI using the DAQ
            Assistant

25. Keep all default settings in the DAQ Assistant window, as shown in Fig. 2.5.8, except
    to uncheck the "Use Waveform Timing" box. If this box is checked, the DAQ
    Assistant Express VI expects both the number of samples and the rate information to

be included in the incoming signal. Since the rate information is not included in the creation of the array in the For Loop, uncheck this box.

Note: The acquisition mode "N Samples" relies on hardware timing using the DAQ on-board clock. This acquisition mode is used in the current VI because it temporarily stores a finite set of samples in a buffer, which is later used to update voltages on a channel in the terminal connector block.

Note: The terminal configuration is referenced single ended (RSE) because the output voltage on channel "ao0" is referenced to the measurement system ground available on the analog output ground channel on the terminal connector block. Read Section 2.1.1 regarding a discussion of reference single-ended terminal configuration. The pin numbers for the analog output channel and the analog output ground channel can be found from the pinout sheet obtained through the Measurement and Automation Explorer (MAX).

26. Select the "Triggering" tab and the triggering values shown in Fig. 2.5.9.

Note: The example VI may be developed without the use of a trigger. If you do not want to use the optional trigger, select "<None>" under the trigger options and skip Steps 26 and 27.

27. Select a channel for the trigger source that is available for your DAQ board if Programmable Function Interface (PFI) channels are not available.

28. Select OK and the DAQ Assistant will generate the appropriate code.

29. Create a constant for the "timeout (s)" input terminal to the DAQ Assistant and enter a value of -1, which means the data generation VI will wait indefinitely.

Note: If you do not enter -1 for the timeout input, data generation must begin before the default timeout limit of 10 seconds elapses, or whatever time limit you selected. Otherwise an error will occur.

30. Wire the array at the tunnel on the right side of the For Loop to the "data" input terminal of the DAQ Assistant.

Note: An Express VI to convert the array, which is initially in the floating point numeric data type, to the dynamic data type expected by the DAQ Assistant will appear automatically. The dynamic data type includes the array values and their attributes.

31. Wire the output terminal of the Multiply function to the "rate" input terminal of the DAQ Assistant, as shown in Fig. 2.5.10.

Note: The VI is complete and the Run arrow should not be broken. If the arrow is broken, click on the broken Run arrow to show the error(s).

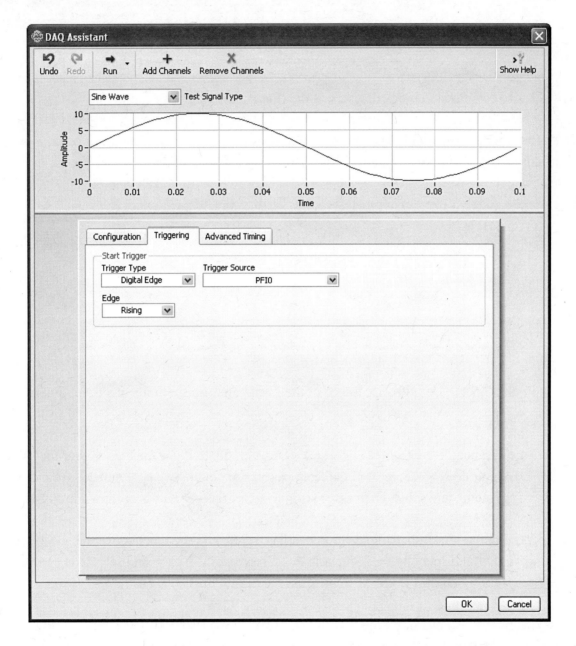

Figure 2.5.9   Trigger settings for the finite analog output VI using the DAQ Assistant

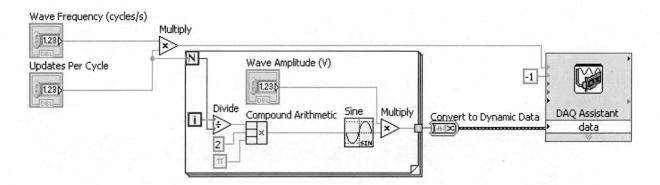

Figure 2.5.10   Completed block diagram of the finite analog output example VI

Note: The front panel should look similar to that shown in Fig. 2.5.11. The front panel may be modified using knobs to give it more of the feel of a function generator. If you choose to include these optional modifications, follow Steps 34-36. Otherwise, you have completed the development of the VI and may proceed to the "Testing the VI" section.

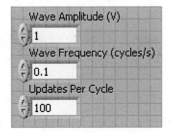

Figure 2.5.11   Default appearance of the front panel for the finite analog output example
                        VI

34. Separate the controls to allow space between them. Place the cursor over the "Wave Amplitude (V)" control in the front panel, right click, select "Replace" from the pop-up menu, and select **Express>>Numeric Controls>>Knob** as shown in Fig. 2.5.12.

35. Enlarge the knob using the blue handles, reposition the label above the knob, and add a digital display by right-clicking the cursor over the knob and selecting **Visible Items>>Digital Display**. Reposition the digital display if desired.

Note: The digital display allows the user to enter precise values for voltages that would otherwise be difficult to enter via the knob.

Warning: The knob's upper limit should be within the range of voltages allowed on the DAQ board to prevent any damage to the hardware.

36. Perform the same steps for the "Wave Frequency (cycles/s)" control so that the front panel looks similar to Fig. 2.5.13.

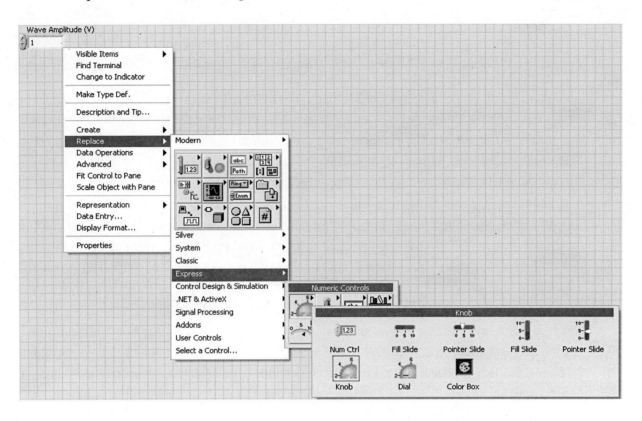

Figure 2.5.12   Sequence to replace a front panel control in the finite analog output example VI

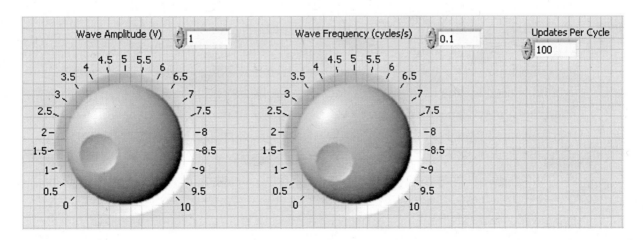

Figure 2.5.13   Modified front panel for the finite analog output example VI

Congratulations! You have developed a single channel, hardware-timed, buffered, and triggered analog output VI that can generate a finite number of updates. The VI may be used to generate one cycle of a sine wave, or other types of waves with appropriate modifications. Be sure to save your program using one of the save options on the "File" pull-down menu.

Testing the VI

Determine the analog output and analog ground pin numbers on the terminal connector block so that a set of leads may be connected to an oscilloscope or multimeter. Unlike with analog input connections, the DAQ Assistant does not have a Connector Diagram tab to show the pin number for the analog output channel, "ao 0", or the analog ground terminal, "ao GND". However, a device pinout diagram for your DAQ board can be found using the Measurement & Automation Explorer (MAX) software program, a National Instruments utility to manage hardware. Select "Measurement & Automation Explorer…" from the "Tools" pull-down menu. A window will appear like the one that is partially shown in Figure 2.5.14. Expand "Devices and Interfaces", right click on the DAQ board that was selected when you configured your channels using the DAQ Assistant, and select "Device Pinouts." Device Pinouts may also be selected in the toolbar at the top of the MAX window. The pinout sheet appears in a new window and the pin number for the analog output and analog ground terminals can be identified. For example, "ao 0" is pin 22 and "ao GND" is pin 55 on the NI PCI/PXI 6221 DAQ board. The pin number for the trigger, PFI 0, or the channel you selected for the trigger source if PFI 0 was not selected, can be identified using the pinout sheet as well. For example, PFI 0 is pin 11 on the NI PCI/PXI 6221 DAQ board.

Attach leads from the terminal connector block to an oscilloscope or a multimeter, if an oscilloscope is not available. Attach the terminal connector block's analog output channel to the oscilloscope's positive terminal and the terminal connector block's analog output ground channel to the oscilloscope's negative terminal. Note that the analog output ground is used for the negative terminal since a referenced single-ended system configuration was specified in the DAQ Assistant as shown in Fig. 2.5.8, which requires that the output signal is referenced to the measurement system ground on "ao GND".

After the leads have been connected, the VI is ready to run. If you are using a multimeter, the wave frequency must be low to display the sine wave, like the value of 0.1 cycles per second recommended in Step 18, because of the integrating effect of the multimeter.

Click on the Run button in the toolbar to begin execution of the VI and apply the trigger before the timeout limit for the data generation VI. An error message, like the one shown in Fig. 2.5.15, will be displayed if the trigger is not activated before the timeout limit. The VI will generate one cycle of the sine wave that can be observed on the oscilloscope or multimeter.

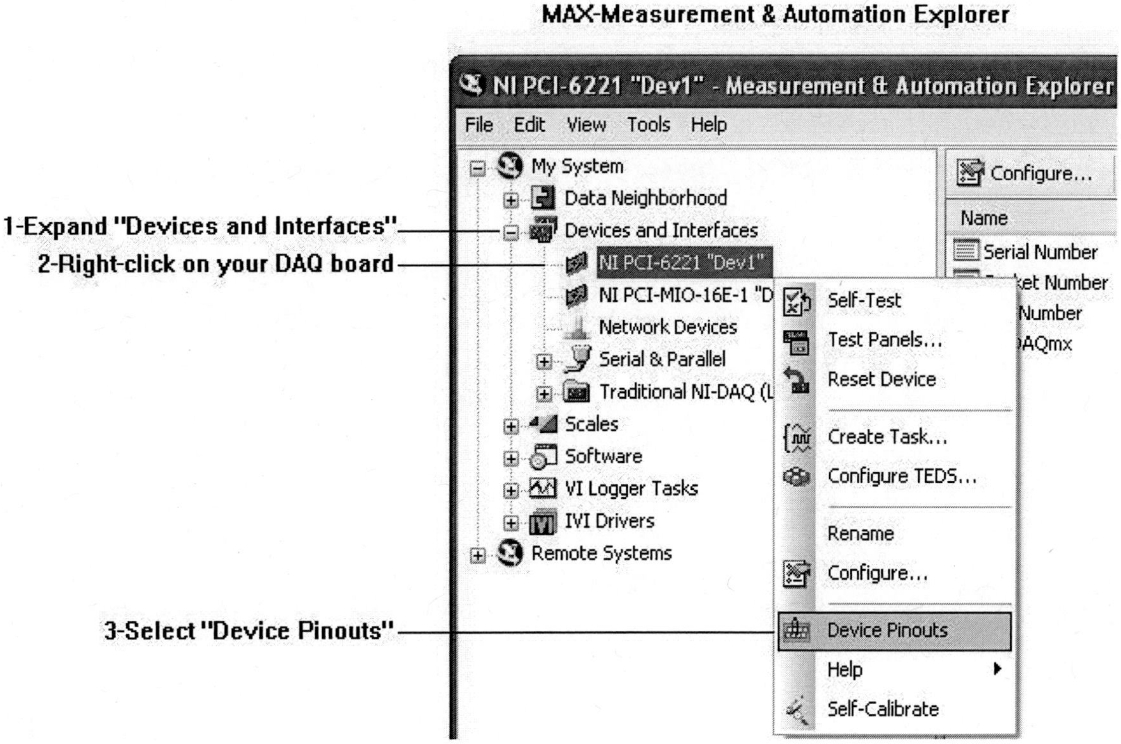

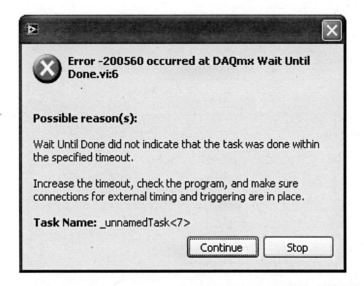

Figure 2.5.14 Using the Measurement &Automation Explorer utility to identify the pin connection for the output and ground channels

Figure 2.5.15 Error message that is displayed if the trigger is not activated within the timeout limit for the finite analog output example VI

As a general practice, you should always ensure that the output voltage on the analog output channel is 0 V when you are done with the VI. One easy way to do this is to set the value of the wave amplitude control in the front panel equal to 0 V on the last run.

Discussion

There are parallels between analog signal generation and measurement, as shown in Fig. 2.5.16. This figure shows the block diagram of two VIs: the top one shows a VI to generate finite analog output while the bottom one shows a VI to measure finite analog input.

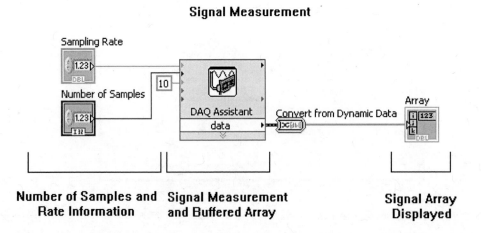

Figure 2.5.16 Comparison between VIs for finite buffered analog output and input

In the case of signal generation, a data array is initially created using LabVIEW functions to represent the signal that we want to generate at the terminal connector block. The data array is temporary since it will not exist after the VI is completed. However, we could have read a data array from a file that is stored on a computer's hard drive or other external memory. In the current example, the data array is created in the For Loop shown in the top block diagram of Fig. 2.5.16. The array happens to be one-dimensional because we are using only one analog output channel but would be a two-dimensional array with multiple channels.

The data array is stored temporarily in a reserved section of the computer's internal memory, called a buffer, once the data array is input into the DAQ Assistant Express VI. Data is read from the buffer according to the specified update rate. A digital-to-analog conversion occurs and a voltage is updated on the DAQ board, which appears at the specified analog output channel on the terminal connector block. During execution of the DAQ Assistant Express VI, the analog voltage signal may be displayed on an oscilloscope or used to control an output device.

For the case of signal measurement, an analog voltage signal is created by an input device, like a sensor, that is connected to the terminal connector block. A sample of the analog signal is taken according to the sampling rate specified by the user when the DAQ Assistant Express VI executes, as shown in the lower block diagram of Fig. 2.5.16. Analog-to-digital conversions are performed on the samples and the resulting array of digital values is stored in the buffer. Once the execution of the DAQ Assistant Express VI is complete, the data array in buffer can be stored temporarily in an array, as shown in Fig. 2.5.16, or stored permanently in a file on the computer's hard drive or other external memory.

The parallels are shown in more general terms in Fig. 2.5.17. Starting at the generation and measurement block diagrams from the left, analog signals exist on channels of the terminal connector block. The analog signal is either received from the DAQ board to an output device, such as a motor driver or an oscilloscope, or the signal is sent to the DAQ board from an input device, such as a sensor or transducer. The signal is converted by the DAQ board, either a digital-to-analog conversion for data generation or an analog-to-digital conversion for data measurement. The data is stored temporarily in the computer's internal memory (buffer) to ensure that the signal can be updated (for data generation) or sampled (for data measurement) fast enough. The data array representing the analog signal can be stored temporarily within the software during VI execution. This could take the form of a data array created by the software for data generation or a data array, chart, or graph for data measurement. The data array may also be stored in a permanent file, either for the purposes of reading data for data generation or storing data after data measurement.

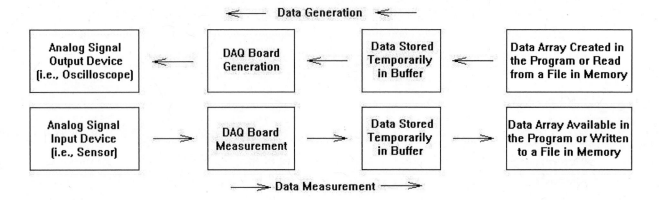

Figure 2.5.17   Illustration to show the parallels between analog signal measurement and generation

2.6   Continuous Analog Output using Circular Buffers and Hardware Timing

This section describes how to write a relatively simple analog output VI to introduce basic data acquisition concepts and develop your skills. The example VI in this section employs data generation with hardware timing and a circular buffer to generate a continuous analog output signal from a single channel. This section is structured so that you can develop the VI as you read the material. The idea is that it will be easier to learn and retain key data acquisition concepts by applying the concepts as you learn them. This VI is most appropriate when you update at relatively fast generation rates, the intervals between updates must be uniform and precise, and the length of time to update is unknown. For example, this VI could be used as a high-frequency function generator. The example VI is used to generate sine waves although other types of waves, like a saw tooth wave, could also be generated.

The material discussed in this section assumes that LabVIEW Professional Version or Student Version software, NI-DAQ software, and a data acquisition board have been installed on your computer.

Equipment

1. An oscilloscope to display the analog output signal or, if an oscilloscope is not available, a multimeter may be used for low frequency signals.

Goals

1. Become acquainted with some basic analog output data acquisition concepts on hardware timing using LabVIEW's configuration approach.

2. Develop the single channel, circular-buffered, hardware-timed analog output VI shown in Figs. 2.6.1 and 2.6.2, which generates a continuous sine wave until stopped by the user.

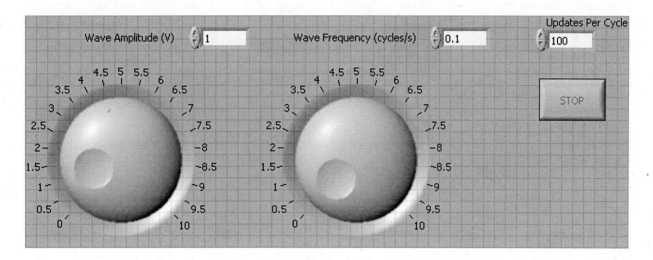

Figure 2.6.1   Front panel of the continuous analog output example VI with hardware timing and circular buffering

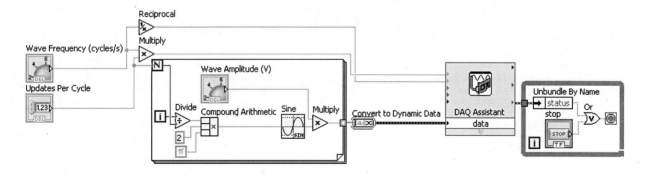

Figure 2.6.2   Block diagram of the continuous analog output example VI with hardware timing and circular buffering

Developing the VI

1. Beginning at the Start Menu, select **All Programs>>National Instruments>>LabVIEW 2012>>LabVIEW 2012**

Note: Read Section 1.3 if you need background on the LabVIEW environment.

2. Select "Blank VI" to open a new file

Note: Sine values are created in Steps 3-19 to represent a function generator's voltage sine wave at the terminal connector block. The sine wave is divided into a number of points, called updates, which will later serve as the locations where the DAQ board generates (updates) a voltage at the terminal connector block. The more points (updates) on the sine wave, the better the resolution to enable the analog voltage signal to represent the intended sine wave. An array consisting of values for one cycle of the sine wave will be created within a For Loop as the number of iterations goes from zero to the total number of updates per cycle. The sine wave is created as shown in the following expression.

$$\text{Wave Amplitude} * \sin\left(2\pi \frac{\text{Iteration Number}}{\text{Number of Updates per Cycle}}\right)$$

3. From the Functions palette, select **Programming>>Structures>>For Loop** and drag the For Loop in the block diagram to create an area large enough to contain the sub diagram shown in Fig. 2.6.2.

Tip: The For Loop can be resized, if needed, at a later time by using the blue handles.

4. From the Functions palette, select **Express>>Arithmetic & Comparison>>Express Numeric>>Divide** and drag the function inside the For Loop.

5. Wire the iteration terminal (box containing the letter "i") to the upper left input terminal of the Divide function and the loop count terminal (box containing the letter "N") to the lower left input terminal.

6. From the Functions palette, select **Express>>Arithmetic & Comparison>>Express Numeric>>Compound Arithmetic** and drag the function to the right of the Divide function in the block diagram.

7. Resize the Compound Arithmetic function by selecting the function and dragging down on the bottom blue handle to add one more input terminal as shown in Fig. 2.6.3 or right-click over an input terminal and select "Add Input" to do the same thing.

8. Right-click on the function and select **Change Mode>>Multiply** as shown in Fig. 2.6.3.

9. Create a constant for the middle input terminal of the Compound Arithmetic function and assign the constant a value of two as shown in Fig. 2.6.4. The value can be changed automatically when the background is black, which occurs immediately after the constant is created. Otherwise, you must use the "Edit Text" cursor or double-click on the constant to change the value.

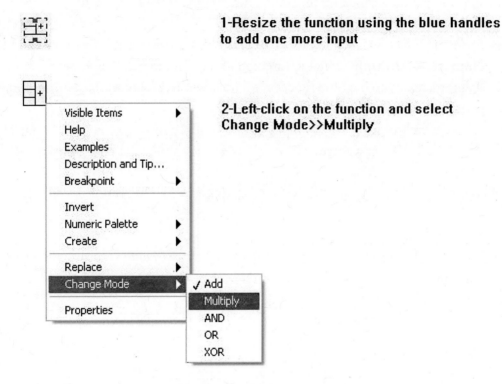

1-Resize the function using the blue handles to add one more input

2-Left-click on the function and select Change Mode>>Multiply

Figure 2.6.3   Resizing and modifying the Compound Arithmetic function for the continuous analog output example VI

10. From the Functions palette, select **Express>>Arithmetic & Comparison>>Express Numeric>>Express Math & Scientific Constants>>Pi** and place the constant to the left of the bottom input terminal of the Compound Arithmetic function.

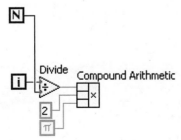

Figure 2.6.4   Wiring the Divide function and constants to the Compound Arithmetic function for the continuous analog output example VI

11. Wire the Divide and Compound Arithmetic functions and constants as shown in Fig. 2.6.4, if any of the wiring did not occur automatically.

12. From the Functions palette, select **Express>>Arithmetic & Comparison>>Express Math>>Express Trigonometric Functions>>Sine**, drag the function to the right of the Compound Arithmetic function, and wire the two functions together.

13. From the Functions palette, select **Express>>Arithmetic & Comparison>>Express Numeric>>Multiply**, drag the function to the right of the Sine function in the block diagram, and wire the Sine function to the lower left input of the Multiply function.

14. Create a control from the top input of the Multiply function, name the control "Wave Amplitude (V)", and enter a value of 1 V in the front panel control.

15. Wire the output of the Multiply function to the border of the For Loop

Note: When the Multiply function is wired to the For Loop, the tunnel appears with indexing enabled, by default. This ensures that a one-dimensional array of sine values will be supplied to the DAQ Assistant.

16. Make sure to wire the sub diagram to create a sine wave as shown in Fig. 2.6.5.

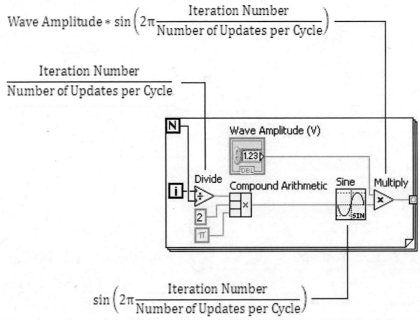

$$\text{Wave Amplitude} * \sin\left(2\pi \frac{\text{Iteration Number}}{\text{Number of Updates per Cycle}}\right)$$

$$\frac{\text{Iteration Number}}{\text{Number of Updates per Cycle}}$$

$$\sin\left(2\pi \frac{\text{Iteration Number}}{\text{Number of Updates per Cycle}}\right)$$

Figure 2.6.5   Wiring diagram of the functions to create the sine wave showing the state of the calculations throughout the sub diagram

Tip: Labels can be added by left-clicking on an icon and selecting **Visible Items>>Labels** to document your VI.

17. From the Functions palette, select **Express>>Arithmetic & Comparison>>Express Numeric>>Multiply** and drag the function to the left and above the For Loop ensuring that the function is sufficiently far from the For Loop to avoid automatic wiring.

18. Create a control for the upper left input of the Multiply function, name it "Wave Frequency (cycles/s)", and enter a value of 0.1 in the front panel as shown in Fig. 2.6.6.

19. Create a control for the lower left input of the Multiply function, name it "Updates Per Cycle", wire it to the loop count terminal (box containing the letter N) on the For Loop, and enter a value of 100 in the front panel. It is also beneficial to move both controls to the left to make room for future wiring.

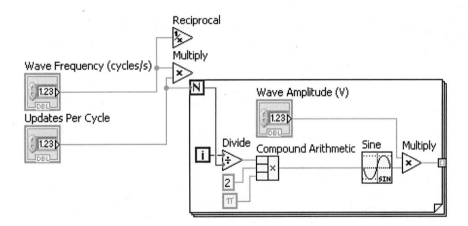

Figure 2.6.6   Intermediate block diagram for the continuous analog output example VI

20. From the Functions palette, select **Express>>Arithmetic & Comparison>>Express Numeric>>Reciprocal,** drag the function above the Multiply function, and wire the "Wave Frequency (cycles/s)" control to the input of the Reciprocal function.

21. From the Functions palette, select **Express>>Output>>DAQ Assistant** and drag the DAQ Assistant to the right of the For Loop.

22. Click on "Generate Signals", "Analog Output", and "Voltage" in the "Create New…" window as shown in Fig. 2.6.7.

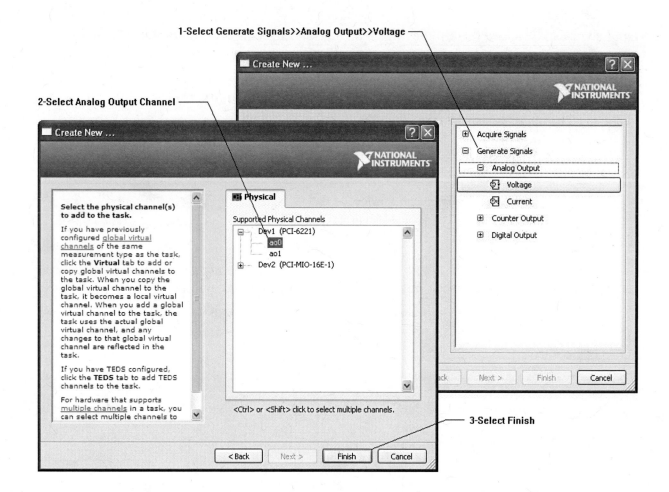

Figure 2.6.7   Steps to use the DAQ Assistant to select the channel for the continuous analog output VI

23. Click on the hardware device to show the channels that are available to generate analog output signals on your DAQ board.

24. Select analog output channel 0 ("ao0"), or another appropriate channel for your DAQ hardware, as shown in Fig. 2.6.7.

25. Select "Finish" and the DAQ Assistant window appears.

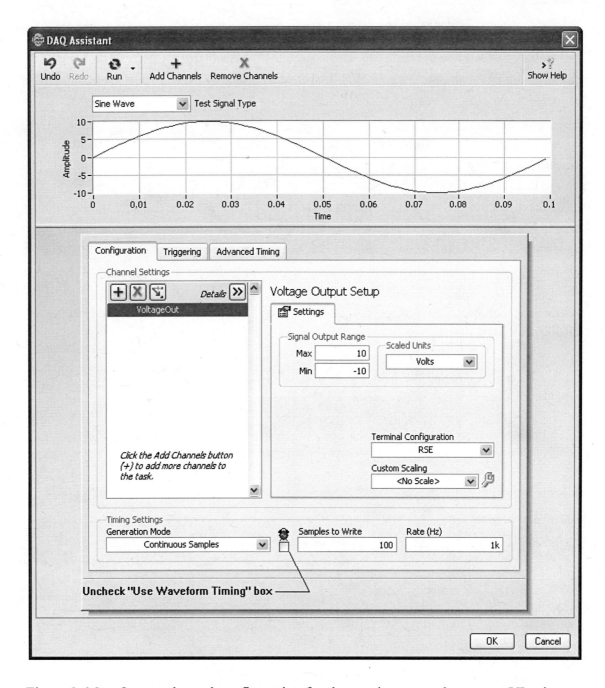

Figure 2.6.8   Output channel configuration for the continuous analog output VI using
the DAQ Assistant

26. Keep all default settings in the DAQ Assistant window, as shown in Fig. 2.6.8, except
to select "Continuous Samples" from the "Generation Mode" pull-down menu and to
uncheck the "Use Waveform Timing" box. If this box is checked, the DAQ Assistant
Express VI expects both the number of samples and the rate information to be
included in the incoming signal. Since the rate information is not included in the
creation of the array in the For Loop, uncheck this box.

Note: The acquisition mode "Continuous Samples" relies on hardware timing using the DAQ on-board clock. This mode continuously reads samples from a circular buffer, which are used to update voltages on an output channel at the terminal connector block. See Section 2.3.1 for information on circular buffers.

Note: The terminal configuration is referenced single ended (RSE) because the output voltage on channel "ao0" is referenced to the measurement system ground available on the analog output ground channel on the terminal connector block. Read Section 2.1.1 regarding a discussion of reference single-ended terminal configuration. The pin numbers for the analog output channel and the analog output ground channel can be found from the pinout sheet obtained through the Measurement and Automation Explorer (MAX).

Note: The example VI may be developed with a trigger. If you want to use the optional trigger, follow Steps 26 and 27 in Section 2.5, Finite Analog Output using Buffers and Hardware Timing.

27. Select OK and the DAQ Assistant will generate the appropriate code.

28. Select "No" when the "Confirm Auto Loop Creation" window appears automatically after the DAQ Assistant window closes. A While Loop will be created at a later time.

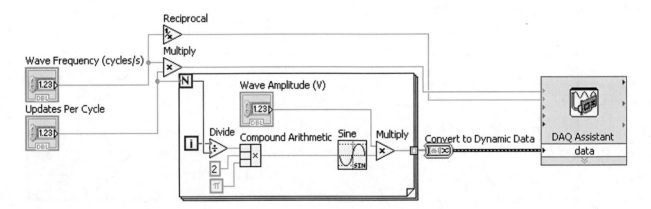

Figure 2.6.9   Intermediate block diagram for the continuous analog output example VI

29. Wire the data array at the tunnel on the right side of the For Loop to the "data" input terminal of the DAQ Assistant as shown in Fig. 2.6.9.

Note: An Express VI to convert the array, which is initially in the floating point numeric data type, to the dynamic data type expected by the DAQ Assistant will appear automatically. The dynamic data type includes the array values and their attributes.

30. Wire the output of the Reciprocal function to the "timeout (s)" input terminal of the DAQ Assistant as shown in Fig. 2.6.9.

31. Wire the output of the Multiply function below the Reciprocal function to the "rate" input terminal of the DAQ Assistant as shown in Fig. 2.6.9.

32. From the Functions palette, select **Express>>Execution Control>>While Loop**, place the structure to the right of the DAQ Assistant, and drag the While Loop to create an area within its borders to contain the sub diagram shown on the right side of Fig. 2.6.10.

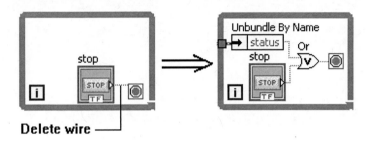

Figure 2.6.10 While Loop as initially created (left) and containing the sub diagram for the continuous analog output example VI (right)

Note: The VI is constructed in Steps 32-37 so that the sine wave will be generated continuously until either the user stops the execution or an error occurs.

33. Place the cursor over the wire between the "stop" control and the conditional terminal, right-click the mouse, and select "Delete Wire Branch" from the pop-up menu.

34. From the Functions palette, select **Programming>>Cluster, Class, and Variant>>Unbundle by Name** and place the function above the "stop" control.

35. Wire the error cluster from the "error out" terminal of the DAQ Assistant to the input terminal of the Unbundle By Name function and notice that the "status" element of the error cluster appears as shown in Fig. 2.6.11.

36. From the Functions palette, select **Express>>Arithmetic & Comparison>>Express Boolean>>Or** and drag the function to the right of the Unbundle by Name function in the block diagram.

37. Wire the outputs of the Unbundle by Name function and the stop control to the inputs terminals of the Or function and the output of the Or function to the conditional terminal, as shown in Fig. 2.6.11.

Note: The VI is complete and the Run arrow should not be broken. If the arrow is broken, click on the broken Run arrow to show the error(s).

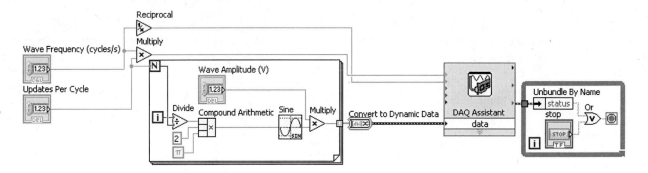

Figure 2.6.11   Completed block diagram of the continuous analog output example VI

Note: The front panel should look similar to that shown in Fig. 2.6.12. The front panel may be modified using knobs to give it more of the feel of a function generator. If you choose to include these optional modifications, follow Steps 38-40. Otherwise, you have completed the development of the VI and may proceed to the **Testing the VI** section.

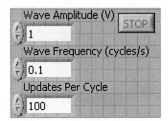

Figure 2.6.12   Default appearance of the front panel for the continuous analog output example VI

38. Separate the controls to allow space between them. Place the cursor over the "Wave Amplitude (V)" control in the front panel, right click, select "Replace" from the pop-up menu, and select **Express>>Numeric Controls>>Knob** as shown in Fig. 2.6.13.

39. Enlarge the knob using the blue handles, reposition the label above the knob, and add a digital display by right-clicking the cursor over the knob and selecting **Visible Items>>Digital Display**. Reposition the digital display if desired.

Note: The digital display allows the user to enter precise values for voltages that would otherwise be difficult to enter via the knob.

Warning: The knob's upper limit should be within the range of voltages allowed on the DAQ board to prevent any damage to the hardware.

40. Perform the same steps for the "Wave Frequency (cycles/s)" control so that the front panel looks similar to Fig. 2.6.14.

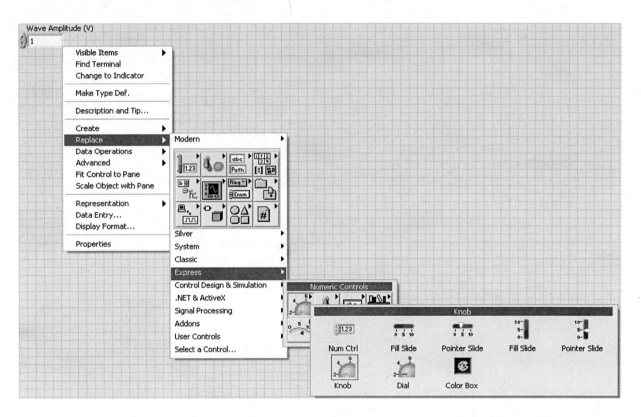

Figure 2.6.13 Sequence to replace a front panel control in the continuous analog output example VI

Congratulations! You have developed a single channel, circular-buffered, hardware-timed analog output VI that can generate updates continuously until stopped by the user. The VI may be used to simulate a function generator continuously generating a sine wave, or other types of waves with appropriate modifications. Be sure to save your program using one of the save options on the "File" pull-down menu.

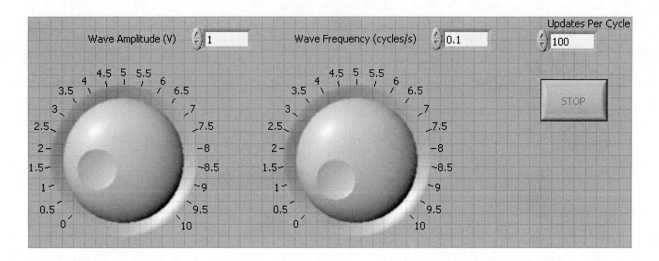

Figure 2.6.14 Modified front panel for the continuous analog output example VI

Testing the VI

Determine the analog output and analog ground pin numbers on the terminal connector block so that a set of leads may be connected to an oscilloscope or multimeter. Unlike with analog input connections, the DAQ Assistant does not have a Connector Diagram tab to show the pin number for the analog output channel, "ao 0", or the analog ground terminal, "ao GND". However, a device pinout diagram for your DAQ board can be found using the Measurement & Automation Explorer (MAX) software program, a National Instruments utility to manage hardware. Select "Measurement & Automation Explorer…" from the "Tools" pull-down menu. A window will appear like the one that is partially shown in Figure 2.6.15. Expand "Devices and Interfaces", right click on the DAQ board that was selected when you configured your channels using the DAQ Assistant, and select "Device Pinouts." Device Pinouts may also be selected in the toolbar at the top of the MAX window. The pinout sheet appears in a new window and the pin number for the analog output and analog ground terminals can be identified. For example, "ao 0" is pin 22 and "ao GND" is pin 55 on the NI PCI/PXI 6221 DAQ board.

Attach leads from the terminal connector block to an oscilloscope or a multimeter, if an oscilloscope is not available. Attach the terminal connector block's analog output channel to the oscilloscope's positive terminal and the terminal connector block's analog output ground channel to the oscilloscope's negative terminal. Note that the analog output ground is used for the negative terminal since a referenced single-ended system configuration was specified in the DAQ Assistant as shown in Fig. 2.6.8, which requires that the output signal is referenced to the measurement system ground on "ao GND".

After the leads have been connected, the VI is ready to run. If you are using a multimeter, the wave frequency must be low to display values of the sine wave, like the value of 0.1 cycles per second recommended in Step 18, because of the integrating effect of the multimeter. Click on the Run button in the toolbar to begin execution of the VI and observe the signal on the oscilloscope or multimeter. The VI will generate data continuously until the user selects the stop control in the front panel.

As a general practice, you should always ensure that the output voltage on the analog output channel is 0 V when you are done with the VI. One easy way to do this is to set the value of the wave amplitude control in the front panel equal to 0 V on the last run.

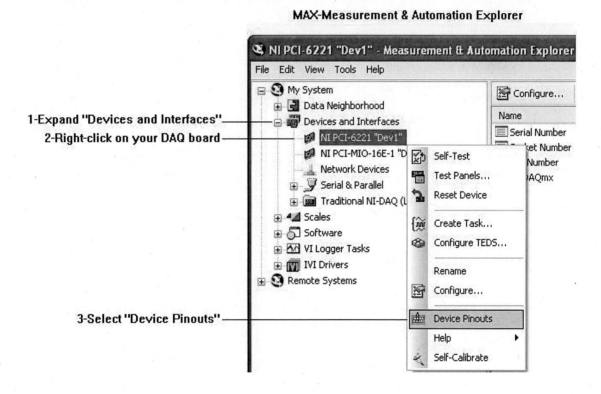

Figure 2.6.15   Using the Measurement &Automation Explorer utility to identify the pin connection for the output and ground channels

Discussion

It is interesting to make a comparison between two VIs that perform the same function but employ software timing versus hardware timing. The block diagrams of the VIs shown in Figs. 2.6.16 and 2.6.17 continuously generate analog output data. The VI shown in Fig. 2.6.16 is a variation of the VI shown in Fig. 2.4.2 and developed in Section 2.4.2, which employs software timing. The main difference between the VI in Fig. 2.6.16 and the one developed in Section 2.4.2 is that the controls for wave resolution and rate are placed outside the While Loop to make a more direct comparison to the VI developed in the current section. This means that the wave frequency cannot be changed after the While Loop execution begins. The VI shown in Fig. 2.6.17 was developed in this section and employs hardware timing.

Because the DAQ Assistant is configured for software timing in Fig. 2.6.16 (i.e., the data generation mode is set to "1 Sample (On Demand)"), data points that represent the intended sine wave must be created point by point since the DAQ Assistant can use only one value each iteration of the While Loop. Because the DAQ Assistant updates only one value when it is called, it must be placed inside the While Loop for continuous generation. The timing between updates is determined by the execution of the "Time Delay" Express VI, which is controlled by the computer's clock and when it is called by the software, hence software timing. The DAQ Assistant will be called repeatedly to continuously generate an output voltage each iteration of the While Loop until stopped by the user or an error occurs.

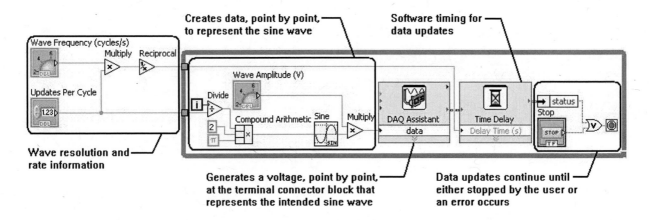

Figure 2.6.16 Functions of the various components on a variation of the Section 2.4.2 example VI to continuously generate voltages on an analog output channel using software timing

On the other hand, when the DAQ Assistant is configured for hardware timing with the use of a circular buffer as shown in Fig. 2.6.17 (i.e., the data generation mode is set to "Continuous Samples"), the entire data array representing the sine wave is created before any values are input to the DAQ Assistant. Once the data array is read by the DAQ Assistant, the data array is stored temporarily in a buffer memory and the DAQ Assistant updates the voltage point-by-point according to the user specified rate. The rate at which updates take place are controlled by the clock on the DAQ hardware, hence hardware timing. From the principle of data flow, execution will then pass to the While Loop and, therefore, the DAQ Assistant will continuously update voltages until the While Loop is stopped by the user or an error occurs.

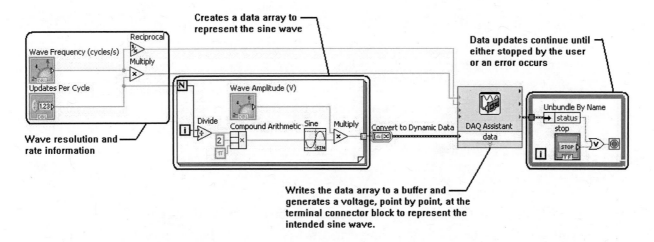

Figure 2.6.17 Functions of the various components of the current example VI to continuously generate voltages on an analog output channel using circular buffers and hardware timing

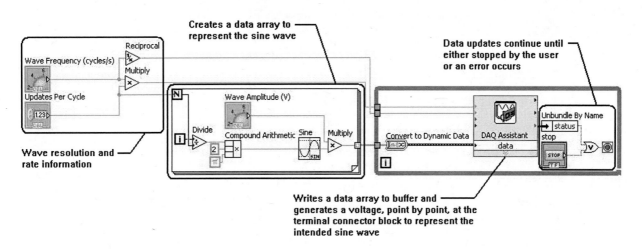

Figure 2.6.18 Functions of the various components of a modified form of the current example VI to continuously generate voltages on an analog output channel using circular buffers and hardware timing

It is informative to look at the block diagram in Fig. 2.6.18, which is a variation of the block diagram in Fig. 2.6.17, to better understand the DAQ Assistant. The DAQ Assistant is placed within the While Loop in the alternate block diagram shown in Fig. 2.6.18. The DAQ Assistant not only configures a data measurement or generation task, it also generates the code to perform the task. Two of the subVIs within the DAQ Assistant write the data array to the buffer and update the voltages. These operations are performed each iteration of the While Loop in Fig. 2.6.18. A continuous sine wave can be generated using the block diagram in Fig. 2.6.18 just like the block diagram in Fig. 2.6.17. However, since you are writing a new array each time the DAQ Assistant executes, you must be careful not to overwrite elements in the buffer that have not been updated. If this happens, the error shown in Fig. 2.6.19 will occur. It is possible to remedy this error by increasing the update rate. This ensures that all data elements will be updated before a new array is written to the buffer. This is equivalent to increasing the "Wave Frequency" control value in the current example. If the update rate is fixed by the physical process you are working with, you can also increase the write timeout. For the current VI, this means you could create a constant or control for the "timeout (s)" DAQ Assistant input instead of using the wired value automatically calculated.

The block diagram shown in Fig. 2.6.17 was used as the example VI in the current section since low frequency waves may need to be generated if an oscilloscope is not available. In this block diagram, the data array is written to buffer once to avoid the error of attempting to overwrite new data into the buffer.

Figure 2.6.19 Error message that is displayed if an attempt is made to overwrite data in the buffer before an update is generated

2.7 Learn by Doing

The problems in this section are offered to help you work on developing proficiency using LabVIEW for data acquisition. The problems may be multi-function in nature and strive to show the practical application of LabVIEW to real-life problems. The presentation of material in this section assumes that you have worked the introductory LabVIEW example problem in Section 1.4, which helps you to learn some basic LabVIEW concepts, and the skill-development problems in this chapter. The hope is that you will be able to complete the

LabVIEW proficiency problems without the need of a guide…the next step to developing LabVIEW VIs on your own.

2.7.1   Proficiency-Development Problem: General Purpose Analog Input

Introduction

The purpose of this problem is to develop a general purpose analog input VI that continuously samples multiple channels, applies linear scaling factors to the samples, displays current data in a chart during acquisition, writes data into a file suitable for a spreadsheet, and displays the entire data collected in a graph at the end of the measurement task. The VI employs software timing so that it is most suitable for moderate to low sampling rates.

This VI is similar to the skill-development problem in Section 1.4 although a new focus of this problem is the application of linear scaling to convert the samples into meaningful physical units. The linear scaling appears explicitly in the block diagram shown in the **Developing the VI** section. However, linear scaling can also be performed during the configuration of the measurement task using the DAQ Assistant, which is covered in the **Discussion** section.

Goals

1. Develop proficiency with single-function data acquisition concepts using LabVIEW's configuration approach.

2. Apply linear scaling to measurements either explicitly through functions in the block diagram or through task configuration using the DAQ Assistant.

3. Develop the software-timed general purpose analog input VI which samples multiple analog input channels and then scales, displays, and records the data continuously until stopped by the user.

Equipment

1. Analog input sources comprising sensors, a function generator, or a power supply, if sensors are unavailable.

Developing the VI

The front panel and block diagram of the general purpose analog input VI are shown in Figs. 2.7.1.1 and 2.7.1.2. All functions that have been employed in this VI have been described in this chapter or Section 1.4, except for Split Signals and Merge Signals. Split Signals splits a dynamic data signal into two or more signals and can be found in the functions palette under **Express>>Signal Manipulation>>Split Signals.** Merge Signals merges two or more dynamic data signals into a single output and can be found in the functions palette under **Express>>Signal Manipulation>>Merge Signals**. Both functions can be resized to add inputs or outputs.

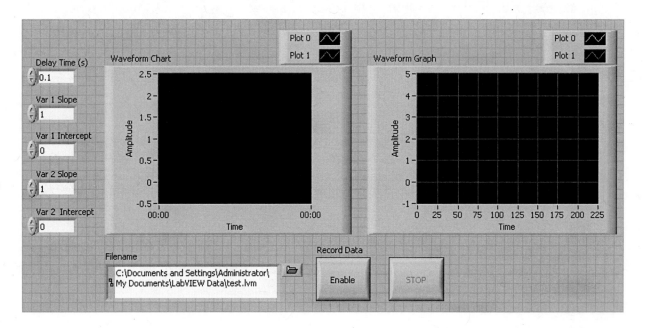

Figure 2.7.1.1   Front panel of the general purpose analog input VI

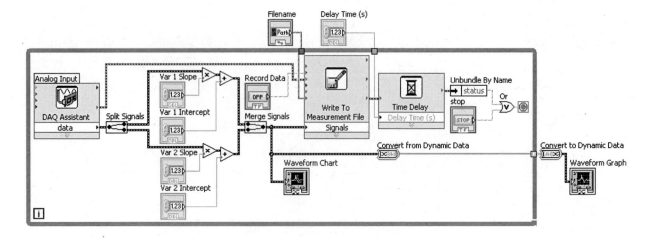

Figure 2.7.1.2   Block diagram of the general purpose analog input VI

The configuration of the task to measure the analog input signals using the DAQ Assistant is shown in Fig. 2.7.1.3. The default configuration values are appropriate if you will be using a function generator or power supply to provide the analog input signals. Otherwise if you are using sensors, the signal input range may need to be modified, depending on the types of sensors that will be used.

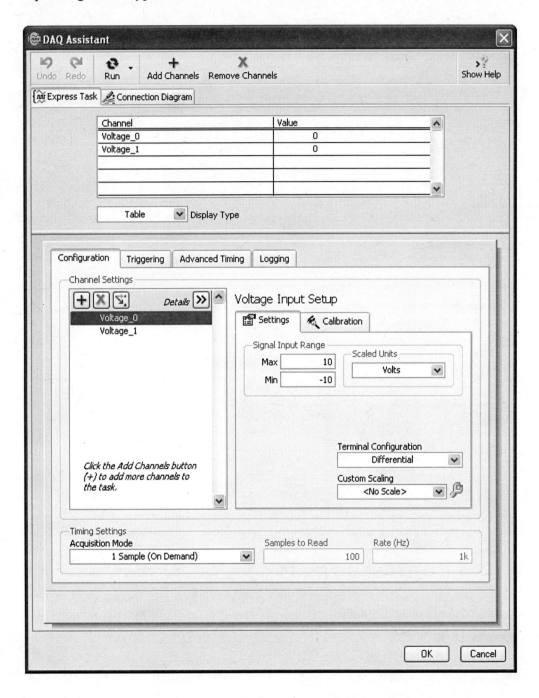

Figure 2.7.1.3   Configuration to measure multiple analog input channels using the DAQ Assistant for the general purpose analog input VI

The configuration of the file to store measurements is shown in Fig. 2.7.1.4. Enter an appropriate filename if the default filename is not suitable. "Append to file" is selected since the Express VI will be called repeatedly within the While Loop and new data will be appended every iteration. Time will be recorded in the first channel followed by the order in which the channels are listed in the DAQ Assistant. For the "Convert from Dynamic Data" Express VI select "1-D array of scalars-automatic" for the resulting data type and "2-D array of scalars-columns are channels" for the input data type for the "Convert to Dynamic Data" Express VI.

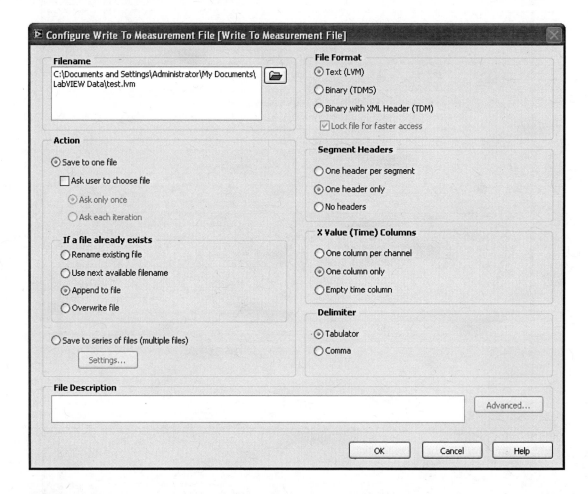

Figure 2.7.1.4   Configuration of the file to store the measured data using the Write to Measurement File Express VI

Fabrication and Testing

Attach the voltage sources, such as sensors, a function generator, or a power supply to the terminal block connector using channel 0 (ai0) and channel 1 (ai1), or any other appropriate channels. The voltage difference between the two leads of the voltage source, the positive and negative leads, will be measured since the channels were configured for a differential measurement system. Use the "Connection Diagram" in the DAQ Assistant to determine the terminals assigned to the designated analog input channels. Alternatively, you may use the device pinout diagram from the Measurement & Automation Explorer (MAX) to determine the terminal numbers on the terminal connector block. For a DAQ board with 16 analog input channels configured for a differential measurement system, the positive leads connect with the first eight channels, <ai0…ai7>, and the negative leads with the next eight channels, <ai8…ai15>, respectively. More specifically, if you selected "ai0" as one of your input channels in the DAQ Assistant, the positive lead connects to "ai0" and the negative lead connects to "ai8."

After the leads for the analog input signals have been connected, the VI is ready to run. The VI displays the analog input signals in the chart continuously but does not record the data in a file until you press "Enable" on the Record Data control in the front panel. This control allows you to reduce the data storage file size by only observing the data until you need to store it. Data storage ends when you press the Record Data control a second time. The entire data sampled is displayed in the graph after the measurement ends.

Discussion

Many sensors have a linear response to a physical stimulus. The electrical output from this type of sensor can be converted to physically meaningful units by linear scaling. The slope and intercept of the linear scaling is generally obtained from a calibration curve provided by the sensor manufacturer. The scaling of the sensor's electrical output through a multiplier and offset can be accomplished explicitly through functions in the block diagram or through the custom scaling option when configuring the measurement task with the DAQ Assistant.

The explicit use of functions in the block diagram to scale the analog input signals is shown in Fig. 2.7.1.5. The measurement task is configured to sample a voltage when the new Express task is created and no scaling is applied in the "Custom Scaling" option in the DAQ Assistant (see, for example, the Voltage Input Setup panel in Fig. 2.7.1.3). Different scaling factors are then applied to each signal (Fig. 2.7.1.5 (a)) or the same scaling factor is applied to all signals (Fig. 2.7.1.5 (b)).

An alternate approach is to apply the scaling factors when configuring the measurement task as shown in Fig. 2.7.1.6. Once again, the measurement task is configured to sample a voltage when the new Express task is created but this time the custom scaling is applied as shown in Fig. 2.7.1.6.

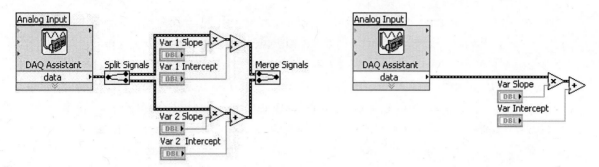

(a) Different linear scaling applied to each signal   **(b) The same linear scaling is applied to all signals**

Figure 2.7.1.5   Linear scaling applied explicitly through functions in the block diagram: (a) different scaling factors applied to each signal and (b) the same scaling factor applied to all signals

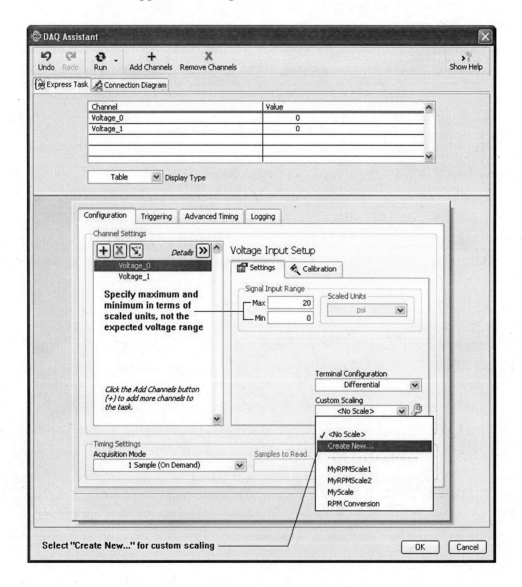

Figure 2.7.1.6 Initial steps to create a custom scale for an analog input channel

The maximum and minimum signal input range is specified in terms of the scaled units, not the anticipated voltage range. For example, let's assume that you have a pressure transducer with a linear calibration curve. The linear scale for the sensor is $y=2x+10$, where x is the voltage (in volts) of the analog input signal and y is the scaled units, like lb/in^2 (psi). You know before the test that the pressure in your process will vary from 0-20 psi, which is then specified as the maximum and minimum of the signal input range, as shown in Fig 2.7.1.6. Based on the signal input range you specified, the software understands that the anticipated voltage range is ±5V that the DAQ board will see and will select an appropriate input range for the board. Typically, a DAQ board with a bipolar range will have ±5V as an available option. However, if not, the next largest range will be automatically selected, likely ±10V.

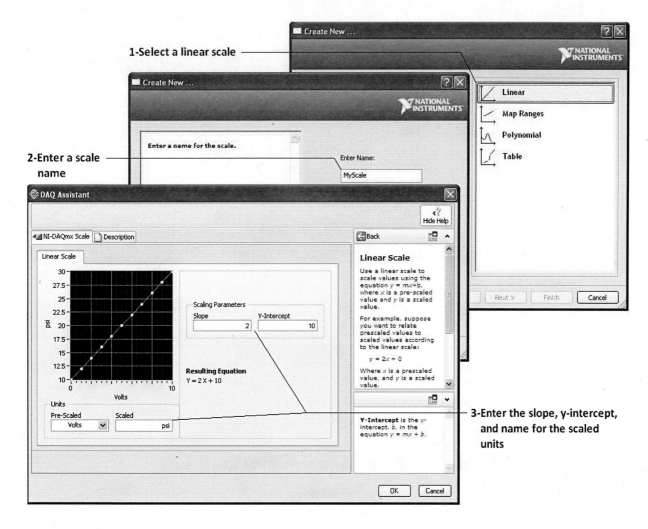

Figure 2.7.1.7 Steps to create a custom scale for an analog input channel

After the "Create New…" option is selected for the custom scaling, a "Create New…" window will appear as shown in Fig. 2.7.1.7. For this example, select a linear scale and give it a name. Then enter the slope, y-intercept, and a name for the scaled units. Repeat the preceding steps for each analog input channel that has a different scale. An existing scale may also be selected for a new channel. Nonlinear scales can also be created using different functions in the block diagram or through the "Create New…" window as shown in Fig. 2.7.1.7.

The scales that you create are available for use in other VIs. For example, the pull-down menu under Custom Scaling in Fig. 2.7.1.6 shows other available scales. You may access these scales to view, modify, or delete using the Measurement and Automation Explorer (MAX). To access the scales, launch MAX under the Tools pull-down menu in the front panel or block diagram and expand Scales and NI-DAQmx Scales as shown in Fig. 2.7.1.8.

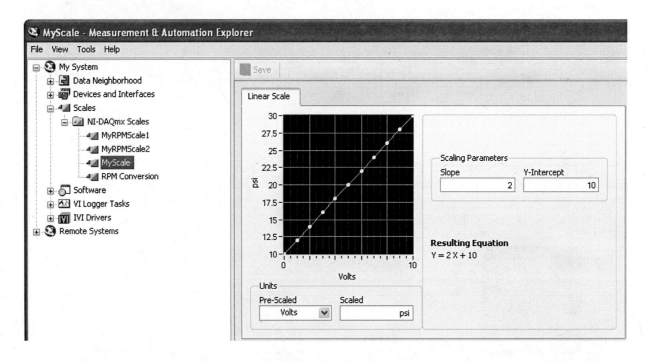

Figure 2.7.1.8   Partial view of the Measurement & Automation Explorer window that displays the available scales for analog input channels

2.7.2   Proficiency-Development Problem: Thermocouple Input

Introduction

Thermocouples are a common means to measure temperature since they are rugged, inexpensive, self-powered, and operate in a wide range of temperatures. They have the disadvantage of being non-linear in their response to temperature changes and require that the temperature of a reference junction be known. Furthermore, thermocouples have relatively low sensitivity, that is, they do not generate much voltage per degree change in temperature so that they generate only small voltage differences over moderate temperature changes, which can be a challenge for data acquisition systems. However, these drawbacks can be addressed.

Signal conditioning is often performed on thermocouple signals, such as signal amplification, filtering, linearization, and cold junction compensation. Signal amplification is common, especially for lower resolution DAQ boards, because of the low voltage output generated by the thermocouple. For example, consider the resolution of a 12-bit DAQ board with an input range of ±50 mV to the board. The smallest change in voltage detectable by the DAQ board is 24.4 μV (Note: resolution is calculated by dividing the board's voltage range by the number of levels on the board, or for this example, $100 \text{ mV}/2^{12}$). Since the typical thermocouple output is on the order of 20-60 μV/°C, this means that the DAQ board would not be able to detect a temperature change less than approximately 0.4-1.2 °C and signal amplification is recommended. However, the resolution of a 16-bit DAQ board with an input range of ±0.2 V is 6.1μV, which allows the board to detect temperature changes down to approximately 0.1-0.3°C. This is a range within the realm of direct measurement of the thermocouple signal. Filtering is often performed to remove the 60 Hz electrical noise that is picked up on the thermocouple leads. A 2-4 Hz low-pass filter will effectively remove this electrical noise. The thermocouple leads typically terminate in hardware with an embedded isothermal junction block, which is at a junction reference temperature. Software can then compensate for a reference temperature that is different from the standard ice-point temperature used as a reference in thermocouple voltage tables.

The purpose of this problem is to develop an analog input VI that makes continuous hardware-timed thermocouple measurements until stopped by the user. The DAQ Assistant has configuration windows set up specifically for many common sensors including thermocouples. Instead of reading in the analog input voltage and calculating the temperature manually through a calibration curve or table, LabVIEW performs this step and others, like cold junction compensation, automatically. This approach will be used in the present problem.

The problem will also explore the use of software filtering. The VI is set up so that the signal is filtered after sampling and compared with the unfiltered signal. A low-pass Butterworth software filter is used with a low-pass cutoff frequency that can be modified during the execution of the VI to observe the effects of the filtered signal.

Goals

1. Develop proficiency with single-function data acquisition concepts using LabVIEW's configuration approach.

2. Take thermocouple measurements and explore the application of a software Butterworth filter on the signal.

3. Develop the hardware-timed buffered analog input VI to sample thermocouple data continuously until stopped by the user.

Equipment

1. Thermocouple (Type J, K, N, R, S, T, B, or E)
2. Pyrex glass beakers (2)
3. Hot plate

Developing the VI

The front panel and block diagram of the analog input VI to take thermocouple measurements are shown in Figs. 2.7.2.1 and 2.7.2.2. All functions that have been employed in this VI have been described in this chapter or Section 1.4, except for the Filter Express VI. The Filter Express VI contains a number of different filters that can be applied to a signal and provides different views of the filtered signal. The Filter Express VI can be found in the functions palette under **Express>>Signal Analysis>>Filter**.

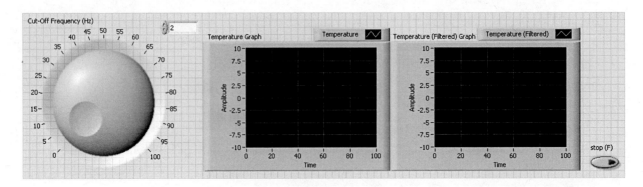

Figure 2.7.2.1   Front panel of the analog input VI to measure a thermocouple signal

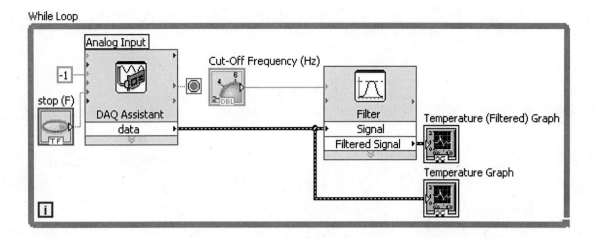

Figure 2.7.2.2   Block diagram of the analog input VI to measure a thermocouple signal

The steps to create a thermocouple measurement task using the DAQ Assistant and the configuration of the task are shown in Figs. 2.7.2.3 and 2.7.2.4, respectively.

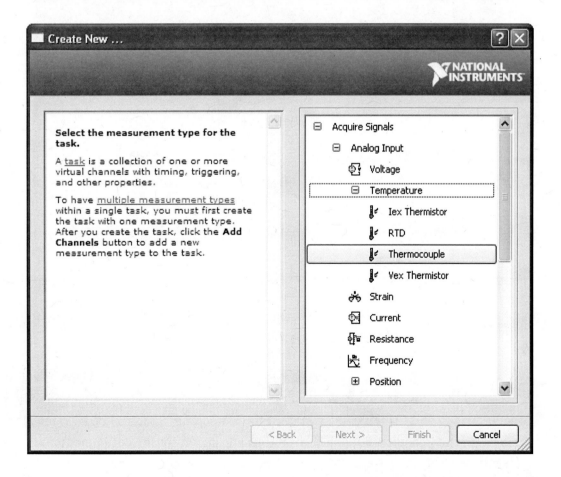

Figure 2.7.2.3   Procedure to create a thermocouple measurement task using the DAQ Assistant

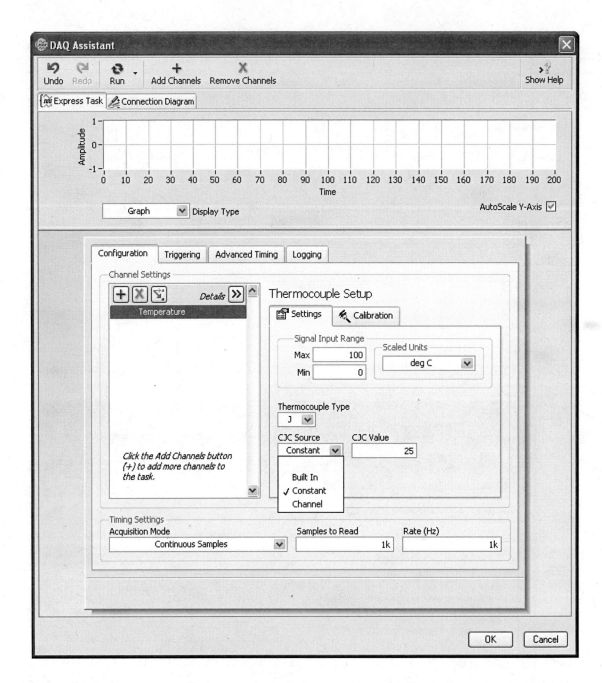

Figure 2.7.2.4   Configuration using the DAQ Assistant to measure a thermocouple
                     channel for the analog input VI

Configure the task to measure the thermocouple according to the values shown in Fig.
2.7.2.4 with two possible exceptions: (1) select the thermocouple type that you will use to
conduct the test and (2) select the source of the temperature that will be used to calculate
the cold junction compensation. Three options are shown for the cold junction
compensation source as shown in Fig. 2.7.2.4: built in, constant, and channel. Some DAQ
hardware has a built-in sensor to measure temperature and the built in option could be
used if you are using this type of hardware. The channel option could be used if you are

using your own sensor, such as an IC temperature sensor to measure the temperature of the junction. Finally, the constant temperature option could be used if the DAQ hardware is located in a room with a stable known temperature.

The configuration of the filter for the thermocouple measurement is shown in Fig. 2.7.2.5. The parameters and values shown are suitable for the initial set of samples. The view mode is configured to show the time-based filtered signal ("Signals" option). Alternatively, you may display the filtered signal based on the frequency spectrum ("Show as spectrum" option), which is informative if you want to observe the attenuation of individual frequency components of the signal.

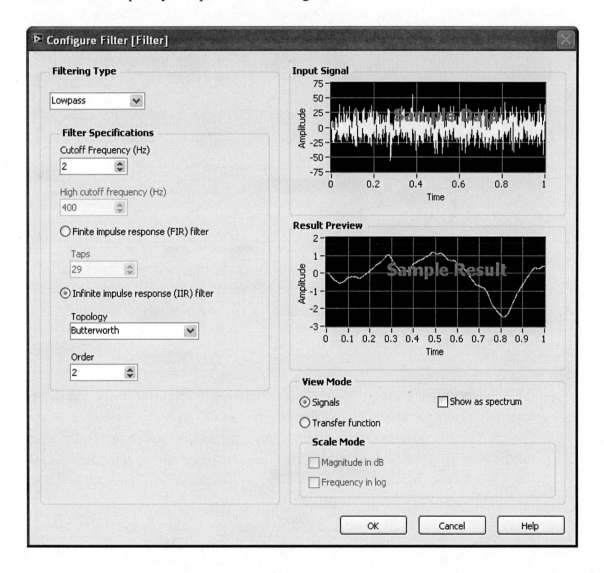

Figure 2.7.2.5   Configuration of the filter for the thermocouple measurement using the Filter Express VI

Fabrication and Testing

Attach the leads of the thermocouple to the terminal connector block. The voltage difference between the two leads, the positive and negative leads, will be measured since the channel was configured for a differential measurement system. Use the "Connection Diagram" in the DAQ Assistant to determine the terminals assigned to the designated analog input channel. Alternatively, you may use the device pinout diagram from the Measurement & Automation Explorer (MAX) to determine the terminal numbers on the terminal connector block. For a DAQ board with 16 analog input channels configured for a differential measurement system, the positive leads connect with the first eight channels, <ai0…ai7>, and the negative leads with the next eight channels, <ai8…ai15>, respectively. More specifically, if you selected "ai0" as one of your input channels in the DAQ Assistant, the positive lead connects to "ai0" and the negative lead connects to "ai8."

Prior to running the VI, fill one beaker with water and heat on the hot plate until the water boils. Fill the other beaker with mostly ice and enough water to saturate the ice. The water in these two beakers will serve as known temperatures for testing the thermocouple.

After the leads for the analog input signals have been connected, the VI is ready to run. Place the thermocouple successively in both beakers of water. The VI displays both the filtered and unfiltered temperature signal. Using the control in the front panel, observe the effect of adjusting the cutoff frequency on the filtered signal. Stop the VI when a range of cutoff frequencies has been tested.

Discussion

After the test is completed, double-click on the Filter Express VI to show the effect of the filter settings on the last block of thermocouple data as shown in the example data in Fig. 2.7.2.6. You can show the effect of the filter on the data by selecting "Transfer function" for the view mode and selecting magnitude and the frequency on a log scale as shown in Fig. 2.7.2.7. You can vary parameter values, such as the cutoff frequency and the order of the Butterworth filter, to see the effects on your data.

This example VI used software filtering although it should be noted that equivalent filtering could have been done with hardware. The filters could also be designed to amplify the signal. The thermocouple signal could have passed through a passive or an active RC or RLC filter to achieve similar effects. Software filtering was used because the software makes it easy to explore variations in the cutoff frequency on the electrical noise. In general, one should be careful when using software filtering because of problems with aliased signals. Aliasing is discussed in Section 2.1.3. However, thermocouple signals will generally have low frequency content unless the temperature of the physical phenomenon is changing rapidly. Software filtering was a viable option in this example because the temperature does not change rapidly and the sampling rate is fast relative to the phenomenon.

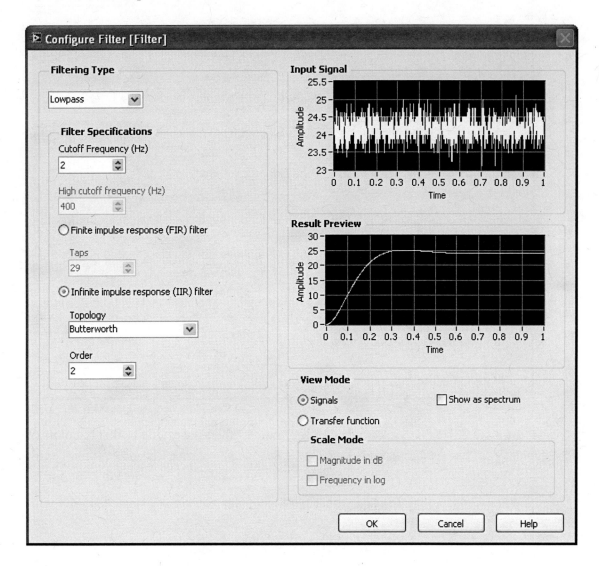

Figure 2.7.2.6   Plots showing the effect of the second-order Butterworth filter on a sample signal

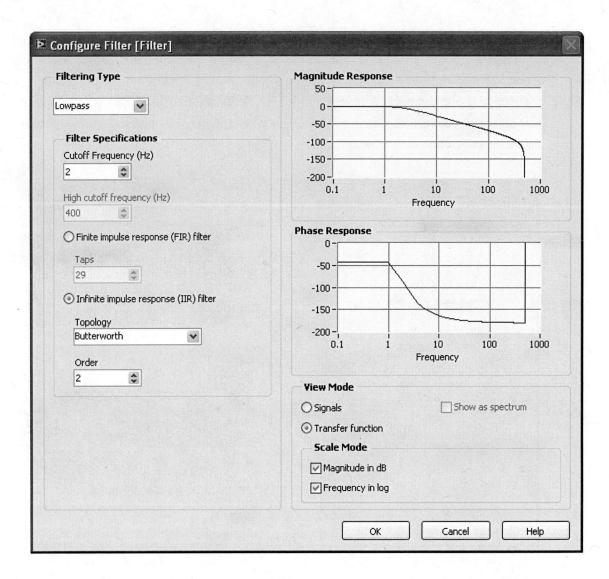

Figure 2.7.2.7.   Alternate configuration of the view mode to display plots of sample data

2.7.3   Proficiency-Development Problem: Strain Gage Input

Introduction

The strain gage is the most common device to measure strain in a material, which is defined as the ratio of the change in length of a body due to an applied force to the total length of the body. The most common type of gage is the bonded metallic strain gage. This type of gage has a thin metallic foil wire arranged in a serpentine pattern bonded to a flexible backing that is affixed to a specimen with a special adhesive. The long axis of the metallic foil wire of the strain gage is mounted parallel to the strain to be measured in the body. The change in cross-sectional area of the metallic foil wire from the strain in the body results in a small change in the resistance of the strain gage. The small changes in resistance of the strain gage are typically measured in a Wheatstone bridge arrangement.

A schematic of a Wheatstone bridge arranged in a quarter-bridge circuit is shown in Fig. 2.7.3.1. The schematic assumes that the lead wires that connect the strain gage to the Wheatstone bridge are short and that the resistance of the lead wires can be neglected. Resistors R_1-R_3 are equal to the resistance of the strain gage, R_G, which is typically 120, 350, or 1000 Ω. A typical mode of operation is to initially adjust the resistance of R_3 using a hardware adjustable or electronically injected counter voltage under a no-load condition to make the output voltage, V_O, across the bridge equal to zero. The bridge is balanced under this condition. When a load is applied to a specimen, the resistance of the strain gage changes and a voltage is generated across the bridge.

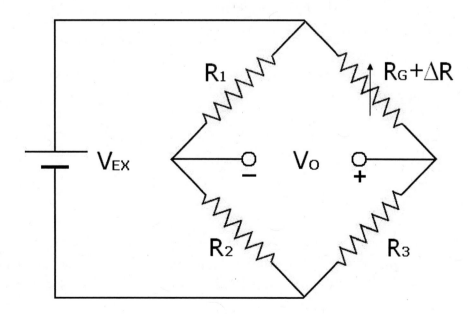

Figure 2.7.3.1   Strain gage used as one arm of a Wheatstone bridge in a quarter-bridge circuit

The change in the resistance of the strain gage is small, generally only a fraction of a percent. This creates only a small imbalance in the bridge and produces changes in output voltage on the order of microvolts to millivolts. Because of this, direct measurement of output voltage is susceptible to electrical noise. Generally, strain is measured with the use of a strain gage indicator, an instrument which allows the bridge to be balanced and filters and amplifies the output voltage signal. The strain is typically shown in an LED display and is often retransmitted as an amplified analog output voltage with or without an offset. However, in spite of the accuracy and ease of use of a strain gage indicator, it does have the disadvantage of appearing as a "black box" when learning the principles of strain gage measurement.

The problem in this section guides the user to develop a simple Wheatstone bridge in a quarter-bridge circuit. With care in the development of the hardware circuit and the use of a software low-pass filter that can be used to attenuate the electrical noise, the simple Wheatstone bridge arrangement can take strain measurements to within approximately ±20 microstrain. While the simple circuit is not recommended for general engineering applications, it is a good tool to learn the general principles of strain gage measurement.

The purpose of this problem is to develop an analog input VI that takes continuous hardware-timed direct strain gage measurements until stopped by the user.

Goals

1. Develop proficiency with single-function data acquisition concepts using LabVIEW's configuration approach.

2. Take strain gage measurements and explore the use of a Butterworth filter on conditioning the signal.

3. Develop the hardware-timed buffered analog input VI to sample strain gage data directly and continuously until stopped by the user.

Equipment

1. Strain gage mounted to an appropriate specimen, which for the purposes of this problem will be assumed to be a flat aluminum bar, 3.18 mm (1/8 inch) thick, 25.4 mm (1 inch) wide, and 305 mm (12 inches) long. Other similar specimens may be used although recommended configuration values may have to be adjusted to accommodate differences in the specimen.
2. Strain gage wire

3. C-clamp
4. Hook and 454 g (1 lb) weight
5. Three resistors each with resistance equal to that of the strain gage and with a 0.5 W power rating or higher.
6. Power supply
7. Prototype board
8. Soldering iron and solder
9. Twisted shielded pair cable
10. Resistor, 10 kΩ

Developing the VI

The front panel and block diagram of the analog input VI to take strain gage measurements are shown in Figs. 2.7.3.2 and 2.7.3.3. All functions employed in this VI have been described in this chapter or Section 1.4, except for the Split Signals function, General Error Handler VI, and the Filter Express VI. Split Signals splits a dynamic data signal into two or more signals and can be found in the functions palette under **Express>>Signal Manipulation>>Split Signals.** The General Error Handler VI returns the description of an error during execution, if one occurs, and can be found under **Programming>>Dialog & User Interface>>General Error Handler**. The Filter Express VI contains a number of different software filters that can be applied to a signal and provides different views of the filtered signal. The Filter Express VI can be found in the functions palette under **Express>>Signal Analysis>>Filter**.

The output voltage across the Wheatstone bridge is sampled two ways. The first channel is configured to sample the voltage and output the unfiltered voltage signal while the second channel samples the same voltage but is configured to output a strain measurement that then passes through a software filter. These two different ways of sampling the voltage allow the user to measure the voltage signal (that will eventually be used as an input to the configuration of the strain gage channel) while displaying the filtered strain measurement. The configuration of the voltage channel is shown in Fig. 2.7.3.4. The largest gain setting (smallest voltage range) available for your DAQ board should be selected since the output voltage is on the order of millivolts.

The steps to create a strain measurement task using the DAQ Assistant and the configuration of the task are shown in Figs. 2.7.3.5 and 2.7.3.6, respectively. The configuration of the strain measurement task requires a number of inputs specific to your experimental setup. The gage factor and gage resistance of the strain gage you are using can be determined from the manufacturer's strain gage data sheet. The initial voltage value specified in Fig. 2.7.3.6 assumes a balanced bridge. However, the initial voltage for an unloaded specimen using your custom-built Wheatstone bridge should be measured with a multimeter and entered. The excitation voltage should also be noted and entered as it can be a voltage other than 2 V, as shown in Fig. 2.7.3.6, as long as the excitation voltage is small enough to avoid self-heating of the resistors. This is discussed in the Fabrication and Testing section. A lead resistance of zero assumes short lead wires. Finally, the expected minimum and maximum range of strain for your specimen should be calculated prior to testing and entered.

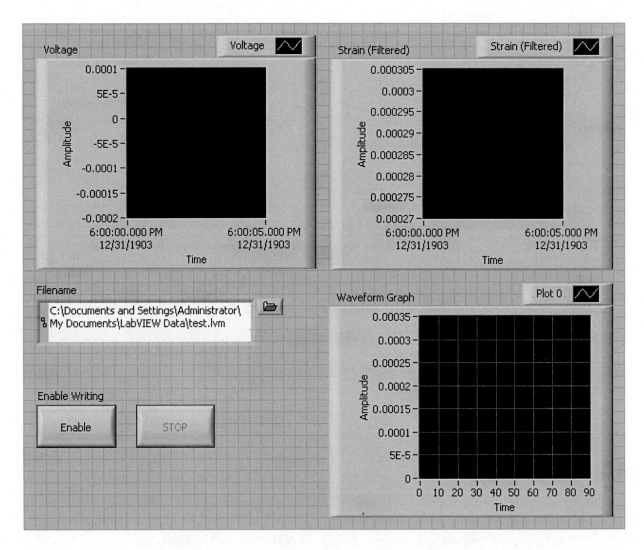

Figure 2.7.3.2   Front panel of the analog input VI to measure a strain gage signal

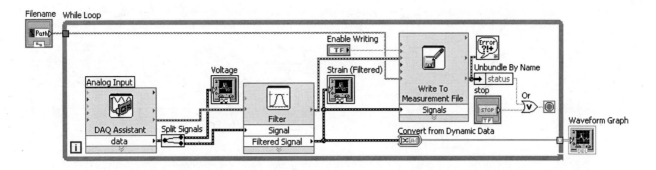

Figure 2.7.3.3   Block diagram of the analog input VI to measure a strain gage signal

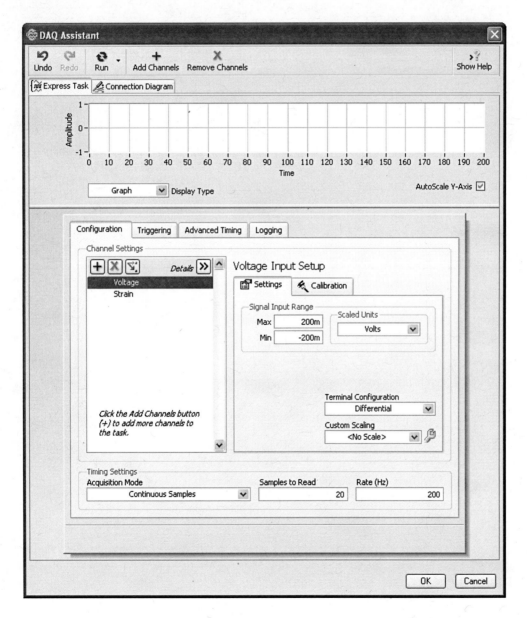

Figure 2.7.3.4   Configuration using the DAQ Assistant to measure the output voltage of the Wheatstone bridge for the analog input VI

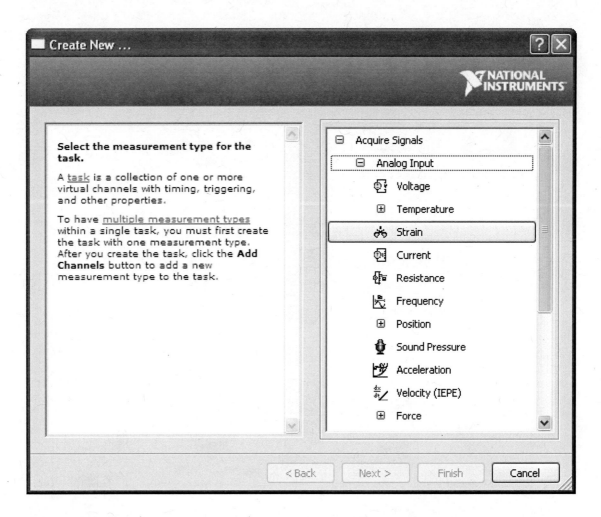

Figure 2.7.3.5   Procedure to create a strain measurement task using the DAQ Assistant

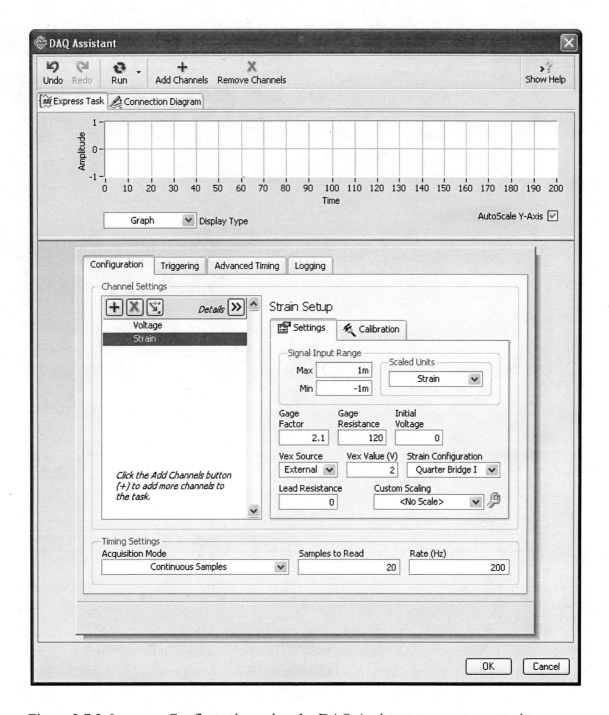

Figure 2.7.3.6   Configuration using the DAQ Assistant to measure a strain gage channel for the analog input VI

The configuration of the filter for the strain measurement is shown in Fig. 2.7.3.7. The parameters and values shown are suitable for the relatively slow changing strain signal expected for this problem. The cutoff frequency will need to be modified for rapidly changing signals as discussed later in the Discussion section. The view mode is configured to show the time-based filtered signal ("Signals" option).

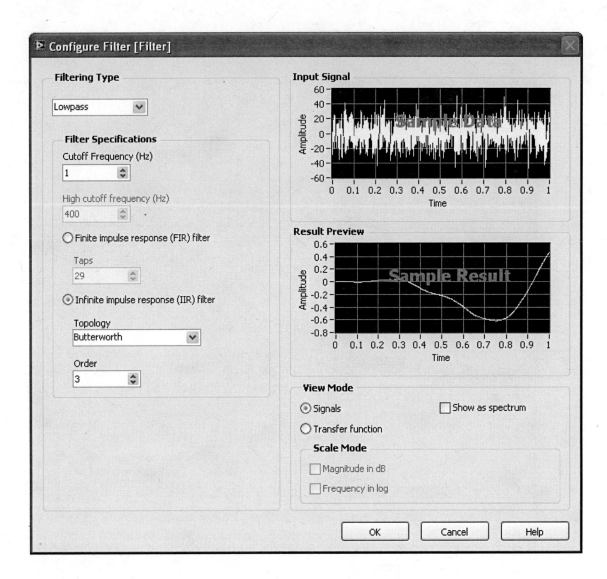

Figure 2.7.3.7   Configuration of the filter for the strain measurement using the Filter Express VI

The configuration of the Convert from Dynamic Data VI is shown in Fig. 2.7.3.8. Enable indexing must be selected at the tunnel in the While Loop to display the entire set of data. You must also transpose the data for proper display on the graph. This is accomplished by right-clicking on the pane of the graph in the front panel and selecting "Transpose Array".

The configuration of the Write to Measurement File VI is shown in Fig. 2.7.3.9. It can be seen from Fig. 2.7.3.3 that a control is placed within the While Loop that allows the user to enable data to be written to the measurement file as the test is conducted. The control allows the user to record and stop recording data during the test to create a file of manageable size.

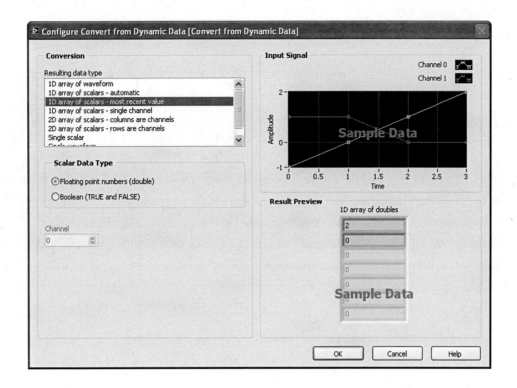

Figure 2.7.3.8   Configuration of the conversion of dynamic data for graphing strain measurements

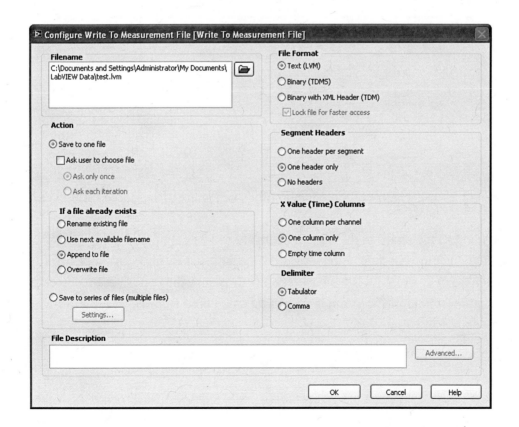

Figure 2.7.3.9   Configuration to write strain measurements to a file

Fabrication and Testing

This section describes the method to measure the strain at the base of a cantilevered beam when a load is attached to the free end of the beam. This problem assumes that an aluminum bar, 3.18 mm (1/8th inch) thick, 25.4 mm (1 inch) wide, and 305 mm (12 inches) long will be the test specimen, which yields a reasonable range of strain for a modest attached weight. Other similarly sized bars may also be used. A strain gage should be affixed to the middle of the 25.4 mm (1 inch) wide bar 25.4 mm (1 inch) from the end that will be clamped. The long axis of the strain gage should be parallel to the long axis of the bar. The bar should be clamped on the lip of a counter or table with the strain gage facing up and the center of the strain gage in line with the edge of the counter. When the test is conducted, an approximately 454 gm (1 lb) weight will be attached to the free end of the beam 254 mm (10 inches) from the center of the strain gage, as shown in Fig. 2.7.3.10.

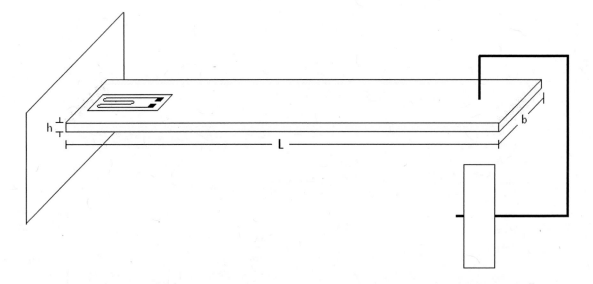

Figure 2.7.3.10   Experimental setup of a strain gage affixed to a cantilever beam

Prior to the test, the strain in the loaded beam should be calculated using analytical methods to enter appropriate values for the "Signal Input Range" parameter in Fig. 2.7.3.6 and to compare with the measurements to ensure the test is set up correctly. The strain, ε, at the center of the strain gage can be calculated from Eq. 2.7.3.1 for a cantilever beam loaded as shown in Fig. 2.7.3.10.

$$\varepsilon = \frac{6PL_P}{Ebh^2}$$

Eq. 2.7.3.1

The load, P, is applied a distance, L_P (not shown in Fig. 2.7.3.10) from the center of the strain gage. In Eq. 2.7.3.1, the modulus of elasticity is E, the beam width is b, and the beam thickness is h.

Build the Wheatstone quarter bridge circuit as shown in Fig. 2.7.3.11. Ideally, all resistors will have the same resistance as the strain gage although small variations are unavoidable unless you are using precision resistors. If there is some variation in the resistance of the resistors, you should match the R_3 resistor as close as possible to the resistance of the strain gage and match the resistance of the R_1 and R_2 resistors. The R_1-R_3 resistors, strain gage leads, and twisted shielded pair cable leads for the DAQ connector block should be soldered to the prototype board to reduce electrical noise. The bias resistor, R_B, should be on the order of 10 kΩ to 100 kΩ and connects the negative analog input channel to the analog input ground on the DAQ terminal connector block.

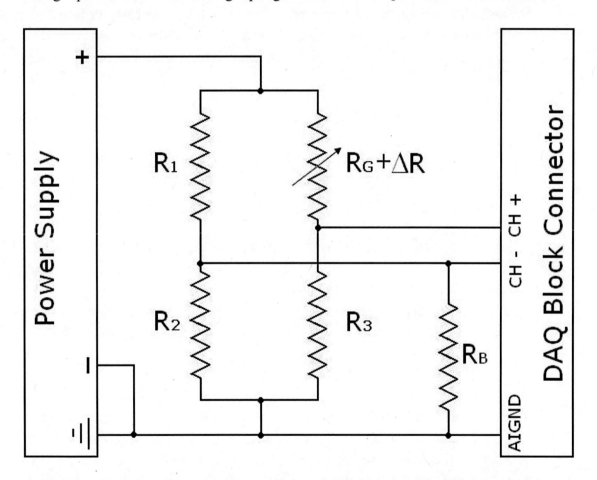

Figure 2.7.3.11   Wheatstone quarter-bridge circuit to measure strain

A small excitation voltage should be applied across the Wheatstone bridge and the output voltage should be measured with a multimeter. The highest possible excitation voltage is desirable from the standpoint of maximizing the output voltage but the excitation voltage must also be small enough to avoid self-heating in the resistors. The power dissipated by each resistor can be calculated with the target dissipated power less than approximately 2% of the power rating for the resistors. For example, an excitation voltage of 2 V is suitable for a 120 Ω resistor with a 0.5 W rating. If the excitation voltage is too large, self-heating of the resistors will manifest itself as drift in the output voltage or a variable output voltage as the resistors are fanned even under otherwise static conditions for the cantilevered beam.

The voltage across both voltage dividers, that is, the output voltage of the Wheatstone bridge, should be measured with a multimeter and entered as the initial voltage in the DAQ Assistant configuration window for the strain gage virtual channel, as shown in Fig. 2.7.3.6. Ideally, the output voltage will be small, say, on the order of a few millivolts. The multimeter may not provide an accurate enough reading of the initial voltage to ensure the unloaded strain in the cantilever beam is zero. If this is the case, the initial voltage used in the DAQ configuration window may need to be updated with a more accurate voltage reading from the DAQ board after a trial test to get the unloaded strain closer to zero. Based on the trial run with an unloaded specimen, the initial voltage across the Wheatstone bridge should be noted on the voltage graph shown in Fig. 2.7.3.2. The displayed voltage will generally be noisy and an average voltage should be estimated. The strain is very sensitive to the voltage across the Wheatstone bridge, even variations on the order of a few microvolts. The estimated average initial voltage across the Wheatstone bridge entered into the strain gage configuration window may need to be adjusted slightly to yield zero strain for the unloaded specimen.

After the initial voltage is adjusted to zero the initial strain, the VI can be executed and the weight can be hung on the free end of the cantilever beam at a location 254 mm (10 inches) from the center of the strain gage. The strain value recorded by the DAQ board should be noted and compared to your theoretical calculations. The test may be repeated using a strain gage indicator, if available, and output values for strain compared.

Discussion

An extension of the previous exercise is to measure the natural frequency and damping ratio of the cantilever beam. If the end of the cantilever beam is depressed and suddenly released, the beam will respond with damped vibrations until it returns to its original (equilibrium) state. The damped vibrations are the response of an under damped second-order system subjected to a step function input.

With only slight modifications, the same VI can be used to measure the strain gage output to calculate the natural frequency and damping coefficient of the cantilever beam. A low cutoff frequency was used for the low-pass filter in the previous example problem because of the quasi-static loading. However, because of the higher frequency content expected for the dynamic loading example described in this discussion section, a higher cutoff frequency will be used. Likewise, because of the dynamic response of the system, the sampling rate must be increased to avoid aliasing and faithfully reproduce the time content of the signal.

There is a challenge to selecting an appropriate sampling rate for an incoming analog signal with unknown frequency content. If the sampling rate is too low, a false digitized signal of lower frequency than the incoming signal may result. This is a phenomenon known as aliasing and is described in Section 2.1.3. To avoid aliasing, the sampling rate must be greater than two times the maximum frequency of the incoming signal.

One option to avoid aliasing of an unknown incoming signal is to establish a sampling rate and then use an analog low-pass hardware filter to attenuate any incoming signal frequencies at or above the Nyquist frequency, which is one-half of the sampling frequency. A conservative approach is to select a sampling rate well beyond what would be expected from the phenomenon, even up to the maximum supported by the DAQ hardware. After the first test is recorded and the frequency content of the physical phenomenon is now known, the sampling rate may adjusted relative to the newly determined signal frequency if the size of the data file is unmanageable.

As is often the case, even though the maximum frequency of our physical phenomenon is unknown a priori, analytical theory can provide an estimate for setting our sampling rate. In this case, the Euler equation from beam theory can be used to predict the natural frequency of a cantilever beam. The natural frequency, ω_i in Hz (cycles/sec), is a solution of Euler's equation.

$$\omega_i = \frac{(\beta_i L)^2}{2\pi} \left(\frac{EI}{\bar{m}L^4}\right)^{\frac{1}{2}}$$
Eq. 2.7.3.2

In Eq. 2.7.3.2, E is the modulus of elasticity of the beam material, I is the moment of inertia of the cross section of the beam, $\bar{m}$ is the mass of the beam per unit length, L is the effective length of the beam, and $(\beta_i L)^2$ is a constant dependent on both the frequency mode and the boundary conditions of the beam. For a cantilever beam (one fixed end and one free end), $(\beta_1 L)^2$ equals 3.51602 for the fundamental (first-mode) frequency.

For a uniform beam of rectangular cross section (b wide by h thick), the moment of inertia is $I = {bh^3}/{12}$ and the mass per unit length is $\bar{m} = \rho bh$, where ρ is the density of the material. The fundamental frequency of a cantilevered uniform beam of rectangular cross section is given in Eq. 2.7.3.3.

$$\omega_1 = \frac{(\beta_1 L)^2}{2\pi}\left(\frac{Eh^2}{12\rho L^4}\right)^{\frac{1}{2}}$$

Eq. 2.7.3.3

An example will now be provided to illustrate the options to select the sampling rate to record the fundamental natural frequency of the beam used in the quasi-static loading problem. For this example, the aluminum beam is h=3.18 mm thick, b=25.4 mm wide, and L=290 mm from the fixed end to the free end of the beam. Assuming a density of ρ=2770 kg/m^3 and a modulus of elasticity of E=70x10^9 N/m^2, the fundamental natural frequency of the cantilevered beam is 30.7 Hz using Eq. 2.7.3.3.

It's understood that the calculated fundamental natural frequency is only an estimate. However, if it was truly the actual frequency, the minimum sampling rate would be twice the natural frequency of the beam to avoid aliasing errors. This minimum sampling rate would preserve the frequency content of the analog input signal but would only provide two digitized points per cycle. The shape of the analog input signal, that is, the time content of the signal, could not be faithfully reproduced by a digitized signal with only two points per cycle. To preserve the time content of the analog input signal, a sampling rate an order of magnitude or more larger than the maximum frequency of the input signal is appropriate. A sampling rate of 1000 samples/sec will be selected since the amplitude of the wave will be used later in the analysis of the data. This will provide approximately 30 samples per cycle and will reasonably capture the peak of the wave.

Since an estimate of the natural frequency of the cantilever beam has been calculated, an analog low-pass filter prior to the DAQ hardware is not indicated for this experiment. If the natural frequency of the cantilever beam was unknown, an analog low-pass filter with a cutoff frequency of 500 Hz would be mandated for the selected sampling rate of 1000 Hz. Since the risk of an aliased signal is minimal, a digital low-pass filter is an option to reduce the 60 Hz electrical noise contained in the digitized signal. However, a digital low-pass filter with a cutoff frequency of 60 Hz is advised only after a preliminary test with a high cut-off frequency shows the natural frequency of the cantilever beam is less than 60 Hz.

Perform the experiment to determine the natural frequency of the cantilever beam. Prior to the experiment, modify the LabVIEW input parameters to appropriate values for this experiment. If you are using an aluminum beam as described in the quasi-static portion of this problem, set the samples to read at 100, the sampling rate to 1000 Hz, and a cut-off frequency of 60 Hz. Depress the end of the beam and release. Record the strain until the beam's vibrations are damped and the beam returns to its original position. The goal of this extended exercise is to determine the fundamental natural frequency and the damping ratio of the cantilever beam. The damping ratio and natural frequency of the beam can be determined using the following data analysis techniques.

The beam oscillates at its damped natural frequency, ω_d, also called its ringing frequency, and is related to the beam's fundamental natural frequency, ω_n, through the solution of a step input to the second order system.

$$\omega_d = \omega_n(1 - \zeta^2)^{\frac{1}{2}}$$
Eq. 2.7.3.4

The damping ratio, ζ, is the ability of the system to absorb or dissipate energy.

The damping ratio can be determined using the logarithmic decrement technique by comparing the amplitude of the peaks at periodic intervals of the recorded wave. The logarithmic decrement, δ, can be calculated from the recorded experimental signal using Eq. 2.7.3.5.

$$\delta = \frac{1}{n} ln\left(\frac{x_1}{x_{n+1}}\right)$$
Eq. 2.7.3.5

The variable x_1 is the maximum amplitude of a wave at an arbitrary point in time and x_{n+1} is the maximum amplitude of a wave n peaks later. Based on the sampling rate, there may not be a reduction in amplitude with each successive peak. Because of this, it is strongly recommended that you use many cycles (for example, $30<n<60$) to calculate the logarithmic decrement using Eq. 2.7.3.5.

An alternate analytical expression for the logarithmic decrement, which is shown in Eq. 2.7.3.6, can be derived by taking the ratio of the equation for the theoretical amplitude of an under damped wave at two different peaks.

$$\delta = \frac{2\pi\zeta}{(1-\zeta^2)^{\frac{1}{2}}}$$
Eq. 2.7.3.6

The damping ratio can then be determined by using the experimental data to calculate the logarithmic decrement, δ, using Eq. 2.7.3.5 and then the damping ratio by manipulating Eq. 2.7.3.6.

$$\zeta = \frac{\delta}{((2\pi)^2+\delta^2)^{\frac{1}{2}}}$$
Eq. 2.7.3.7

Once the damping ratio has been determined, the natural frequency of the beam can be determined from Eq. 2.7.3.4 given that the damped natural frequency, ω_d, is the reciprocal of the period of the recorded oscillatory experimental wave.

2.7.4   Proficiency-Development Problem: Signal Conditioning Using Filters

Introduction

Filters are commonly used to attenuate undesirable frequency content in a time-varying signal. For example, signals from instruments often contain unwanted electrical noise. This proficiency-development problem employs a software filter, which requires the selection of a number of filter parameters in its configuration window. The remainder of this introduction section provides a description of the filter concepts that are associated with the filter configuration window.

An ideal filter has pass band and stop band frequency regions with sharp demarcations between these regions occurring at a cutoff frequency. An ideal filter passes incoming signal information for wave frequencies within the frequency range of the pass band but does not permit any information of the signal to pass through the range of frequencies of the stop band. The filter may be designed to allow low-frequency signal content to pass (low-pass filter), to allow high frequency signal content to pass (high-pass filter), to allow signal content to pass in only a range of frequencies (band-pass filter), or to allow signal content to pass for all frequencies other than a specified range of frequencies (band-stop or notch filter). A low-pass filter is commonly applied to experimental measurements since changes in physical processes often vary slowly relative to the frequency of electrical noise.

Unlike an ideal filter that passes no signal information through the stop band, a real filter will only attenuate (as opposed to remove) a signal in the transition band, which is analogous to the stop band in ideal filters. In real filters, the cutoff frequency is defined as the frequency in which the filter attenuates the power of the incoming signal by one half. This corresponds to a magnitude ratio of 0.707 in the amplitude of the signal. In the transition band, components of the incoming signal having frequencies farther from the cutoff frequency have correspondingly larger reductions in signal amplitude. The rate at which the amplitude decreases with frequency is referred to as the filter roll off.

A filter may be designed to amplify the incoming signal that passes through the pass band. These types of filters incorporate an operational amplifier, which requires excitation from an external power supply, and hence are called active filters. A passive filter does not amplify the signal through the pass band and does not require an operational amplifier or, therefore, an external power source.

An example of a low-pass passive filter is shown in Fig. 2.7.4.1. For incoming signals containing frequencies that are low relative to the cutoff frequency, the capacitor can quickly charge or discharge as the incoming voltage, V_i, varies and essentially match the incoming voltage. Since the voltage at the junction between the resistor and the capacitor is at the same voltage as the source, no current passes through the resistor and the capacitor behaves as an open circuit. Since the output voltage, V_o, is in parallel with the capacitor, the signal passes through the filter without attenuation in the pass band. For incoming signals that contain frequencies that are high relative to the cutoff frequency, the capacitor can neither charge nor discharge fast enough to respond to the incoming signal. The voltage at the junction between the resistor and the capacitor is only a fraction of the incoming voltage, which is increasingly attenuated with higher incoming signal frequencies. Because the voltage across the capacitor is only a small fraction of the incoming voltage, it continues to charge even after the incoming voltage has peaked and is decreasing, as long as the decreasing voltage of the incoming signal is still larger than the voltage across the capacitor. Eventually, the voltage of the incoming signal drops below the voltage across the capacitor. The voltage across the capacitor then peaks and begins to drop. This lag in peaks between the incoming voltage and the voltage across the capacitor manifests itself as a phase shift in the output voltage relative to the input voltage.

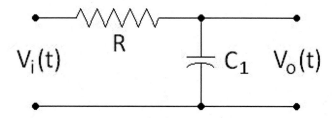

Figure 2.7.4.1   First-order passive low-pass RC filter circuit

There are many different types of filters and they are characterized by their response features, which influence the filter's behavior in the pass band and transition band. One type of filter referred to as an infinite impulse response (IIR) filter, yields a non-zero response to an impulse over an infinite period of time. For example, the RC filter in Fig. 2.7.4.1 has an exponential response to an input, which is characterized by the time constant of the circuit. An IIR filter commonly used in experimental measurements is the Butterworth filter. With an appropriate filter design and proper selection of component values, the Butterworth filter transmits an input signal with minimal change in magnitude to the output signal in the pass band (a feature often termed maximally flat) and rolls off linearly in the transmission band when the signal frequency is plotted on a logarithmic scale.

The rate of roll off for a Butterworth filter is determined by the order of the filter: the higher the filter order, the more rapid the roll off. The order of the filter is determined by the number of reactive elements, such as, the number of capacitors and inductors, in the filter. For example, Fig. 2.7.4.1 is a first-order passive low-pass RC Butterworth filter circuit since it contains one capacitor. Additional reactive elements to the circuit increase the order of the filter and also increase the roll-off slope. With proper selection of resistive, capacitive, and inductive values, the circuit shown in Fig. 2.7.4.2 can behave as an nth-order Butterworth filter. The order of the Butterworth filter can be both odd and even numbered values.

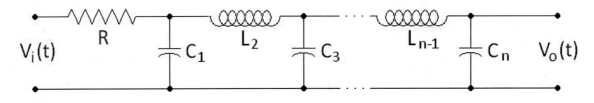

Figure 2.7.4.2 n^{th}-order passive low-pass RLC filter circuit

Goals

1. Explore the use of a passive first-order low-pass Butterworth filter on signal attenuation as the wave frequency is increased.

2. Explore the effects of sampling rate on aliasing of signals.

Equipment

No equipment is required to perform the proficiency-development problem. However, the extended proficiency-development problem described in the discussion section requires the following equipment.

1. Function generator and appropriate wire lead
2. A 1μF capacitor and a 4 kΩ resistor or any other capacitor-resistor pair that yields a 40 Hz cutoff frequency
3. Breadboard
4. Resistor, 10 kΩ

Developing the VI

The front panel and block diagram of the VI to process a simulated signal using a software filter are shown in Figs. 2.7.4.3 and 2.7.4.4. All functions employed in this VI have been described in this chapter or Section 1.4, except for the Simulate Signals VI, the Filter Express VI, the Tone Measurements VI, and the Bundle function. The Simulate Signals VI simulates a function generator's ability to generate sine, triangle, square, and sawtooth waves and can be found in the functions palette under **Express>>Signal Analysis>>Simulate Signal.** The Filter Express VI contains a number of different filters that can be applied to a signal and provides different views of the filtered signal. The Filter Express VI can be found in the functions palette under **Express>>Signal Analysis>>Filter**. The Tone Measurements VI reports the amplitude, frequency, and phase of the single tone with the largest amplitude of a wave and can be found in the functions palette under **Express>>Signal Analysis>>Tone Measurements**. The Bundle function assembles different elements into a cluster and can be found in the function palette under **Programming>>Cluster, Class &Variant>>Bundle**. Meter is an indicator and can be found in the controls palette under **Modern>>Numeric>>Meter**.

The configuration to simulate the sine wave using the Simulate Signal VI is shown in Fig. 2.7.4.5. The sine wave is configured to have amplitude of 1 with no offset in amplitude or phase. The frequency was entered at 10 Hz but ultimately will be determined by the user through the frequency control in the front panel. The sampling of the wave was configured to simulate continuous acquisition with a DAQ board. The sampling rate was set at 1000 samples/second to satisfy the Nyquist frequency requirement since the frequency control in the front panel permits the simulation of waves up to 500 Hz.

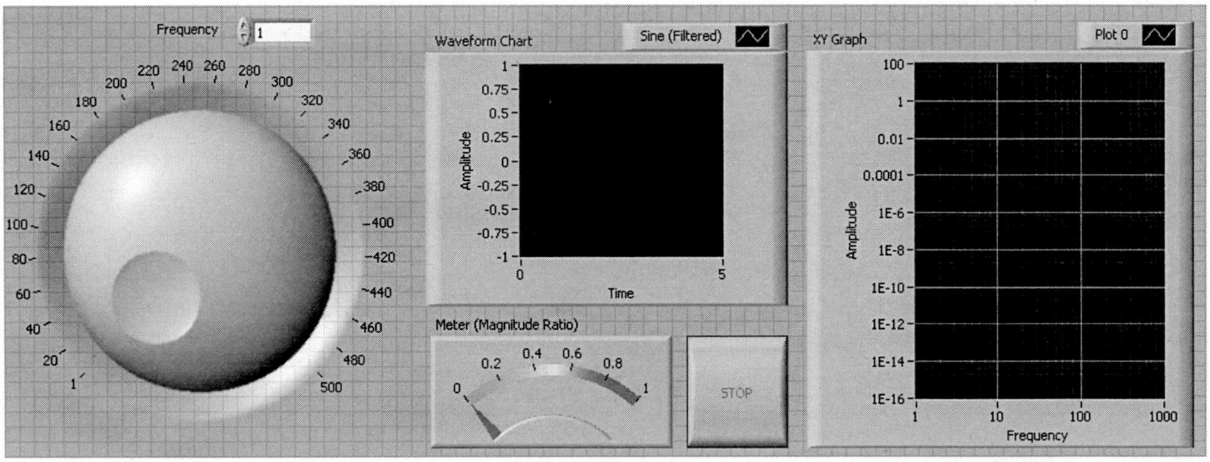

Figure 2.7.4.3 Front panel of the VI to process a simulated signal using a software filter

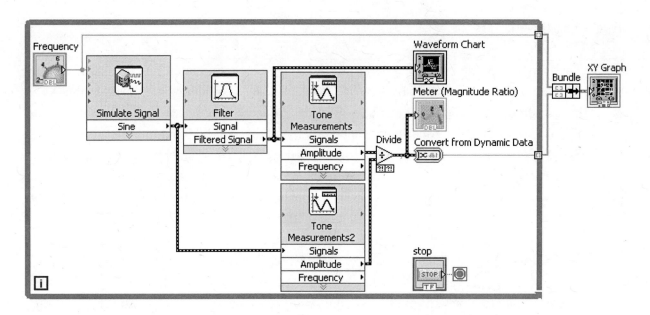

Figure 2.7.4.4   Block diagram of the VI to process a simulated signal using a software filter

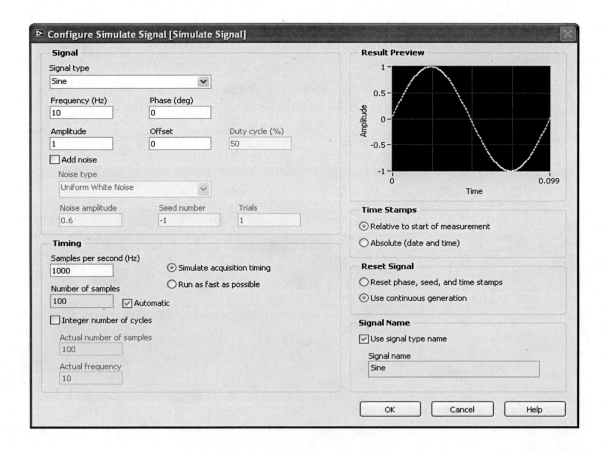

Figure 2.7.4.5   Configuration to simulate a sine wave for the VI to condition signals using a software filter

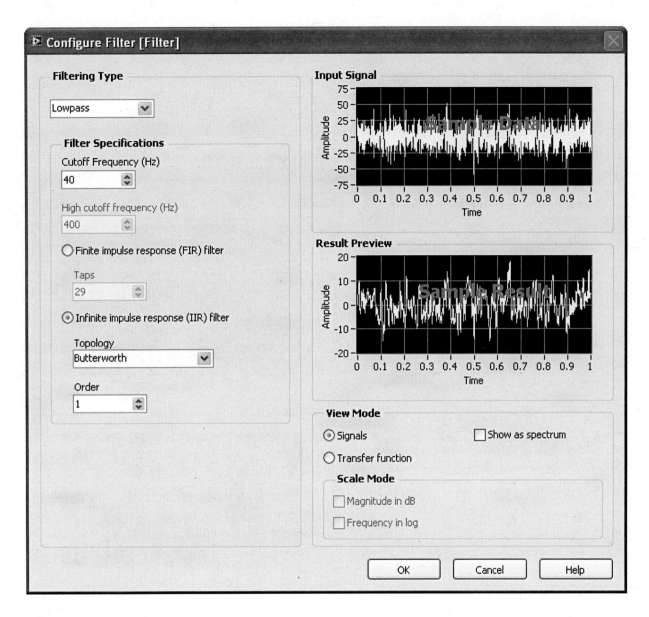

Figure 2.7.4.6   Configuration of the filter for the VI to condition signals using a software filter

The simulated signal then passes through a software filter, which was configured as a first-order passive low-pass Butterworth filter with a cutoff frequency of 40 Hz. A description of a first-order passive low-pass Butterworth filter is given in the introduction section of this proficiency-development problem. The configuration of the software filter is given in Fig. 2.7.4.6.

The amplitude and frequency of the filtered and unfiltered signals are determined by the Tone Measurements VIs. Both the Tone Measurements and Tone Measurements2 VIs have the same configuration as shown in Fig. 2.7.4.7. The amplitude of the filtered signal is then divided by the amplitude of the unfiltered signal to show the attenuation of the signal by the filter as the frequency of the signal is increased. The magnitude ratio of the filtered to unfiltered signal is displayed during the execution of the VI on the Meter indicator and plotted on the graph as a function of wave frequency after simulation of the signal ends.

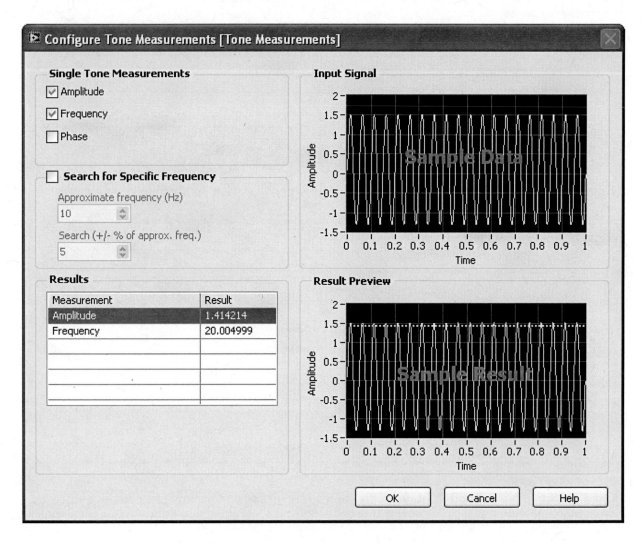

Figure 2.7.4.7   Configuration of the Tone Measurements VI for both the filtered and non-filtered simulated signals to report the amplitude and frequency of the wave component with the largest amplitude

The configuration of the Convert from Dynamic Data VI is shown in Fig. 2.7.4.8. Enable indexing must be selected at the tunnel in the While Loop to display the entire set of data. Be sure to select XY Graph, not Waveform Graph since you are plotting one variable as a function of another. Select **Mapping>>Logarithmic** for both X and Y scales of the XY Graph.

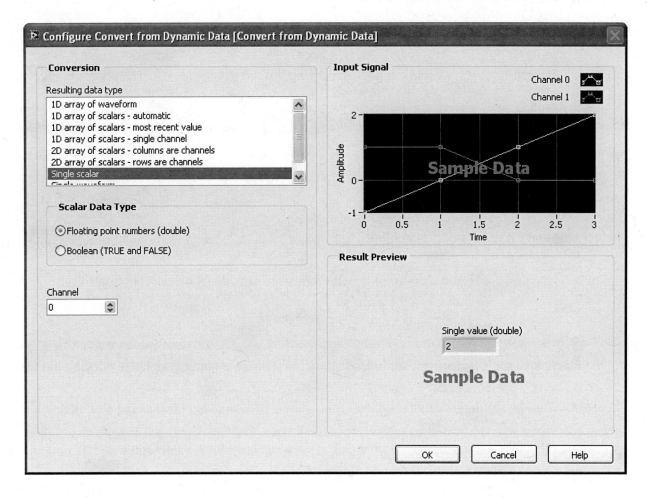

Figure 2.7.4.8   Configuration of the conversion of dynamic data to graph the ratio of the magnitude of the filtered to unfiltered signals as a function of wave frequency

Fabrication and Testing

This section describes the procedure to examine the attenuation of the input signal by the software filter. No hardware is required to perform this procedure.

A sine wave, whose frequency varies continuously from 1 to 500 Hz, will be used as the simulated signal. Prior to the execution of the VI, ensure that the value of the frequency control is set at 1 Hz. Start execution of the VI and slowly increase the frequency of the wave from 1 to 500 Hz while noting the reduction in relative magnitude of the filtered signal on the meter and chart. After stopping the execution of the While Loop, the magnitude ratio should appear as a function of wave frequency in the XY graph similar to that shown in Fig. 2.7.4.9.

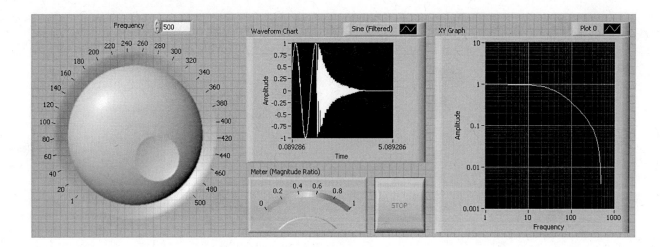

Figure 2.7.4.9   Magnitude ratio of the filtered to unfiltered signal as a function of the frequency of the simulated wave

Another point to note is that to avoid aliasing of the signal, the sampling rate must be at least twice the frequency of the highest frequency of the incoming signal according to the Nyquist criterion. Aliasing is discussed in Section 2.1.3. Since the sampling rate was set at 1000 Hz, the maximum frequency of the simulated signal is 500 Hz. The Simulate Signal VI will not permit any generated signal with frequencies greater than one-half the sampling rate. For example, if you try to generate a wave with a frequency of 501 Hz by changing the value in the digital display of the frequency control, you will get an error message from the Simulate Signal VI indicating that the wave frequency must be less than or equal to one-half of the sampling rate. However, in real-life applications, no error message will appear and the user must be aware of the limitations imposed by the Nyquist criterion. The extended proficiency-development problem in the **Discussion** section explores this topic.

Discussion

The purpose of this extended proficiency-development problem is to explore the use of a passive first-order low-pass Butterworth *hardware* filter and to demonstrate the potential problems of the sampling rate on aliasing the signal. In the proficiency-development problem presented earlier, filtering was performed by a software filter after "sampling" of the signal; the "sampling" that would normally occur in the DAQ hardware, of course, was simulated in the Simulate Signal VI. The current problem is similar to the previous problem except that hardware filtering occurs *before* the signal is digitized by the DAQ hardware.

The electrical circuit for the passive first-order low-pass Butterworth filter is shown in Fig. 2.7.4.10. The filter will be designed to have a cut-off frequency of 40 Hz as was used in the previous problem. This occurs when $f_c = \frac{1}{2\pi RC}$ (Hz) or, in other words, with any RC time constant that equals 0.003979 seconds. One possible combination is a 1 µF capacitor and approximately a 4000 Ω resistor (3979 Ω resistor, to be exact!). The function generator should be configured to generate a sine wave with a ±1 V amplitude, no offset, and with a frequency that varies from 3 to 3000 Hz or similar range. Both the filtered and non-filtered signals are recorded to calculate the magnitude ratio of the two signals.

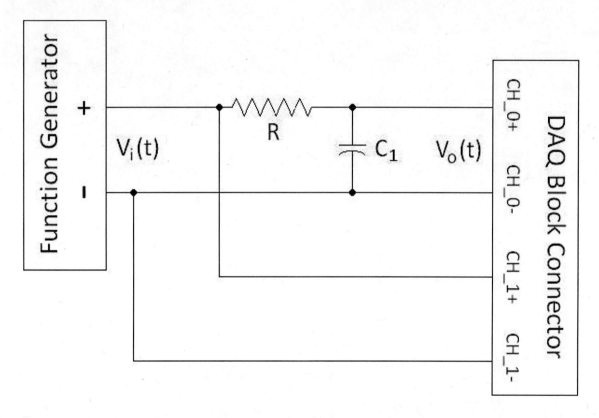

Figure 2.7.4.10   Electrical circuit for a passive first-order low-pass hardware filter

The VI in the proficiency-development problem must be modified as shown in Figs. 2.7.4.11 and 2.7.4.12 to perform the same objectives using the hardware filter. The function generator and the analog input measurement task configured and generated by the DAQ Assistant replace the need for the Simulate Signals VI to generate and "sample" a signal. Likewise, the hardware filter replaces the software filter configured using the Filter VI.

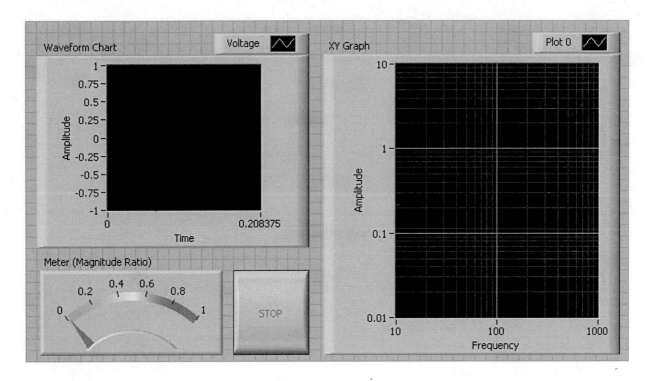

Figure 2.7.4.11   Front panel of the VI to process a signal using a hardware filter

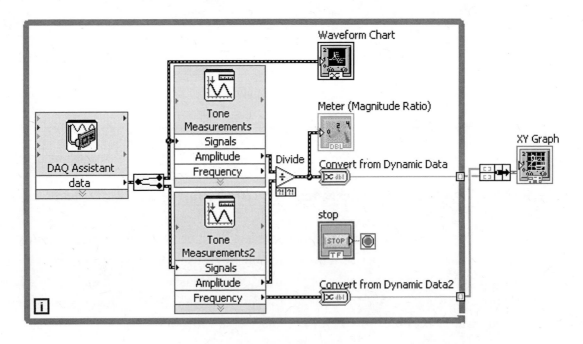

Figure 2.7.4.12   Block diagram of the VI to process a signal using a hardware filter

Both analog input channels are configured using the DAQ Assistant as shown in Fig. 2.7.4.13. Even though the input wave frequency will vary up to 3000 Hz, the sampling rate is intentionally set at 1000 Hz. This sampling rate is lower than dictated by the

Nyquist criterion to illustrate the potential problems that can arise with aliasing of a signal. The Convert from Dynamic Data2 VI is configured as shown in Fig. 2.7.4.8.

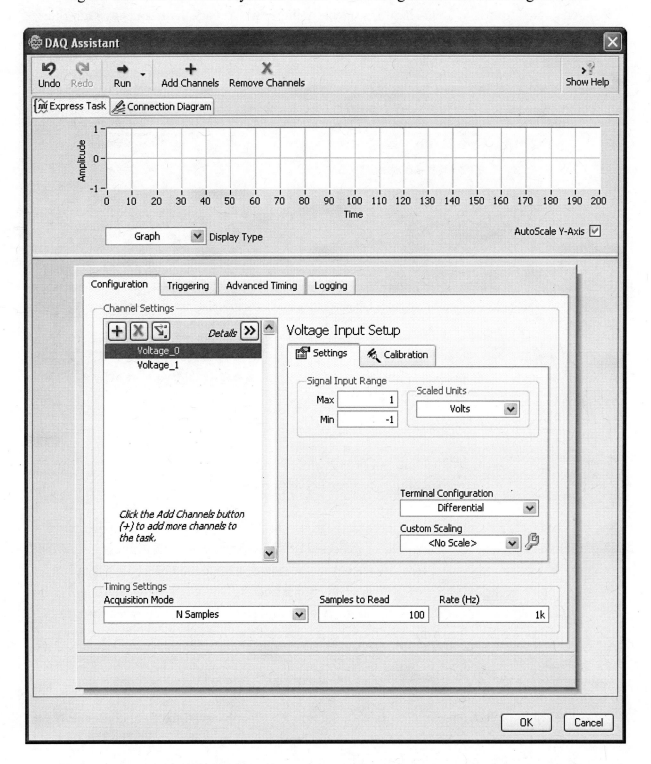

Figure 2.7.4.13   Configuration of the DAQ Assistant for the analog input channels to measure the signal from the function generator and hardware filter

Once the electrical circuit shown in Fig. 2.7.4.10 is complete, execute the VI in Figs. 2.7.4.11 and 2.7.4.12 and *slowly* vary the frequency of the sine wave from the function generator from 3 to 3000 Hz. It is especially important to vary the frequency with fine resolution near multiples of 500 Hz, the Nyquist frequency, to get a response similar to that shown in Fig. 2.7.4.14.

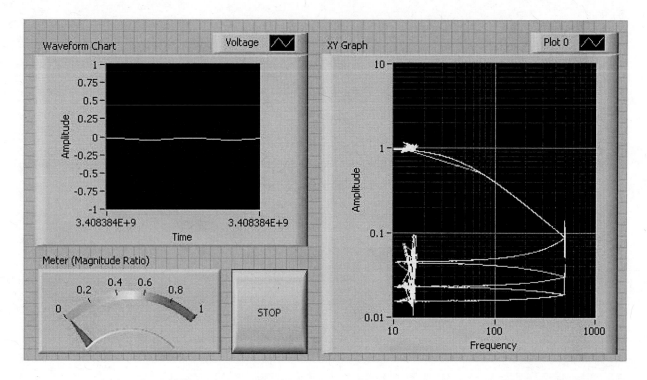

Figure 2.7.4.14   Magnitude ratio of the filtered to unfiltered signal as a function of the frequency of the digitized wave (including alias frequencies)

The results for the magnitude ratio with respect to the frequency of the digitized wave behave similarly to what would be expected of a low-pass filter with a cutoff frequency of 40 Hz for input wave frequencies below the Nyquist frequency of 500 Hz. Except for the noise at the extremes of the frequency range and the lower line between roughly 10-70 Hz, which is an artifice of switching decade scales on the function generator, the magnitude ratio is unity for low frequencies, has a value near 0.7 at the 40 Hz cutoff frequency, and rolls off linearly in the transition band. However, above the Nyquist frequency of 500 Hz, the impact of alias frequencies is observed.

The folding phenomenon discussed in Section 2.1.3 is observed for frequencies above the Nyquist frequency. As the frequency of the input signal increases above the Nyquist frequency, the apparent frequency of the digitized wave approaches zero at twice the Nyquist frequency and so on. Of course, the attenuated wave that passed through the hardware filter still has the same frequency as the input wave. The problem lies in the sampling rate used to digitize the data.

Once the sampling rate is modified to exceed twice the maximum frequency of the input signal, results that would be expected for a low-pass filter are generated, as shown in Fig. 2.7.4.15. The results shown in Fig. 2.7.4.15 were generated using the same VI and hardware that were used to produce the results shown in Fig. 2.7.4.14 except that the sampling rate was increased to 10,000 samples/second and the samples to read were increased to 1000.

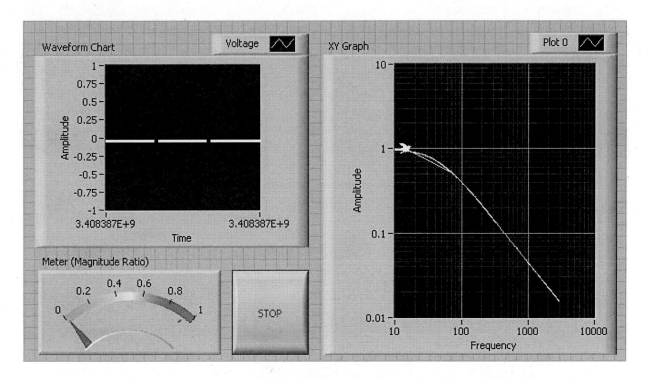

Figure 2.7.4.15   Magnitude ratio of the filtered to unfiltered signal as a function of the frequency of the digitized wave using a sampling rate that satisfies the Nyquist criterion

2.7.5   Proficiency-Development Problem: Analog PID Compensator

Introduction to PID Control Theory

This problem uses a proportional-plus-integral-plus-derivative (PID) compensator to demonstrate the use of the analog output function. The PID compensator can be used to control hardware, such as the position of a servomotor. However, if appropriate hardware is not available, you can still create the VI described in this section to observe how the analog output function works by using the output of the DAQ board as an input to the same DAQ board to match a software set point.

PID is a second-order controller and is widely used in feedback control systems. The proportional component is pure gain, that is, the compensation is proportional to the instantaneous error. The error is the difference between the set point and the output of the plant (system that is being controlled) and is the compensator input. A pure proportional compensator cannot provide zero steady-state error. The integral component is proportional to the accumulated error and provides dynamic compensation. Because the integral component is based on the integrated effect of the error, it is a slow reaction control mode. Integral control has a potential problem called reset windup or integral windup. If there is a large step input, the integral component can accumulate a large output, one that is larger than the physical limits of the actuator (actuator saturation). This can create a large overshoot during the delay while the compensator winds down and can create severe oscillations. One means to mitigate this effect is to clamp the integrator output to lie between a high and low value. The derivative component is based on the rate of change of the error and also provides dynamic compensation. One limitation of the derivative component is that it can yield large responses to high-frequency control errors.

The output, $u(t)$, of a PID compensator in the time domain is given in Equation 2.7.5.1.

$$u(t) = K_p e + K_i \int_0^t e\, dt + K_d \frac{de}{dt} \qquad \text{Eq. 2.7.5.1}$$

In Eq. 2.7.5.1, K_p, K_i, and K_d are the compensator gains for the proportional, integral, and derivative components, respectively, and $e(t)$ is the input error to the compensator. Equation 2.7.5.1 may also be expressed in the differential form.

$$\frac{du}{dt} = K_i e + K_p \frac{de}{dt} + K_d \frac{d^2 e}{dt^2} \qquad \text{Eq. 2.7.5.2}$$

The velocity algorithm, a finite-difference approximation of Eq. 2.7.5.2 that yields the change in value of the compensator input, can be obtained using backward difference approximations and an average value of the input error. The backward difference form of the first derivative is given in Eq. 2.7.5.3, where Δt is the difference in time between the two time steps at t_k and t_{k-1}.

$$\frac{de}{dt} \approx \frac{e_k - e_{k-1}}{\Delta t}$$

Eq. 2.7.5.3

The form of Eq. 2.7.5.3 will also be applied to the $\frac{du}{dt}$ term in Eq. 2.7.5.2. The backward difference form of the second derivative is given in Eq. 2.7.5.4.

$$\frac{d^2 e}{dt^2} \approx \frac{e_k - 2e_{k-1} + e_{k-2}}{(\Delta t)^2}$$

Eq. 2.7.5.4

Finally, using the finite-difference approximations, Eqs. 2.7.5.3 and 2.7.5.4, in Eq. 2.7.5.2 and using the average value for the error, $e = \frac{e_k + e_{k-1}}{2}$, in the integral component yields the velocity algorithm form of Eq. 2.7.5.2.

$$u_k = u_{k-1} + K_p(e_k - e_{k-1}) + K_i \Delta t \frac{e_k + e_{k-1}}{2} + K_d \frac{(e_k - 2e_{k-1} + e_{k-2})}{\Delta t}$$

Eq. 2.7.5.5

Eq. 2.7.5.5 will be the basis of the basic PID compensator described in this section. Velocity algorithms are often used because they provide a smooth transition between manual and automatic control.

In this problem, a PID compensator VI is developed to illustrate the use of the analog output function. The compensator provides continuous scanning of a single process variable through an analog input channel and compares the variable's value to a software set point. The compensator program calls on a basic PID algorithm as a subVI and updates the compensator's output to an analog output channel that drives the hardware the user wants to control. When using the analog output function, the user should ensure that the amperage requirements of the hardware do not exceed the ratings on the DAQ board or computer power supply.

Goals

1. Develop proficiency with multi-function data acquisition concepts using LabVIEW's configuration approach.

2. Develop the multi-function, software-timed analog input/output VI which both samples and updates analog channels continuously until stopped by the user.

3. Learn how to create subVIs

Equipment

Hardware that can be controlled by the software may be used but is not necessary to construct and execute the following VI. If you do not have any hardware for automatic feedback control, you can still observe the performance of the analog output function using only the DAQ board.

Developing the Basic PID Algorithm subVI

This section shows how to develop the basic PID algorithm and to create a subVI. The front panel and block diagram of the Basic PID subVI are shown in Figs. 2.7.5.1 to 2.7.5.5.

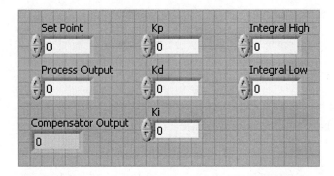

Figure 2.7.5.1   Front panel for the Basic PID subVI

Since the basic PID algorithm will be called as a subVI, values must be stored from one call to the next. This will be accomplished using a While Loop and a special type of variable called a shift register, which retains the variable's value from the previous iteration of the loop. Shift registers may be used with While Loops and For Loops and are discussed in Section 1.4.5.

The While Loop executes only once when the basic PID subVI is called from the PID compensator program since the conditional terminal assumes the logical FALSE by default. The Shift Registers are used to store the variables' values from one call to the next.

It is convenient to calculate the PID compensator output one component at a time. This can be done using a sequence structure, which executes one frame at a time starting with frame 0. The sequence of executing frame by frame with numerically increasing order is called control flow. Data is passed out of the sequence structure after the last frame is completed as part of LabVIEW's overall dataflow approach.

Under the functions palette, select **Programming>>Structures>>Stacked Sequence Structure** and place the function inside the While Loop, and drag the Sequence Structure to cover an area large enough to contain the functions shown in Fig. 2.7.5.2. There is only one frame when the structure is first placed in the block diagram. Right click on the border of the structure and select "Add Frame After" or "Add Frame Before" to create additional frames.

The error, e_k, of the proportional component, $K_p(e_k - e_{k-1})$, is the difference between the set point and the output of the process variable of the plant. For example, if you were controlling the temperature of an oven (plant), the error would be the difference between the thermostat setting (set point) and the actual temperature of the oven (process variable). Since the PID algorithm will be a subVI, the set point and process variable will be created as controls in the Front Panel. Later, these controls will be terminals for the subVI and actual readings from the DAQ board will be connected to these terminals.

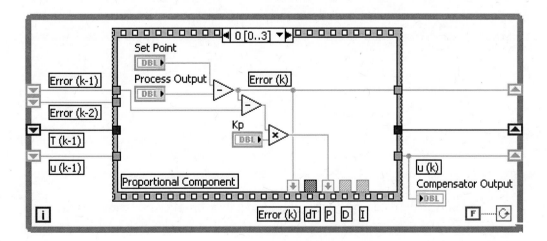

Figure 2.7.5.2   Block diagram showing the proportional component of the Basic PID subVI

The values of "Error(k)" and the proportional component will be passed to other frames of the Sequence Structure through sequence local terminals. Right click on the lower border of the Sequence Structure and select "Add Sequence Local". Wire the "Error(k)" output to the box and add the label "Error(k)" below the terminal. Repeat the same process for the proportional component and label it "P". The outward-pointing arrow shows the terminal is a data sink in this frame. In subsequent frames, the terminal will contain an inward-pointing arrow indicating the terminal is a data-source for those frames. The frame should appear like that shown in Fig.2.7.5.2.

The second frame of the Sequence Structure contains the functions to calculate the derivative component, $K_d \dfrac{e_k - 2e_{k-1} + e_{k-2}}{\Delta t}$, as shown in Fig. 2.7.5.3. To add the second frame, right click on the frame and select "Add Frame After". The Compound Arithmetic function can be found in the functions palette under **Express>>Arithmetic & Comparison>>Express Numeric>>Compound Arithmetic**. The Tick Count function can be found in the functions palette under **Programming>>Timing>>Tick Count (ms)**.

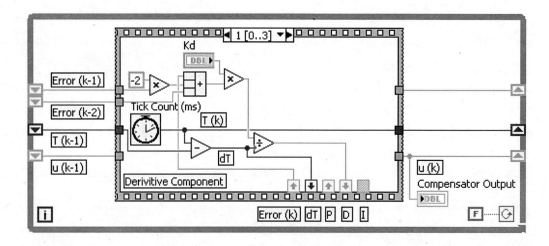

Figure 2.7.5.3   Block diagram showing the derivative component of the Basic PID subVI

The third frame of the Sequence Structure contains the functions to calculate the integral component, $K_i \Delta t \dfrac{e_k + e_{k-1}}{2}$, as shown in Fig. 2.7.5.4. As discussed earlier in this section, the integral component can be clamped to prevent integral windup error, that is, values that would exceed the physical limits of the actuator. Clamping can be accomplished using the "In Range and Coerce" function, which is found in the functions palette under **Programming>>Comparison>>In Range and Coerce**.

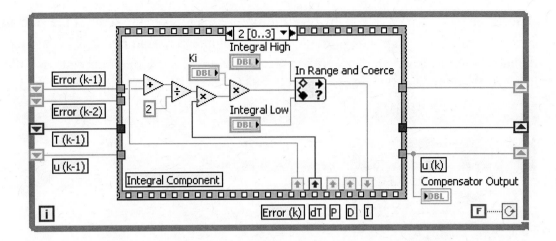

Figure 2.7.5.4   Block diagram showing the integral component of the Basic PID subVI

The last frame adds all four PID components to implement the PID algorithm from Eq. 2.7.5.5: the previous compensator output, u_{k-1}, and the proportional, derivative, and integral components. To pass the compensator output through a terminal out of the subVI, create an indicator and wire the output, u_k, to this indicator.

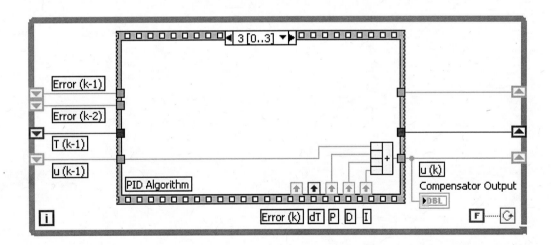

Figure 2.7.5.5   Block diagram showing the PID algorithm of the Basic PID subVI

Creating the subVI

SubVIs are like subroutines in other programming languages. The modular nature of SubVIs aid debugging and create less cluttered block diagrams.

To create a subVI, you must create an icon and assign connectors. Right click on the icon in the upper right corner of the front panel or block diagram and select "Edit Icon", as shown in Fig. 2.7.5.6. While in the Icon Editor, use the tools to the right of the icon and create a new icon to represent your VI. For the example shown in Fig. 2.7.5.7, all items in the interior of the original icon were selected using the Select tool on the right and then deleted. Then "Basic PID" was typed under the "Icon Text" tab and the icon was saved. However, you can be as creative as you like for your icon.

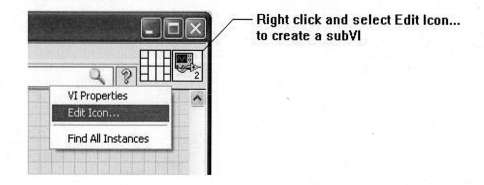

Figure 2.7.5.6   Initial step to create a subVI

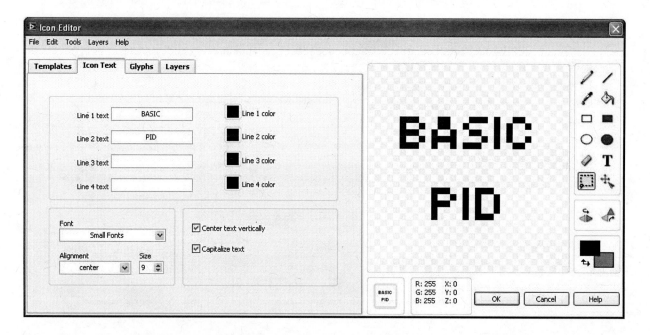

Figure 2.7.5.7   Creating a new icon for the subVI

Next, right click on the new icon in the upper right corner of the Front Panel and select "Show Connector" as shown in Fig. 2.7.5.8. If the pattern is not suitable for your inputs and output, you can view other options by right-clicking on the icon and selecting "Patterns". In this example, there are seven inputs and one output so choose a pattern that has at least eight connectors.

Right-click on the connector icon, select "Patterns", and then select an appropriate pattern for your VI

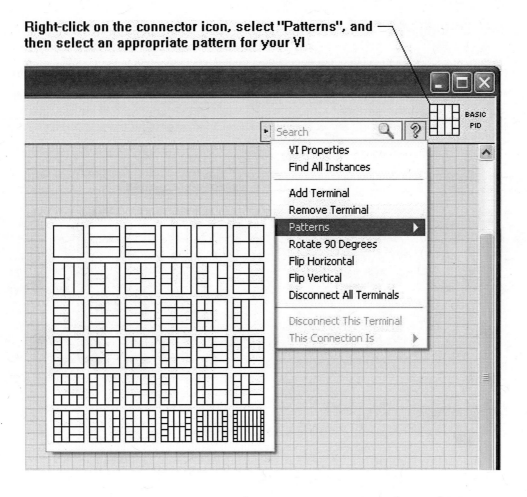

Figure 2.7.5.8   Process to select a connector pattern for a subVI

You must assign a connector terminal to each control or indicator in the front panel. Using the "Connect Wire" (solder) cursor, click on one of the terminals in the connector and then click on the control or indicator that you want to assign to this terminal. The terminal changes from black to the data type of the control or indicator. Repeat this process for all of the controls and indicators that are in the Front Panel. When you have finished the last control or indicator, click on an open area of the Front Panel. You may make a terminal required, recommended, or optional by right clicking on the specific terminal and selecting "This Connection Is".

Developing the PID Compensator VI

The PID Compensator VI continuously samples the process variable in a plant on an analog input channel, calls the Basic PID subVI to determine the error between the process variable and the set point and calculate compensation output, and outputs a signal on an analog output channel to the actuator to compensate for the error. The front panel and block diagram of the PID Compensator VI are shown in Figs. 2.7.5.9 and 2.7.5.10, respectively.

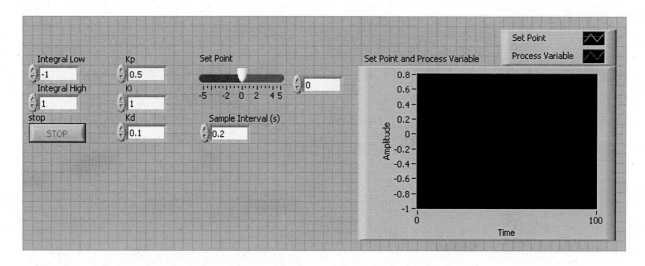

Figure 2.7.5.9   Font panel for the PID Compensator VI

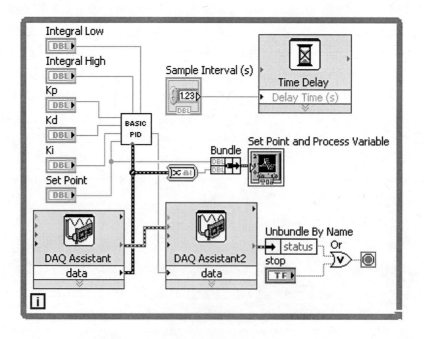

Figure 2.7.5.10   Block diagram for the PID Compensator VI

The Basic PID subVI can be included in the block diagram by choosing "Select a VI…" from the functions palette. When you choose "Select a VI…", a dialog box appears. You may have to browse for the directory where BasicPID.vi is stored. Values must be supplied to all of the *input* terminals. If you right-click on the PID Basic icon and select **Visible Items>>Terminals**, you can easily create controls for all of the required inputs.

The process output from the plant is measured with an analog input channel configured by the DAQ Assistant as shown in Fig. 2.7.5.11.

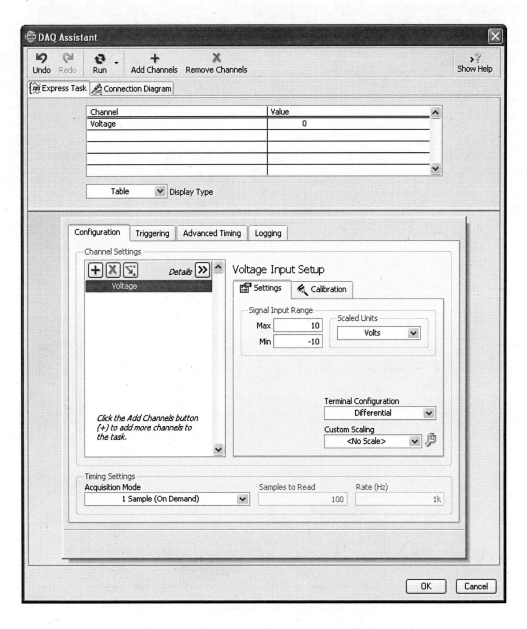

Figure 2.7.5.11   Configuration of an analog input channel using the DAQ Assistant to measure the process variable for the PID compensator

In the current example, a software-timed, single-point analog output function is appropriate since an actuator compensation value will be calculated after every reading of the process variable. The configuration of the analog output channel by the DAQ Assistant2 is shown in Fig. 2.7.5.12.

Select "Single scalar" as the resulting data type in the configuration window of the "Convert from Dynamic Data" Express VI.

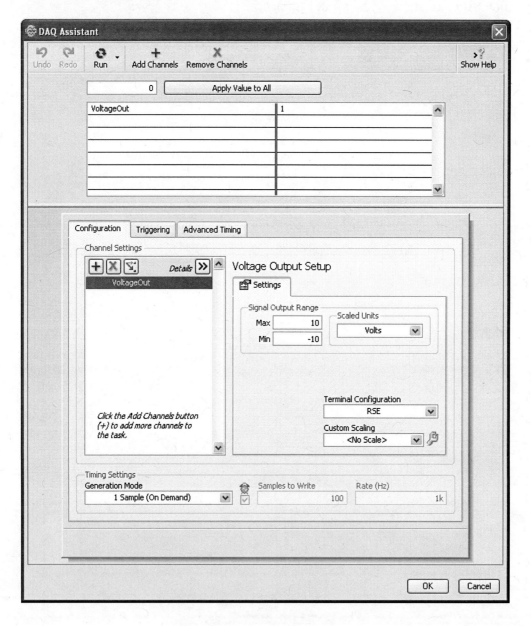

Figure 2.7.5.12   Configuration of an analog output channel using the DAQ Assistant2 to output compensation to the process variable based on the PID compensator

Fabrication and Testing

You can use your DAQ board to demonstrate the PID compensator VI if you do not have other hardware for a feedback control system. This can be accomplished by physically wiring the PID compensator output directly to the input for the process variable. In this example, the input is assumed to be analog input channel 0 with a differential input. The output is assumed to be analog output channel 0 and is configured as a referenced single-ended terminal. This means that the voltage on the analog output channel is referenced to the analog output ground on the DAQ board. Physically connect the analog output channel 0 to the analog input channel 0. Since the analog input channel is configured as a differential input, an analog output ground channel must be connected to the differential pair of analog input channel 0, which is analog input channel 8 for a 16-input analog input DAQ board.

Before executing the program, enter values as shown in Fig. 2.7.5.9 for the controls. After execution begins, you may move the slider on the set point control and observe the process variable on the chart. By adjusting the PID parameters, you can explore the range of values that create a stable feedback control. The stability of the control is also affected by the sampling rate. Once you have a set of parameters that work, select "Make Current Values Default" from the Operate pull-down menu in the front panel and save the program.

Notes:

Chapter 3   Digital Signal Measurement and Generation

3.1. Digital Signal Basics

A digital, or binary, signal is defined by two voltage states, which may be characterized as high or low, true or false, 0 or 1, and on or off. Common voltage pairs, for example, include 0-5 VDC for the transistor-transistor logic (TTL) family and 0-3.3 VDC for the low voltage transistor-transistor logic (LVTTL) family for single-ended signals.

However, because of electrical noise on the lines, the voltages do not have to be exactly those specified in the logic pair to be interpreted as a high or low signal by the DAQ board or digital devices. For example, consider the digital input example shown in Fig. 3.1.1. The digital output device generates a voltage to represent a logical high, V_{OH}, or a logical low, V_{OL}. The signal may then transmit over an electrically noisy cable to a DAQ board configured for digital input. The voltage at the DAQ board must be at or above an input high voltage threshold, $V_{IH,DAQ}$, for the DAQ board to interpret the voltage as a logical high or at or below a low input voltage threshold, $V_{IL,DAQ}$, for the DAQ board to interpret the voltage as a logical low. National Instruments DAQ boards use TTL logic and, for example, the PCI/PXI 6221 DAQ board interprets a voltage at or above 2.2 V as logic high and a voltage at or below 0.8 V as logic low. A similar situation occurs when the DAQ board is configured for digital output as shown in Fig. 3.1.1.

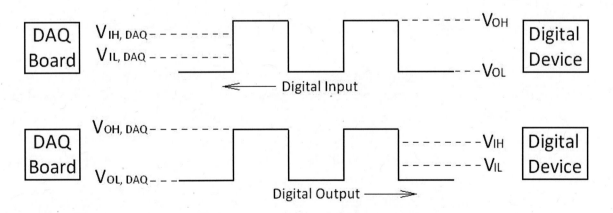

Figure 3.1.1   Voltage margins for interpreting digital signals

Digital signals can have the voltage on one wire referenced to system ground (referenced single-ended signals) or the voltage on one wire referenced to the voltage on another wire (differential). Single-ended digital signals are more common than differential digital signals. For example, most DAQ boards generate referenced single-ended digital signals. However, differential digital signals have the advantage that they are less susceptible to electrical noise, which allows for lower voltage signals and tighter threshold ranges.

A single digital channel is called a line and a group of lines is called a port. Generally four to eight lines are grouped into a port but the number is specific to each device. Each line can transmit a binary value so a port can transmit a digital pattern. Typically, all lines in a port are configured for one direction, either digital input or output.

Static digital acquisition or generation refers to the situation when a single sample or update is performed when called by the software. With static acquisition, a single sample is taken of the state of a digital line. Likewise, with static generation, a single update is performed when called by the software and the updated voltage remains on the line until the next call by the software. The calling function can be placed in a loop to take repeated samples or make repeated updates using software timing. Because static acquisition and generation depend on software timing, it is best suited for low-speed applications.

Dynamic digital acquisition or generation refers to the situation when a waveform is acquired or generated through buffers and hardware timing. A waveform is an array of samples or updates that have uniform time spacing between elements. With dynamic digital data acquisition, the rate of waveform acquisition is controlled by a clock on the DAQ board or an external device. As the data is acquired, it is stored temporarily in the DAQ board's FIFO buffer and then into the computer's buffer. Finite samples can be taken with a simple buffer or continuous samples can be taken with a circular buffer. With dynamic digital data generation, data can be generated within the software and eventually stored on the DAQ board memory as digital voltage patterns are generated. Because of hardware timing, dynamic data acquisition and generation are best suited for high-speed applications.

Typical applications for digital input and output operations include monitoring and controlling processes or external devices. For example, the state of an alarm may be used to monitor a process. Likewise, a process may be controlled by opening or closing a switch or a relay. Controlling a process may also involve mixed-mode data acquisition, such as controlling a process component with digital output based on the measurement of analog signals. Digital output may also be used to control an external device, such as a stepper motor, usually through a driver since the DAQ hardware cannot generate the required power.

3.2. Continuous Digital I/O with Software Timing

This section describes how to write a general-purpose program to read and write digital data for low-speed applications. This section is structured so that you can develop the VI as you read the material. The idea is that it will be easier to learn and retain key data acquisition concepts by applying the concepts as you learn them. In the digital acquisition mode, this program would be suitable when an experiment or process involves the need to read simultaneous digital signals, for example from switches or LEDs (Light Emitting Diodes). In the data output mode, the program would be suitable to control equipment via solid state or mechanical relays or display an alarm through an LED. The front panel contains virtual LED displays and switches that allow the user to manually monitor and control the state of the digital lines. This allows the user to continuously turn on and off relays or other equipment connected directly or indirectly to the DAQ board until the execution of the program stops. However, the user is cautioned not to drive the equipment directly from the DAQ board unless the maximum current rating on the DAQ board is not exceeded. You must consult the DAQ hardware specifications to determine the maximum current ratings.

The material discussed in this section assumes that LabVIEW Professional Version or Student Version software, NI-DAQ software, and a data acquisition board have been installed on your computer.

Equipment

1. Digital input sources comprising a sensor, function generator, or power supply.

2. An oscilloscope to display the digital output signal or, if an oscilloscope is not available, a multimeter may be used for low frequency signals.

Goals

1. Become acquainted with some basic digital input/output data acquisition concepts using LabVIEW's configuration approach.

2. Develop the multi-channel, software-timed digital input/output VI shown in Figs. 3.2.1 and 3.2.2, which both samples and updates digital lines continuously until stopped by the user.

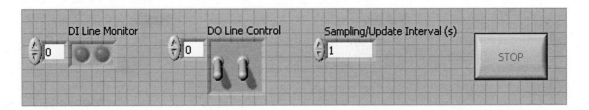

Figure 3.2.1   Front panel of the digital I/O example VI with software timing

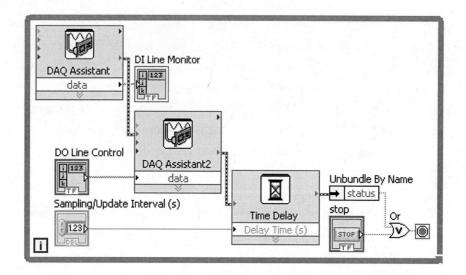

Figure 3.2.2   Block diagram of the digital I/O example VI with software timing

Developing the VI

1. Beginning at the Start Menu, select **All Programs>>National Instruments>>LabVIEW 2012>>LabVIEW 2012**

Note: Read Section 1.3 if you need background on the LabVIEW environment.

2. Select "Blank VI" to open a new file

3. From the Functions palette, select **Express>>Execution Control>>While Loop** and drag the While Loop over an area in the block diagram large enough to contain the sub diagram shown in Fig. 3.2.2.

Tip: The While Loop can be resized, if needed, at a later time by using the blue handles.

4. From the Functions palette, select **Express>>Input>>DAQ Assistant** and drag the DAQ Assistant inside and to the upper left corner of the While Loop.

5. Click on "Acquire Signals", "Digital Input", and "Line Input" in the "Create New…" window as shown in Fig. 3.2.3.

6. Click on the hardware device to show the channels that are available to acquire digital input signals on your DAQ board.

7. Select digital input line 0 ("port0/line0") and line 1("port0/line1"), or other appropriate lines for your DAQ hardware, as shown in Fig. 3.2.3.

1-Select Acquire Signals>>Digital Input>>Line Input

2-Select Digital Input Lines

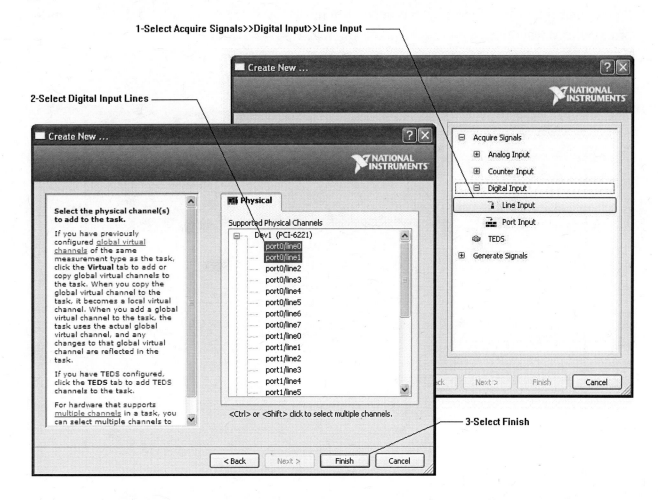

3-Select Finish

Figure 3.2.3   Steps to use the DAQ Assistant to select the digital input lines for the continuous digital I/O example VI

8. Select "Finish" and the DAQ Assistant window appears.

9. Keep all default settings in the DAQ Assistant window, as shown in Fig. 3.2.4.

Note: Software timing is employed when "1 Sample (On Demand)" is selected as the acquisition mode. A sample is taken when the DAQ Assistant Express VI is executed and the timing between samples is controlled by a LabVIEW timing function and the clock controlling the computer's CPU.

Note: The terminal configuration is referenced single ended because the input voltages on channels "port0/line0" and "port0/line1" are referenced to the DAQ board system ground, which is available on the digital ground channel on the terminal connector block. Read Section 2.1.1 regarding a discussion of reference single-ended terminal configuration. The pin numbers for the digital input channels and the digital ground channel can be found from the pinout sheet obtained through the Measurement and Automation Explorer (MAX) software.

10. Select OK and the DAQ Assistant will generate the appropriate code.

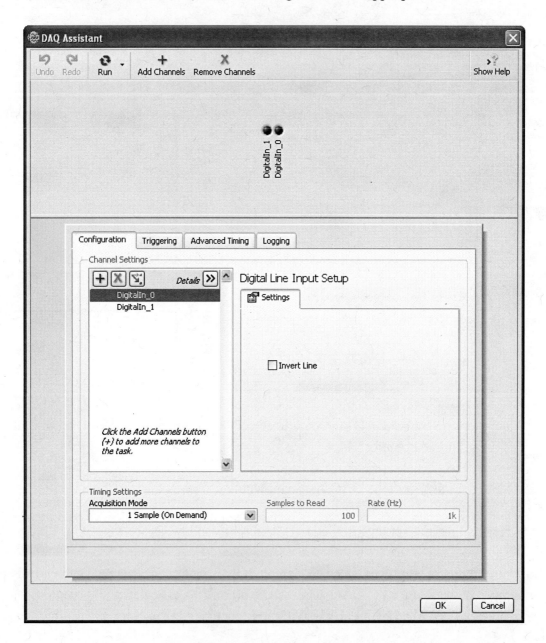

Figure 3.2.4   Input channel configuration for the continuous digital I/O example VI using the DAQ Assistant

.11. Place the "Connect Wire" (solder spool) cursor over the "data" output terminal of the DAQ Assistant, right click on the mouse, select **Create>>Indicator**, and rename the indicator in the front panel "DI Line Monitor" using the "Edit Text" (letter A) cursor.

12. From the Functions palette, select **Express>>Output>>DAQ Assistant** and drag the DAQ Assistant below and to the right of the first DAQ Assistant.

13. Click on "Generate Signals", "Digital Output", and "Line Output" in the "Create New Express Task…" window as shown in Fig. 3.2.5.

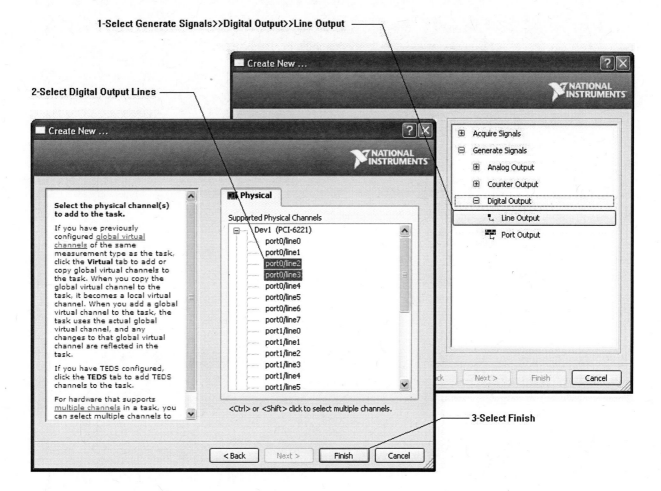

Figure 3.2.5   Steps to use the DAQ Assistant to select the digital output lines for the continuous digital I/O example VI

14. Click on the hardware device to show the channels that are available to generate digital output signals on your DAQ board.

15. Select digital input line 2 ("port0/line2") and line 3("port0/line3"), or other appropriate lines for your DAQ hardware, as shown in Fig. 3.2.5.

16. Select "Finish" and the DAQ Assistant window appears.

17. Keep all default settings in the DAQ Assistant window, as shown in Fig. 3.2.6.

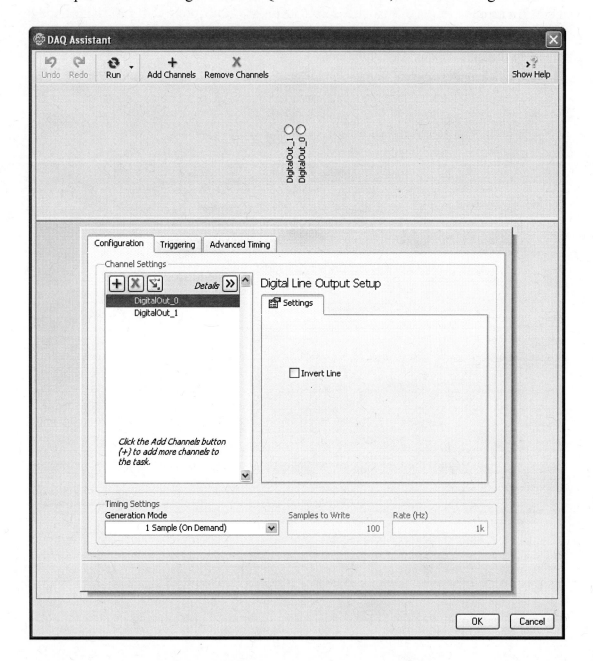

Figure 3.2.6   Output channel configuration for the continuous digital I/O example VI
using the DAQ Assistant

18. Select OK and the DAQ Assistant will generate the appropriate code.

19. Place the "Connect Wire" (solder spool) cursor over the "data" input terminal of the DAQ Assistant, right click on the mouse, select **Create>>Control**, and rename the control in the front panel "DO Line Control" using the "Edit Text" (letter A) cursor.

Warning: Do not click on any of the elements of the data array, which enters a state value for an element. An error will occur later when the VI attempts to run if any of the elements other than the first two elements have a value. The digital output task created by the DAQ Assistant expects inputs from the data array for two lines (port0/line2 and port0/line3). An error will occur if the digital output data array ("DO Line Control" array) has more than two elements with values.

20. Select **Express>>Execution Control>>Time Delay** and drag the Express VI to the right of the digital output DAQ Assistant Express VI in the block diagram. Click OK for the default time setting of 1 second in the "Configure Time Delay" window as the time delay between updates will be determined automatically in a later step.

21. Place the "Connect Wire" (solder spool) cursor over the "Time Delay (s)" input terminal of the Time Delay Express VI, right click on the mouse, select **Create>>Control**, and rename the control "Sampling/Update Interval (s)."

22. Place the cursor over the wire between the "stop" control and the conditional terminal, right-click the mouse, and select "Delete Wire Branch" from the pop-up menu. Move the stop control to add space between the control and the conditional terminal.

23. From the Functions palette, select **Programming>>Cluster, Class, and Variant>>Unbundle by Name** and place the function above the "stop" control.

24. Wire the error cluster from the "error out" terminal of the Time Delay Express VI to the input terminal of the Unbundle By Name function and notice that the "status" element of the error cluster appears as shown in Fig. 3.2.7.

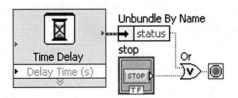

Figure 3.2.7   Wiring diagram for the conditional terminal of the continuous digital I/O example VI

25. From the Functions palette, select **Express>>Arithmetic & Comparison>>Express Boolean>>Or** and drag the function to the right of the Unbundle by Name function in the block diagram

26. Wire the outputs of the Unbundle by Name function and the stop control to the inputs terminals of the Or function and the output of the Or function to the conditional terminal, as shown in Fig. 3.2.7.

27. Wire the "error out" terminal of the first DAQ Assistant to the "error in" terminal of the second DAQ Assistant and the "error out" terminal of the second DAQ Assistant to the "error in" terminal of the Time Delay Express VI as shown in Fig. 3.2.8.

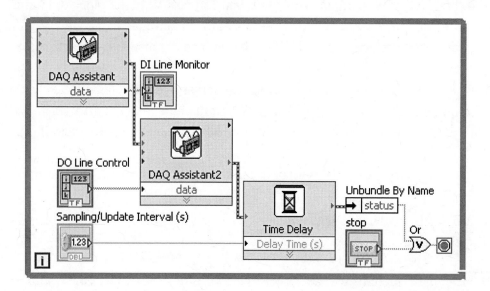

Figure 3.2.8   Completed block diagram of the continuous digital I/O example VI

Note: The VI is complete and the Run arrow should not be broken. If the arrow is broken, click on the broken Run arrow to show the error(s).

Note: The front panel should look similar to that shown in Fig. 3.2.9. The front panel will be modified to resize the front panel objects and to include toggle switches.

28. The "DI Line Monitor" indicator contains an array showing the state (logical on or off) of one port (8 lines) of LEDs. Use the blue handles to reduce the display to two LEDs to represent the state of the two digital input lines selected for this example VI.

29. Separate the front panel objects to allow space between them. Place the cursor over the "DO Line Control" control in the front panel, right click, select "Replace" from the pop-up menu, and select **Express>>Buttons & Switches>>Vertical Toggle Switch** as shown in Fig. 3.2.10

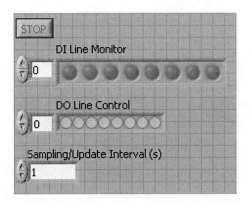

Figure 3.2.9   Default appearance of the front panel for the continuous digital I/O
example VI

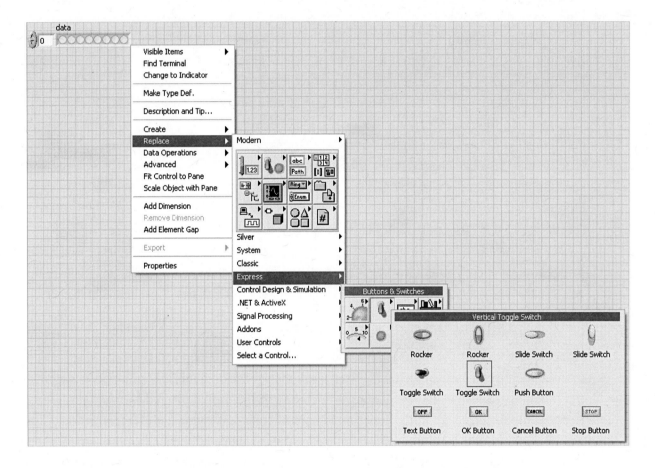

Figure 3.2.10   Sequence to replace a front panel control in the continuous digital I/O example VI

30. The "DO Line Control" control contains an array showing the state (logical on or off) of one port (8 lines) of toggle switches. Use the blue handles to reduce the display to two toggle switches to represent the state of the two digital output lines selected for this example VI.

Note: The left-most element of the array is the first element, which represents the first line (port0/line2) selected when the data output task was configured using the DAQ Assistant. The next element to the right represents the second line (port0/line3) selected when the data output task was configured using the DAQ Assistant.

Congratulations! You have developed a software-timed VI that can acquire or generate digital signals on multiple lines continuously until stopped by the user. Be sure to save your program using one of the save options on the "File" pull-down menu.

Testing the VI

Determine the digital input, output, and ground pin numbers on the terminal connector block so that a set of leads may be connected to the digital input and output devices. A device pinout diagram for your DAQ board can be found using the Measurement & Automation Explorer (MAX) software program, a National Instruments utility to manage hardware. Select "Measurement & Automation Explorer…" from the "Tools" pull-down menu. A window will appear like the one that is partially shown in Figure 3.2.11. Expand "Devices and Interfaces", right click on the DAQ board that was selected when you configured your channels using the DAQ Assistant, and select "Device Pinouts." Device Pinouts may also be selected in the toolbar at the top of the MAX window. The pinout sheet appears in a new window and the pin number for the digital I/O and ground terminals can be identified. For example, the lines configured as digital input lines, P0.0 (port0/line0) and P0.1 (port0/line1), are pins 52 and 17, respectively, and one of the digital grounds, D GND, is pin 4 on the NI PCI/PXI 6221 DAQ board. The lines that are configured as digital output lines, P0.2 (port0/line2) and P0.3 (port0/line3), are pins 49 and 47, respectively, and a separate digital ground, D GND, is pin 7 on the NI PCI/PXI 6221 DAQ board.

Attach the lead(s) of the digital input line(s) (port0/line0 and/or port0/line1) on the terminal connector block to a positive terminal on a function generator or a power supply, if a function generator is not available. Attach one of the digital ground leads on the terminal block connector to the function generator's negative terminal. Note that the digital input ground is used for the negative terminal since a referenced single-ended system configuration is used for digital I/O signals, which requires that the input signal is referenced to the DAQ board system ground on D GND.

Attach the lead(s) of the digital output line(s) (port0/line2 and/or port0/line3) on the terminal connector block to the positive terminal of an oscilloscope or a multimeter, if an oscilloscope is not available. Attach the second digital ground on the terminal connector block to the oscilloscope's negative terminal because the digital output signal is referenced single ended.

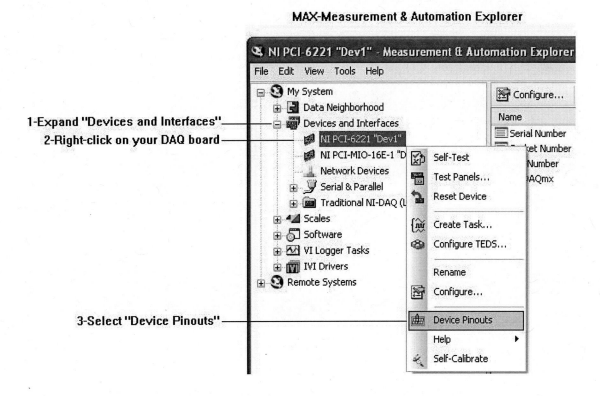

Figure 3.2.11 Using the Measurement &Automation Explorer utility to identify the pin connection for the digital input, output, and ground channels

After the leads have been connected, the VI is ready to run. Set the interval between samples and updates at 0.1 seconds in the front panel control "Sampling/Update Interval (s)", since this should be sufficiently fast to sample manual application of the signals. Click on the Run button in the toolbar to begin execution of the VI. Apply a 5 V signal to one or both of the digital input lines and observe the signal on the "DI Line Monitor" LED indicators in the front panel. Flip the "DO Line Control" vertical toggle switch(es) in the front panel and observe the signal on the oscilloscope or the multimeter. The VI will acquire and generate data continuously until the user selects the stop control in the front panel. As a general practice, you should always ensure that the output voltage on the digital output channel is 0 V when you are done with the VI.

If the VI does not show a broken arrow but runs for only a short time, the problem may be that the data array has too many elements (lines) containing state values. An error reporting function may be used to provide a description of the error.

Select **Programming>>Dialog & User Interface>>Simple Error Handler**, place the function above the "Unbundle by Name" function, connect it to the error cluster line as shown in Fig. 3.2.12.

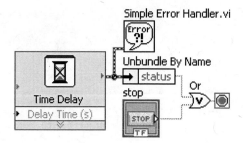

Figure 3.2.12 Sub-diagram of the digital I/O example VI showing how to display errors

If the data array has too many elements with state values, an error message will be displayed as shown in Fig. 3.2.13.

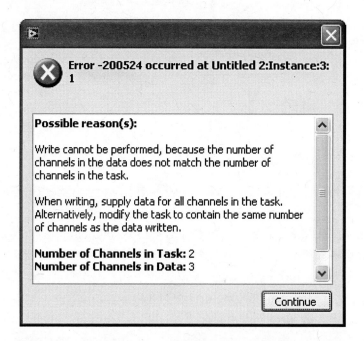

Figure 3.2.13 Error message when the number of elements in the data array do not match the number of digital output lines in the generation task

The error can be corrected by emptying the data array and then assigning values to only two elements to supply state values to the two digital output lines. For example, three state values were provided to the first three elements of the data array in Fig. 3.2.14. The first two elements, corresponding to port0/line2 and port0/line3 in the current example, are assigned the state value "off" and the third element, which does not correspond to any lines in the current generation task, is arbitrarily assigned the state value "on". The error shown in Fig. 3.2.13 would occur if the VI was run. However, the array can be emptied using the pop-up menu sequence shown in Fig. 3.2.14. It is important to note that when you right-click the mouse to get the pop-up menu, the cursor must be placed within the shell of the array that contains the toggle switches but cannot be over a toggle switch. A different set of options occur in the pop-up menu when the cursor is over the toggle switch.

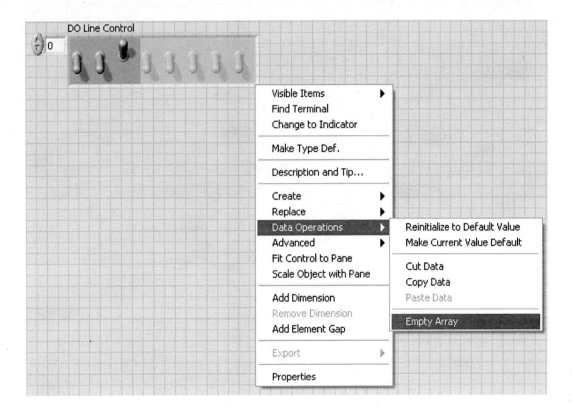

Figure 3.2.14 Procedure to empty the data array for the digital I/O example VI

Discussion

The current digital I/O VI shown in Fig. 3.2.15 is an example of a multi-function VI since it employs both digital input and output tasks. The DAQ Assistant is used to create, configure, and save generation or measurement tasks. However, the task can only be configured for either generation or measurement but not both. Therefore, to have a multi-function VI, two or more DAQ Assistants must be used. In the current VI, the first DAQ Assistant is configured for digital signal measurement and the second DAQ Assistant is configured for digital signal generation.

The current digital I/O VI employs the principle of data flow, which means that functions and subVIs execute only after they have received all inputs. The use of the error cluster lines force the execution of the Express VIs and functions sequentially from 1 through 4, as shown in Fig 3.2.15. For example, the second DAQ Assistant cannot begin execution until the first DAQ Assistant completes execution because it must wait until it receives the error data. The VI could also run without the error cluster lines if the task error was not used as a conditional stop input, although the order in which each Express VI executed would be undermined.

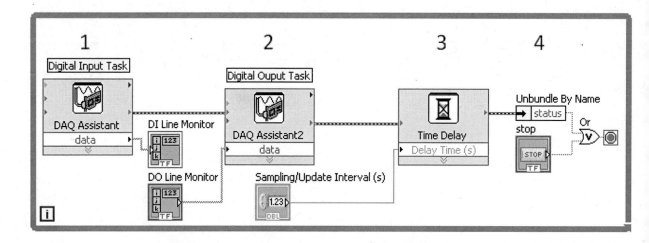

Figure 3.2.15   Block diagram of the digital I/O example VI

The current digital I/O VI employs software timing. The digital signal measurement and generation tasks are configured for an immediate single sample or update. The sample or update occurs immediately after called by the code generated by the DAQ Assistant. Because only a single sample or update is performed, a While Loop must be used for continuous sampling and updating. Without the Time Delay Express VI, sampling and updating would occur as fast as the While Loop could be executed by the computer's CPU. The Time Delay Express VI imposes a time delay that is controlled by the computer's clock, hence software timing. The precision of the time interval is sufficient for low-speed requirements although hardware timing is more appropriate for high-speed applications. The time intervals may vary slightly since the computer may have higher priority requests competing for the CPU.

It should be noted that when lines are grouped as a port, data on all lines within the port can be configured in only one direction, either as signal measurement or generation. However, since each DAQ Assistant configured the task as line, not port, input or output, this restriction does not apply. For example, in the current VI, "port0/line0" and "port0/line1" were configured for digital input lines and "port0/line2" and "port0/line3" were configured for digital output lines.

3.3. Learning by Doing

The problems in this section are offered to help you work on developing proficiency using LabVIEW for data acquisition. The problems are often multi-function in nature and strive to show the practical application of LabVIEW to real-life problems. The presentation of material in this section assumes that you have worked the introductory LabVIEW example problem in Section 1.4, which helps you to learn some basic LabVIEW concepts, and the skill development problem in this chapter. The hope is that you will be able to complete the LabVIEW proficiency problems without the need of a guide…the next step to developing LabVIEW VIs on your own.

3.3.1. Proficiency-Development Problem: Digital Input/Digital Output Control

Introduction

The purpose of this problem is to develop a VI that reads a signal from a digital line, such as from a sensor or a switch, and, based on the state of the digital input, writes a signal to a second digital line to control a device. For example, consider the situation when a door is to be opened when an object breaks a light beam striking a photodiode. Let's say the state of the photodiode controls a relay to supply power to a motor that operates the door. For the purposes of this example, assume the state of the digital signal changes from low to high and back to low again as the light beam is interrupted. Also assume the state of the digital output changes to high to supply power to the motor during the interruption of the beam. Furthermore, after the object passes through the light beam, you would like for the door to remain open for a period of time to allow the object to pass through the opening before the door closes. In other words, the digital output should remain in the high state for a specified time delay.

Goals

1. Develop proficiency with multi-function data acquisition concepts using LabVIEW's configuration approach.

2. Develop the multi-function, software-timed digital input/output VI which both samples and updates digital lines continuously until stopped by the user.

Equipment

1. A digital input source such as a photodiode and light source or, if these items are not available, a function generator or power supply to provide a digital pulse.

2. A multimeter to display the digital output signal.

Developing the VI

The front panel and block diagram of a digital input/output VI to monitor a sensor that is used to control an electrical device are shown in Figs. 3.3.1.1 and 3.3.1.2. The block diagram shows all cases of the Case Structure. All functions that have been employed in this VI have been described in this chapter or Section 1.4, except for the Index Array function, which returns the element of an n-dimensional array at the specified index. The function can be found in the function palette under **Programming>>Array>>Index Array**.

The following tips may be helpful in constructing the VI. See Section 1.4.1 for more information on Case Structures. The Case Structure cases may be constructed in any order shown in Fig. 3.3.1.2; however, all tunnels must have an input or output from every case or the tunnel will not be a solid color. See Section 1.4.5 for information on shift registers on the While Loop.

The configuration of the digital input and output tasks using the DAQ Assistant are shown in Figs. 3.3.1.3 and 3.3.1.4, respectively. The configuration employs software timing by selecting "1 Sample (On Demand)" for the data acquisition mode.

Figure 3.3.1.1   Front panel of the digital input/output VI to monitor a sensor that is used to control an electrical device until stopped by the user

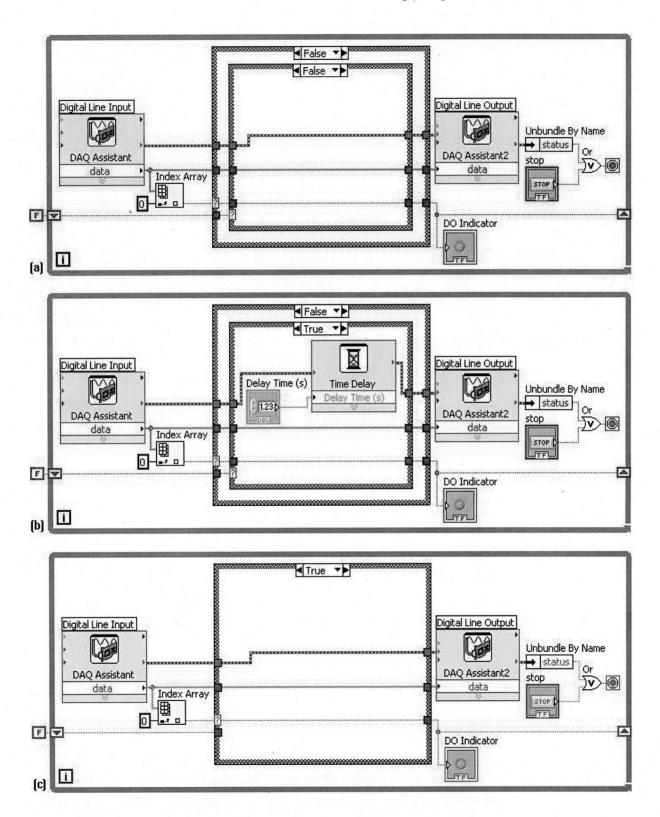

Figure 3.3.1.2   Three cases of the same block diagram of the digital input/output VI to monitor a sensor that is used to control an electrical device until stopped by the user

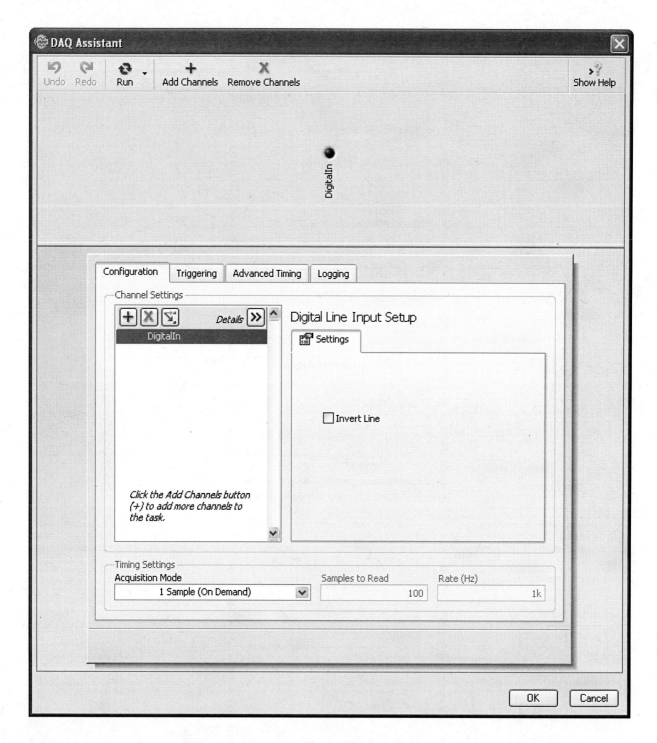

Figure 3.3.1.3   Digital input measurement task configuration using the DAQ Assistant for the digital input/output VI to monitor a sensor that is used to control an electrical device until stopped by the user

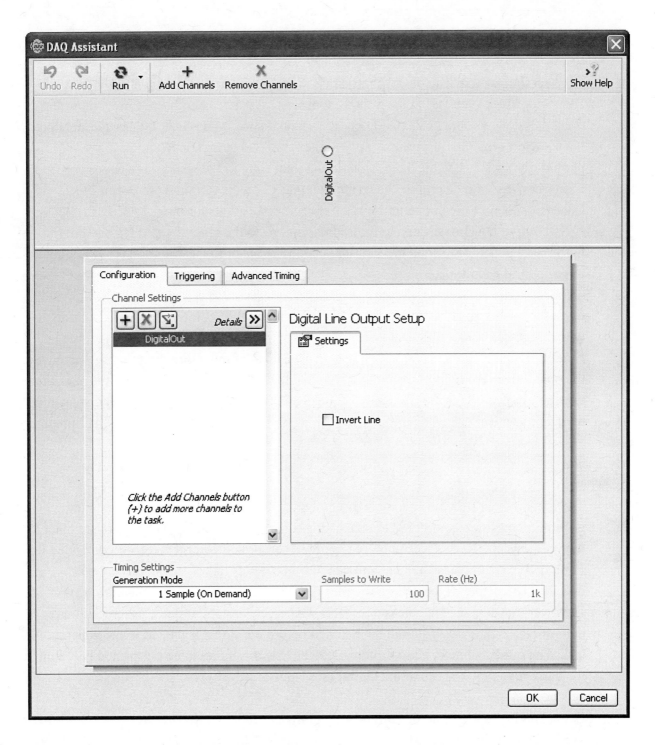

Figure 3.3.1.4   Digital output generation task configuration using the DAQ Assistant for the digital input/output VI to monitor a sensor that is used to control an electrical device until stopped by the user

Fabrication and Testing

Connect the positive lead of the photodiode to the input terminal on the terminal connector block specified in the digital input DAQ Assistant configuration window and the photodiode ground to a D GND on the terminal connector block. Otherwise, connect the function generator or power supply to the same two terminals to simulate the photodiode output. Use the device pinout diagram from the Measurement & Automation Explorer (MAX) to determine the terminal numbers on the terminal connector block. Likewise, connect the output terminal on the terminal connector block specified in the digital output DAQ Assistant configuration window to the voltage input terminal of the multimeter and a D GND on the terminal connector block to the common (COM) terminal of the multimeter.

Once the connections have been made, the VI is ready to run. Interrupt the light beam with an opaque object and observe that the "DO Indicator" software LED in the front panel illuminates and the output voltage, as measured by the multimeter, is 5 V. Remove the object from the light beam and observe that the LED in the front panel dims after the time delay specified in the front panel control and the voltage drops to 0 V as displayed on the multimeter. The VI continues to monitor the input signal until stopped by the user.

Discussion

The logic to create the time delay is discussed in this section. The measurement and generation tasks are configured to take a single sample on demand. Both tasks are placed within the While Loop to continually monitor a sensor and control an electrical device. LabVIEW calls the measurement and generation tasks as fast as the While Loop can execute. The output of the measurement task provides the input to the generation task. However, the output of the measurement tasks passes through nested Case Structures to determine if a time delay should be included before the signal is passed to the generation task. The outer and inner Case Structures determine the action to be performed based on the current and prior states of the digital line inputs, respectively.

For example, assume that the current state of the digital input line is low (false), as shown in Fig. 3.3.1.5, corresponding to the condition prior to the object breaking the light beam. No time delay is required since the object has not passed through the beam and the digital input signal is passed directly to the generation task. It should be noted that the output of the digital input measurement task is a 1-D array, that is, a port of 8 Boolean values. The only element of the array that has a value is the first element, corresponding to the logical state of the line specified in the configuration of the measurement task. The index array function is required since the selector terminal on the Case Structure accepts only a scalar

Boolean value. The "Index Array" function strips the first Boolean element (since the zeroth index was specified) from the 1-D array and passes that along to the Case Structure.

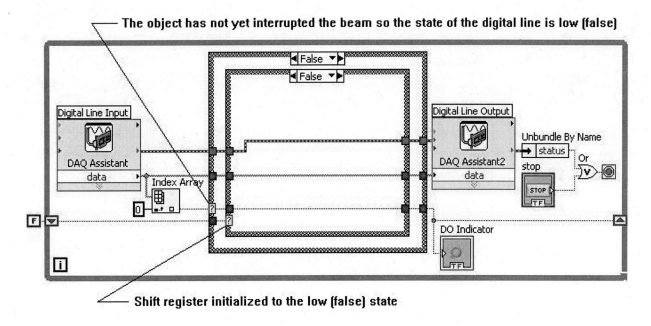

Figure 3.3.1.5   Block diagram of the digital input/output control VI when the current and previous states of the digital line are low

The object is assumed to be interrupting the light beam in Fig 3.3.1.6. The digital input signal passes directly to the digital generation task. No time delay is required since the object has not passed completely through the light beam. There are no nested Case Structures within the "True" case of the outer Case Structure. The value of the shift register is irrelevant since it is not connected to a selector terminal.

Finally, consider the case when the object has just passed through the light beam, as shown in Fig. 3.3.1.7. The current state of the digital input line is low but the previous state of the digital line was high, since the object was still interrupting the light beam. The "True" case of the inner Case Structure is selected since the shift register stores the previous value of the digital input line. The object is moving towards the door and a time delay is required to give the object enough time to pass through the door. The digital output line keeps the value from the previous iteration, which was the high state, until the time delay is complete and the low state passes through the Case Structure.

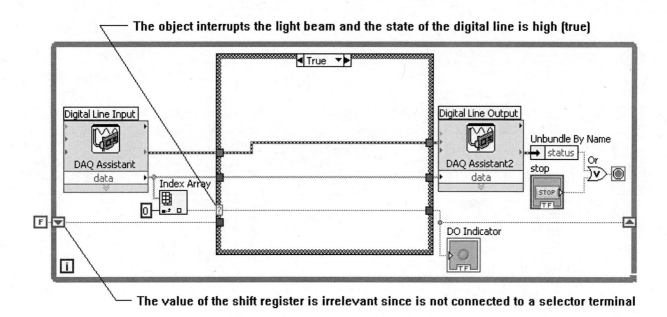

Figure 3.3.1.6   Block diagram of the digital input/output control VI when the current state of the digital line is high

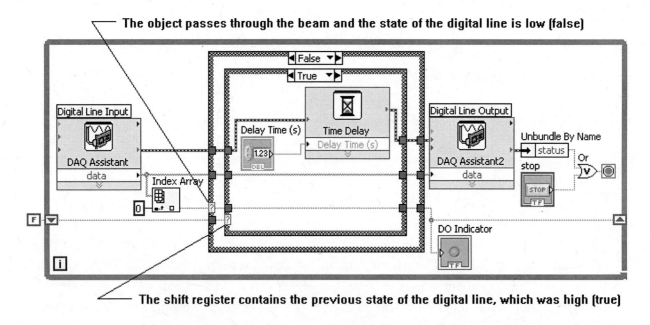

Figure 3.3.1.7   Block diagram of the digital input/output control VI when the current state of the digital line is low and the previous state was high

3.3.2. Proficiency-Development Problem: Analog Input/Digital Output Control with Minimum and Maximum Set Points

Introduction

The purpose of this problem is to develop a VI that reads a signal from an analog input channel, such as from a sensor, and, based on the state of the analog input, writes a signal to a digital line to control a device. For example, consider an experiment that requires a heated test chamber. A sensor, such as a thermistor or a thermocouple, is used to monitor the temperature inside the test chamber. Because of heat loss to the environment, the test chamber will need to be heated periodically using resistive heat strips. If the sensor detects a temperature inside the test chamber below a minimum set point, a relay provides power to the resistive heat strips. The relay should provide power until the temperature inside the test chamber exceeds a maximum set point. Once the power is turned off, the temperature in the test chamber will drop again slowly due to heat loss to the environment. The power will remain off until the temperature falls below the minimum set point. This type of control works for a number of practical applications, such as maintaining water level in a storage tank or pressure in an air compressor tank.

The VI in this section is set up in the following manner. Minimum and maximum set points are established before running the VI. If the analog input signal is below the minimum set point, a 5 V (high) signal is written on the digital output line, which could turn on an electrical device through a set of relays. The signal on the digital output line remains high until the analog input signal exceeds the maximum set point. Once the maximum set point is exceeded, a 0 V (low) signal is written to the digital output line, which would shut off the electrical device. The digital output would remain low until the analog input signal falls below the minimum set point.

Goals

1. Develop proficiency with multi-function data acquisition concepts using LabVIEW's configuration approach.

2. Develop the multi-function, software-timed analog input/digital output VI which samples an analog input channel and updates a digital output line continuously until stopped by the user.

Equipment

Of course, this problem could be performed using a heated test chamber, a compressed air tank, or equivalent, as described earlier. However, to reduce setup time to test the VI, the sensor input signal and the output signal to a relay can be simulated and observed using a power supply and a multimeter.

1. A power supply to provide an analog input signal.

2. A multimeter to display the digital output signal.

Developing the VI

The front panel and block diagram of an analog input/digital output VI to monitor a sensor that is used to control an electrical device are shown in Figs. 3.3.2.1 and 3.3.2.2. The block diagram shows all cases of the Case Structure. All functions that have been employed in this VI have been described in this chapter or Section 1.4, except for the Index Array function and the Comparison Express VI. The Index Array function returns the element of an n-dimensional array at the specified index. The function can be found in the functions palette under **Programming>>Array>>Index Array**. The Comparison Express VI performs one of a number of different comparison options between input items that you provide. The Comparison Express VI can be found in the functions palette under **Express>>Arithmetic & Comparison>>Express Comparison>>Comparison**.

The configuration of the Comparison Express VI is shown for the "In Range" option in Fig. 3.3.2.3 and the "Less" option in Fig. 3.3.2.4. The minimum and maximum values are arbitrary and other appropriate values may be selected.

The configuration of the analog input and digital output tasks using the DAQ Assistant are shown in Figs. 3.3.2.5 and 3.3.2.6, respectively. These configuration values should be appropriate for your VI if you are using a power supply to simulate a sensor signal.

Select "1-D array of scalars-most recent value" for the resulting data type in the "Convert from Dynamic Data" Express VI.

Figure 3.3.2.1   Front panel of the analog input/ digital output VI to monitor a sensor that may be used to control an electrical device until stopped by the user

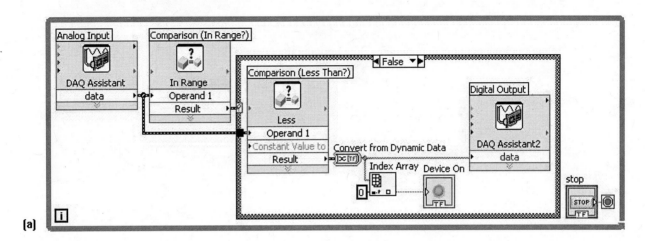

[a]

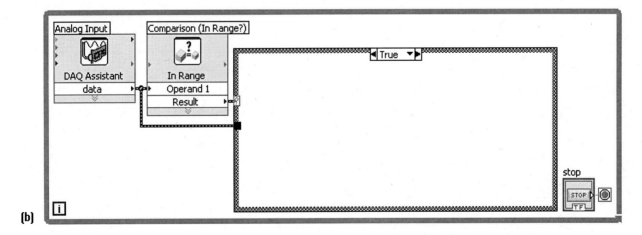

[b]

Figure 3.3.2.2   Block diagram of the analog input/digital output VI to monitor a sensor that may be used to control an electrical device until stopped by the user

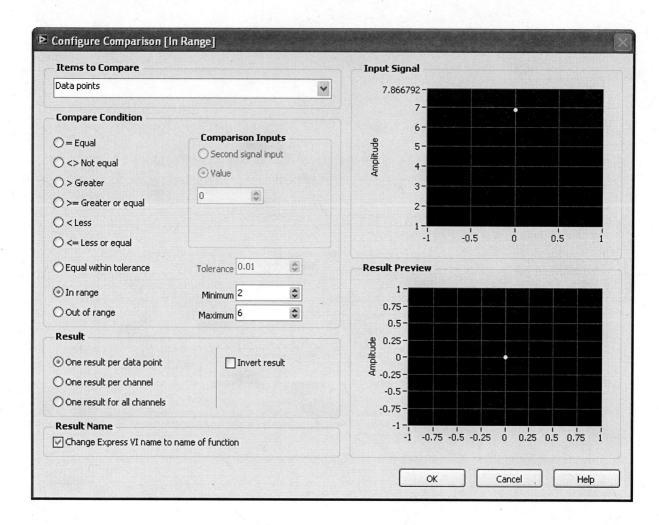

Figure 3.3.2.3   Comparison [In Range] Express VI configuration for the analog input/digital output VI to monitor a sensor that may be used to control an electrical device until stopped by the user

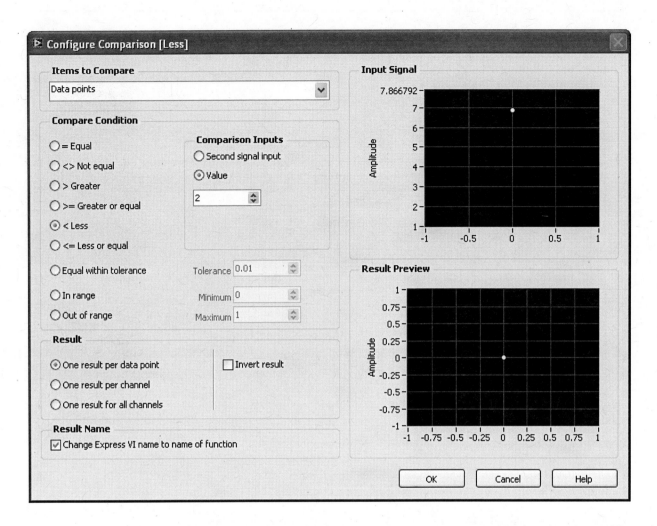

Figure 3.3.2.4   Comparison [Less] Express VI configuration for the analog input/digital output VI to monitor a sensor that may be used to control an electrical device until stopped by the user

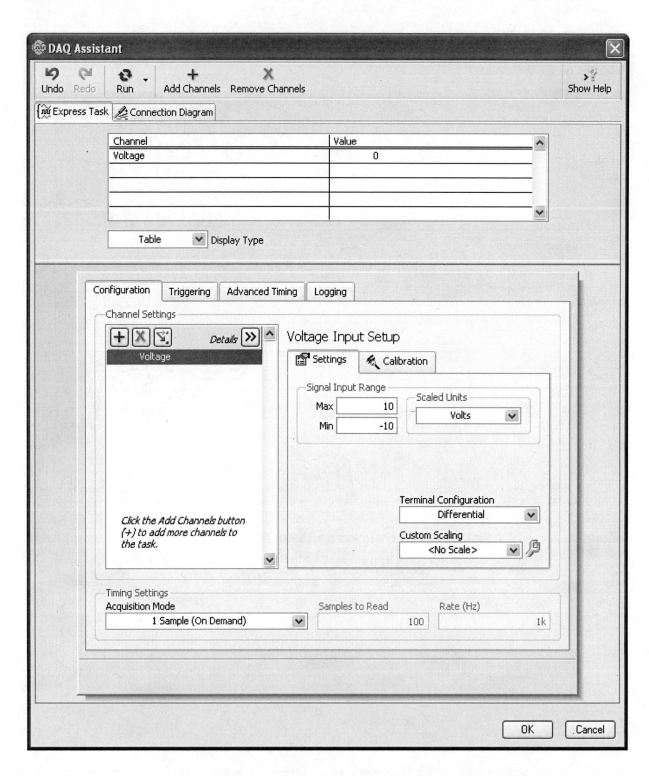

Figure 3.3.2.5   Analog input measurement task configuration using the DAQ Assistant for the analog input/digital output VI to monitor a sensor that may be used to control an electrical device until stopped by the user

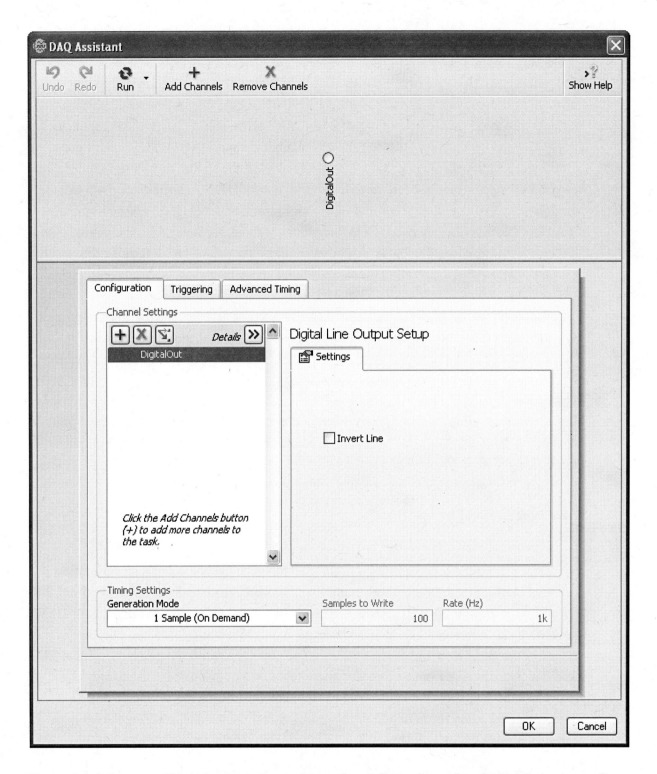

Figure 3.3.2.6   Digital output generation task configuration using the DAQ Assistant for the analog input/digital output VI to monitor a sensor that may be used to control an electrical device until stopped by the user

Fabrication and Testing

Connect the positive lead of the power supply to the positive input terminal on the terminal connector block specified in the analog input DAQ Assistant configuration window and the negative lead to the negative input terminal on the terminal connector block. Use the Connection Diagram tab of the analog input DAQ Assistant configuration window to identify the connections. Likewise, connect the digital output terminal on the terminal connector block specified in the digital output DAQ Assistant configuration window to the voltage input terminal of the multimeter and a D GND on the terminal connector block to the common (COM) terminal of the multimeter. Use the device pinout diagram from the Measurement & Automation Explorer (MAX) to determine the terminal numbers on the terminal connector block.

Once the connections have been made, the VI is ready to run. Start with an analog input voltage below the minimum set point. Notice the "Device On" software LED is illuminated and 5 V appears on the multimeter. Increase the analog input voltage above the maximum set point and observe the LED turns off and 0 V is displayed on the multimeter. The digital output voltage will remain the same until the analog input voltage drops below the minimum set point. The VI continues to monitor the input signal until stopped by the user. As a general practice, you should always ensure that the output voltage on the digital output line is 0 V when you are done with the VI. One easy way to do this is to apply an analog input voltage above the maximum set point.

Discussion

The logic behind the VI is discussed in this section. The measurement and generation tasks are configured to take a single sample on demand. Both tasks are placed within the While Loop to continuously monitor a sensor and control an electrical device. LabVIEW calls the measurement and generation tasks as fast as the While Loop can execute. The output of the measurement task provides input to the logic used to update the generation task. The signal value from the measurement tasks passes through a Case Structure to determine the digital output value. The example of controlling the temperature of a test chamber given in the introduction to this problem will be used to describe the VI logic. It will be assumed that a high (low) digital output signal turns on (off) the heater.

The analog input signal first passes through the Comparison Express VI as shown in Fig. 3.3.2.7 to determine if it is in range, that is, if the analog signal is between the minimum and maximum set points. If the analog signal is in range, there is no need to update the digital output signal. For example, if the heaters are on because the temperature was below the minimum set point at an earlier time, then the heaters will remain on, at least until the temperature exceeds the maximum set point. Likewise, if the heaters are off because the temperature exceeded the maximum set point at an earlier time, the heaters will remain off until the temperature drops below the range. The digital output signal does not change until a new update is generated. However, if the analog input signal is out of range, the digital output task will generate an update.

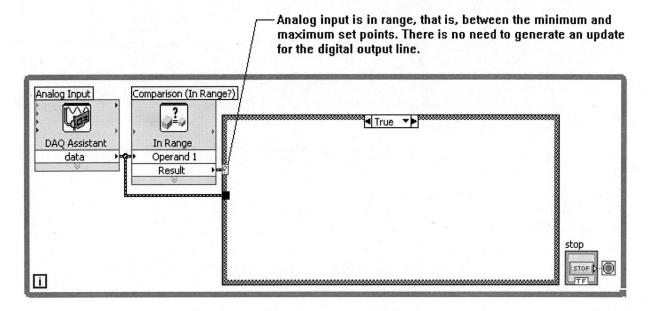

Figure 3.3.2.7   Block diagram of the analog input/digital output control VI when the analog input signal is between the minimum and maximum set points

If the analog input signal is out of range, the signal is then compared to the minimum set point as shown in Fig. 3.3.2.8. If the analog input signal is below the minimum set point, that is, the comparison operation is true, a logical high is output, which is the update value for the digital output generation task. This logic turns on the heater when the chamber temperature is below the minimum set point. If the analog input signal is out of range but not below the minimum set point, it must be above the maximum set point. The comparison operation is false and a logical low is output to update the digital output generation task. This logic turns off the heater when the chamber temperature is above the maximum set point.

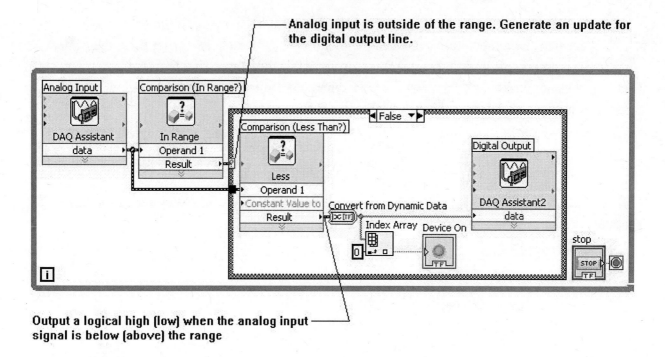

Output a logical high (low) when the analog input
signal is below (above) the range

Figure 3.3.2.8   Block diagram of the analog input/digital output control VI when the
                      analog input signal is outside of the minimum and maximum set points

3.3.3. Proficiency-Development Problem: Stepper Motor Control

Introduction

A bipolar stepper motor with an H-bridge driver is used to demonstrate an application of
the digital output function. If you do not have this hardware, you can still create the VI to
see how the digital output function is used and measure the output of the digital lines with
a multimeter or oscilloscope.

The bipolar stepper motor is constructed of two coil windings around magnetically
conductive stators and a multi-pole permanent magnet rotor as shown in Figure 3.3.3.1.
When a coil is energized, a north and south magnetic pole are created in the stator at the
positive and grounded ends, respectively, of the coil. By reversing the electrical current
through the coil winding, the north and south poles of the stator are reversed.

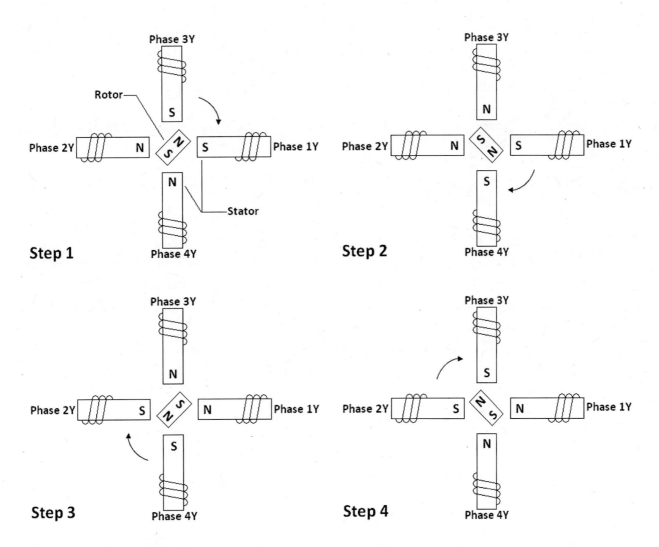

Figure 3.3.3.1 Stepping sequence for a stepper motor with a bipolar coil winding

The stepper motor generates rotary motion by sequentially energizing the coil windings. For example, a "two-phase on" sequence is shown in Figure 3.3.3.1. The Step 1-4 sequence shown in Table 3.3.3.1 will produce a clockwise rotation of the rotor shown in Figure 3.3.3.1. Reversing the steps produces counterclockwise rotation. The "1" and "0" in Table 3.3.3.1 refer to the application of the supply voltage to drive the motor at each of the four motor terminals. For example, the 5 V applied (represented by a 1) to the H-driver terminals 2A and 4A in Step 1 of Table 3.3.3.1 allows the supply voltage to create the north poles at terminals 2Y and 4Y in the stator shown in Figure 3.3.3.1. The opposite poles of the rotor align themselves between the two north and two south poles of the stator. In Step 2, the supply voltage is applied to H-driver terminals 2A and 3A and the rotor rotates 90° to align with the new direction of the magnetic poles in the stator. The resolution of the stepper motor depends on the number of poles on the rotor. By applying the supply voltage to terminals 1A and 3A (Step 3) and then 1A and 4A (Step 4), the sequence for energizing the coils in the stator is complete.

Step	Decimal Pattern	4A	3A	2A	1A
1	10	1	0	1	0
2	6	0	1	1	0
3	5	0	1	0	1
4	9	1	0	0	1

Table 3.3.3.1   Step sequence for a bipolar stepper motor

An H-bridge control circuit is used to drive the motor. It is best not to use the DAQ board to drive hardware directly for at least two reasons: (1) the supply voltage for the hardware may be different than that produced by the DAQ board and (2) the amperage requirements of the device may damage the power supply in the computer or the DAQ board. This is true for both digital output and analog output. In this example, a Texas Instruments SN754410 quadruple half-H driver is used. The inputs are compatible with TTL (transistor-transistor logic) signals, which will be supplied from the DAQ board, and the outputs are designed to drive currents up to 1 A at voltages between 4.5 V and 36 V. The power to drive the output current will be supplied by a separate power supply. The H-bridge will supply a high-level (low-level) voltage as output to the stepper motor terminals when the input voltage from the DAQ board is high-level (low-level) as long as the enable pins are at a high-level TTL signal.

The TTL sequence to step the motor is determined from Table 3.3.3.1. The high- and low-level TTL signal in Table 3.3.3.1 can be viewed as a four-bit pattern of a binary number if you are writing to 4 digital lines. The binary numbers in the rows of Steps 1-4 represent the number sequence 10, 6, 5, and 9 in decimal if you are writing to a port. For example, the binary number 1010 is the decimal number 10. This sequence will be stored in an array that will supply the pattern to the digital output function in the LabVIEW program. If the steps are executed from 1 through 4, then the rotation of the rotor is clockwise. The rotation is counterclockwise if the steps are reversed.

Goals

1. Develop proficiency with digital output data acquisition concepts using LabVIEW's configuration approach.

2. Develop the software-timed VI which generates digital output to continuously control a stepping motor until stopped by the user.

Equipment

The VI may be developed and tested using only a multimeter or oscilloscope to observe the digital output lines. However, the following generic list of equipment is necessary if you want to test the VI with a stepper motor.

1. A bipolar stepper motor
2. H-bridge driver
3. Power supply

Developing the VI

The front panel and block diagram of the digital output VI to control a stepper motor are shown in Figs. 3.3.3.2 and 3.3.3.3. The block diagram shows both cases of the Case Structure.

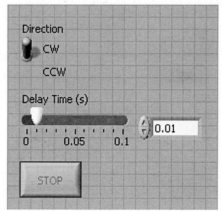

Figure 3.3.3.2   Front panel of the digital output VI to continuously control a stepper motor until stopped by a user

All functions that have been employed in this VI have been described in this chapter or Section 1.4, except for the Quotient & Remainder function, the Index Array function, and the Simple Error Handler subVI. The Quotient & Remainder function computes the integer quotient and the remainder of the inputs. The function can be found in the function palette under **Programming>>Numeric>>Quotient & Remainder**. Note that one of the inputs to the Quotient & Remainder function is the iteration terminal (blue box containing the letter "i") of the While Loop. The Index Array function returns a row or column of an n-dimensional array at the specified index. The function can be found in the function palette under **Programming>>Array>>Index Array**. The Simple Error Handler subVI indicates if an error has occurred and, if so, provides a description of the error. This subVI can be found in the function palette under **Programming>>Dialog & User Interface>>Simple Error Handler**. Its use is optional.

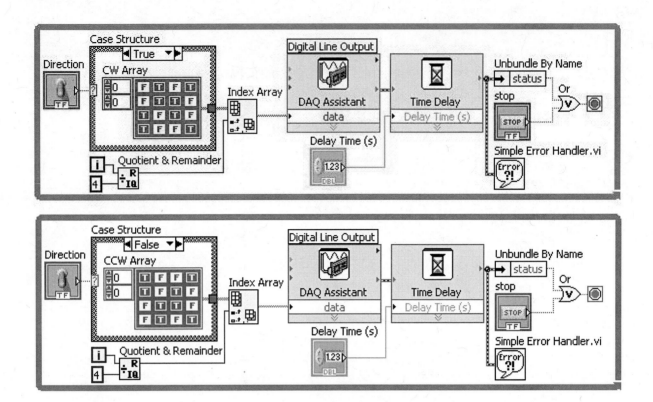

Figure 3.3.3.3   Block diagram of the digital output VI to continuously control a stepper motor until stopped by a user

The sequence shown in Table 3.3.3.1 will be stored as logical elements in a 2-D array. LabVIEW requires a two-step process to store data in an array. First you must create an array shell. The array shell simply tells LabVIEW to set up an array structure for the variable. The second step tells what type of data exists in the array. Arrays can store numbers, logical (Boolean) values, character strings, etc. The logical arrays shown in Fig. 3.3.3.3 supply update values to the digital output task, which will be used to control the rotation of the stepper motor.

The first step is to create an array shell. From the function palette, select **Programming>>Array>>Array Constant** and place the shell in the true case of the Case Structure. Perform the second step by letting LabVIEW know the array will be filled with logical values. From the functions palette, select **Programming>>Boolean>>True Constant** and place it inside the array box. Place the cursor over the index, right click, and select "Add Dimension" from the pop-up menu. Use the Position (arrow) cursor to enlarge the logical value box to view a four by four array. Place the position cursor over the constant box until the resizing brackets (stacked corners) cursor appears and then drag the box to resize. Right-click over the index, select

Visible Items>>Label, and name the array "CW Array." Using the Operate Value (pointing hand) cursor, select the logical values shown in Fig. 3.3.3.3. Repeat the same procedure for the counterclockwise array. The array in the Case Structure will provide the pattern for the digital output function. However, to supply one row at a time, you must extract each row using the Index Array function.

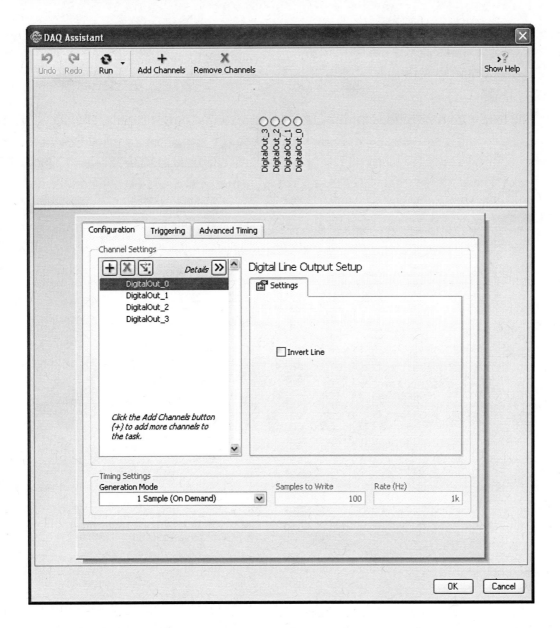

Figure 3.3.3.4 Digital output generation task configuration using the DAQ Assistant for the digital output VI to continuously control a stepper motor until stopped by the user

The configuration of the digital output task using the DAQ Assistant is shown in Fig. 3.3.3.4. Note that "Line Output" was selected for the digital output generation task when the task was created. The output lines, DigitalOut_0 through DigitalOut_3, were selected as "port0/line0" through "port0/line3." Obviously, other appropriate digital output lines could be selected.

Fabricating and Testing

If you do not have a stepper motor and an H bridge driver, you may skip to the testing procedure at the end of this section and use a multimeter or oscilloscope to observe the output of the digital lines.

The hardware connections for the DAQ board, external power supply, H-bridge driver, and stepping motor are shown in Figure 3.3.3.5. The stepper motor used was a 6-lead-wire, bipolar, stepper motor (TEAC part No. 14769070-00, 4302E, Shinano Electric Co. Ltd.). The H bridge driver used was a Texas Instruments SN754410 quadruple half-H driver. A National Instruments PCI-6221 was used for the DAQ board. The connection diagram in Fig. 3.3.3.5 is for the equipment used in the current demonstration. ***You must confirm connections for other equivalent equipment before you proceed with different hardware.***

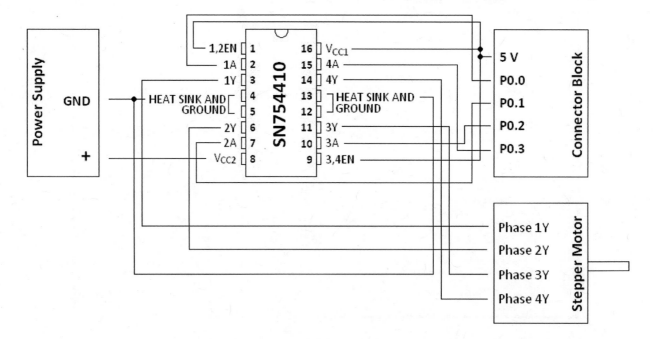

Figure 3.3.3.5   Connection diagram to connect a TEAC 14769070-00 stepper motor to a NI PCI 6221 data acquisition board and a Texas Instruments SN754410 quadruple half-H driver

The LabVIEW VI supplies the TTL sequence to the DAQ board. For the current demonstration, the digital output channels, port0/line0 through port0/line3, pass the TTL signal to 1A-4A, respectively, of the H-bridge driver. Use the device pinout diagram from the Measurement & Automation Explorer (MAX) to determine the terminal numbers on the terminal connector block. Pins 1Y-4Y of the H-bridge driver supplies power to INPUT1-INPUT4 leads, respectively, of the stepper motor. The 5 V source to power the H-bridge driver (V_{CC1}) and to provide the high-level TTL signal for the 1,2 ENABLE and 3,4 ENABLE pins is provided from the DAQ board. The supply voltage for the stepping motor (V_{CC2}) and the ground for the H-bridge driver are provided by the external power supply. The supply voltage for the stepper motor is model dependent and must be determined from hardware data sheets.

Once the connections are made, the VI is ready to run. The rotational speed and the direction of rotation of the stepper motor are controlled by the "Direction" and "Delay Time" controls in the front panel. If you are not using a stepper motor, you can display individual line voltages on an oscilloscope or multimeter. Each of the four lines can be tested separately by comparing the sequence shown in Table 3.3.3.1 to the observed output. This is best done with long time delays (1-2 seconds) so that the sequence at the start of the VI execution can be observed. The VI continues to update the output signals until stopped by the user. As a general practice, you should always ensure that the output voltage on the digital output lines is 0 V when you are done with the VI. One quick method is to open the DAQ Assistant window and run a test of the lines with a logical low (0 V) signal, which is the default value.

Discussion

Since the digital output generation task was configured for line output, a row array of four logical values for each of the four lines must be supplied every iteration. The least significant element, that is, the bit going to pin 1A of the H bridge driver, is the first element of the row. Since one full rotation is completed every four steps, a four by four array of logical values is constructed. Rows are extracted each iteration using the Index Array function. The Quotient & Remainder function determines what row is extracted. By dividing the iteration count by four, the remainder will always be in a repeating sequence of 0, 1, 2, and 3. The clockwise array shows updates from Table 3.3.3.1 for 1A through 4A in the first column through the fourth column, respectively, and Steps 1-4 in the first through fourth rows, respectively. The counterclockwise array lists Steps 4-1 (row order is reversed to that of the clockwise direction) in the first through fourth rows, respectively.

Alternatively, the digital output generation task could have been configured for port output, as shown in Fig. 3.3.6. The NI 6221 DAQ board has three ports, each port consisting of 8 lines. For example, port 0 consists of port0/line0-port0/line7 with the update to pin 1A for the H bridge driver (see Table 3.3.3.1) on port0/line0 being the least significant bit of the 8-bit word. The pattern for Step 1 in Table 3.3.3.1 for the 8-bit word is the binary number, 00001010, which is equivalent to the decimal number, 10. With digital port output, a 2-D integer array provides updates for the digital output generation task. Columns in the array represent different ports that are available on the DAQ board while the rows represent Steps 1-4 of the stepping sequence for the stepper motor. Only one column, representing port 0, is used in the current VI. Port output was selected for digital output when the generation task was configured using the DAQ Assistant, as shown in Fig. 3.3.3.7.

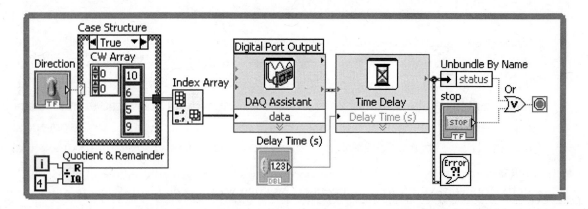

Figure 3.3.3.6   Block diagram showing the use of digital port output in the VI to continuously control a stepper motor until stopped by a user

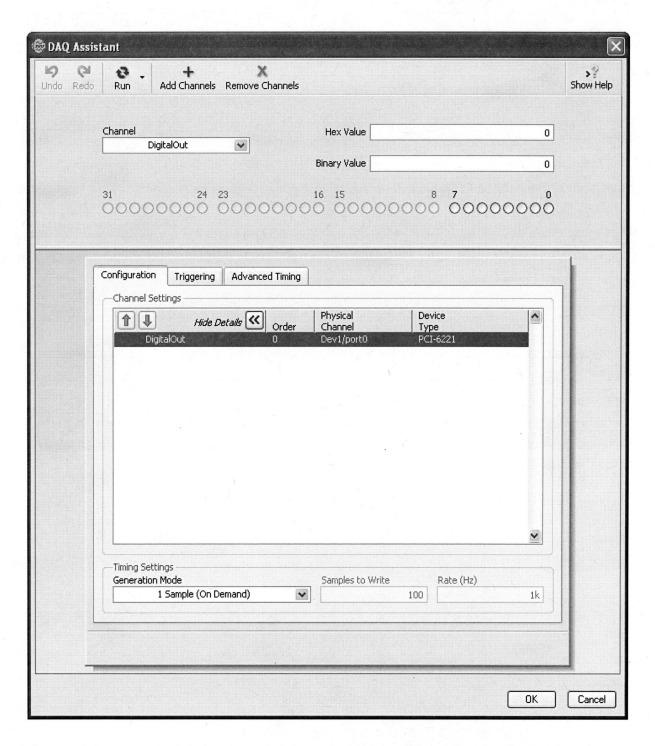

Figure 3.3.3.7   Digital port output generation task configuration using the DAQ Assistant for the digital output VI to continuously control a stepper motor until stopped by the user

3.3.4. Proficiency-Development Problem: Keypad Scanning

Introduction

The technique to represent symbols from symbol-input devices, such as a joystick, keypad, or keyboard, depends on the number of keys or buttons on the device. For a device with few keys or buttons, digital input lines can be dedicated to individual keys. Since the keys are merely switches, the status of the key can be encoded as a bit, such as a logical 0 (0 V) that the key has been pressed and a logical 1 (5 V) that it has been released, for example. However, when a device contains a number of keys, this technique becomes impractical. A technique called scanning (or polling) is employed in this case.

The scanning technique is employed when the keys are arranged in a matrix, such as columns and rows of keys. A known digital pattern is sent out on one direction (say, the columns) of the matrix and the status of the other direction (the rows) is scanned to determine if any key was pressed. The known digital output pattern sent to the columns can be combined with the scanned digital input pattern acquired from the rows to create a unique digital pattern for each key when pressed. This digital pattern can be encoded to represent a character on a device's display or computer monitor that is the same as the depressed key's symbol. The scanning technique works if the scan rate is faster than successive key strokes.

Figure 3.3.4.1 Photograph of a standard telephone keypad

The standard telephone keypad shown in Fig 3.3.4.1 will be used to illustrate the scanning technique. Fig. 3.3.4.2 shows the disassembled keypad exposing the back side of the keys and the printed circuit board. When the keypad is assembled, the back side of the keys and the circuit board are in contact with each other. A closer inspection of the circuit board shows that the keys are wired in rows and columns although the rows and columns are not electrically connected. The rows and columns terminate at each key with an interwoven set of leads arranged like fingers. The electrical connection between a row and column is completed when the key is depressed and a graphite pad covers the interwoven leads.

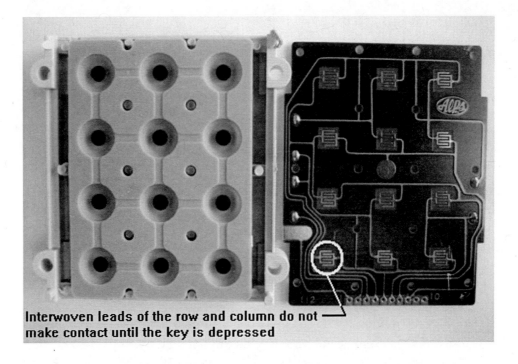

Interwoven leads of the row and column do not make contact until the key is depressed

Figure 3.3.4.2   Photograph of the back side of the keys and printed circuit board of a standard keypad

A schematic showing the wiring for keypad scanning is illustrated in Fig. 3.3.4.3. The numbers and symbols normally found on a keypad are overlaid on the schematic. The horizontal and vertical wires represent the rows and columns shown in Fig. 3.3.4.2. The graphite contact of the key that electrically connects the rows and columns is represented by the symbol ⌎. The contact is shown open because a row and column are not connected until the key is depressed. Pull up resistors are added to the rows to reduce current through the keypad to a level within the acceptable range of the DAQ board.

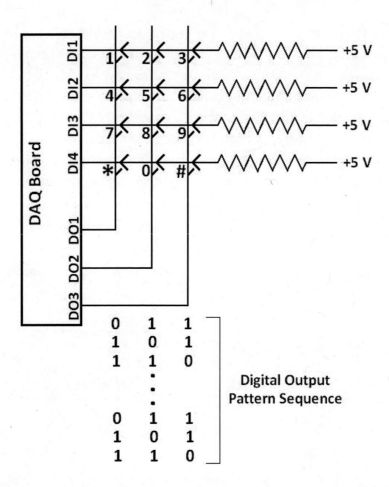

Figure 3.3.4.3   Schematic showing the keypad scanning technique

The keypad scanning technique involves sending out a repeated sequence of digital patterns on the columns and sampling the digital signals on the rows. The sequence of digital patterns involves outputting a logical 0 on alternating columns as shown in Fig. 3.3.4.3 and a logical 1 on the remaining columns. After the digital output lines connected to the columns are updated, the digital states of rows are sampled. When no key is depressed, the rows do not make electrical contact with the columns and all rows are at a logical 1 (+5V). However, when a key is depressed while a column is at the low state (0V), the voltage on the row at the key will also drop to 0V. If the known states of the digital output lines (columns) are combined with the acquired states of the digital input lines (rows), a unique sequence is obtained for each key.

For example, if the "7" key is depressed, a connection between the first column and third row of the keypad is made. A binary number is formed from the state of the columns and rows. For this example, the binary number will be ordered listing columns first, in reverse order from the third column to the first, followed by rows in reverse order from the fourth row to the first. When the first column is updated with a logical 0, the digital output of the combined columns and rows is 1101011, which is equivalent to decimal number 107.

This unique binary or decimal number can then be encoded to display a "7" on the device's display or computer monitor. The digital patterns of all of the keypad symbols are shown in Table 3.3.4.1. C1 through C3 represent the first through third columns, respectively, and R1-R4 represents the first through fourth rows. The last three rows of the table represent the digital patterns when there are no key strokes.

Keypad Symbol	C3	C2	C1	R4	R3	R2	R1	Decimal Number
1	1	1	0	1	1	1	0	110
4	1	1	0	1	1	0	1	109
7	1	1	0	1	0	1	1	107
*	1	1	0	0	1	1	1	103
2	1	0	1	1	1	1	0	94
5	1	0	1	1	1	0	1	93
8	1	0	1	1	0	1	1	91
0	1	0	1	0	1	1	1	87
3	0	1	1	1	1	1	0	62
6	0	1	1	1	1	0	1	61
9	0	1	1	1	0	1	1	59
#	0	1	1	0	1	1	1	55
No Key Pressed	1	1	0	1	1	1	1	111
No Key Pressed	1	0	1	1	1	1	1	95
No Key Pressed	0	1	1	1	1	1	1	63

Table 3.3.4.1   The binary number and decimal equivalent of the digital states of the keypad rows and columns for each symbol during keypad scanning

The scanning must be faster than the keystrokes to be a successful technique since the digital output lines must be updated with three distinct digital patterns to cycle through all of the columns. A scan rate on the order of a few milliseconds ensures that each column is sampled during a keystroke. As stated earlier, when no key is depressed all rows are at the high logical state and the displayed value on the monitor should not change.

Goals

1. Develop proficiency with multi-function data acquisition concepts using LabVIEW's configuration approach.

2. Develop the multi-function, software-timed, digital input/digital output VI to scan a keypad, which updates digital output lines and samples digital input lines continuously until stopped by the user.

Equipment

1. Standard telephone keypad
2. Resistors, 10,000 Ω, one for each row of keys

Developing the VI

The front panel and block diagram of the digital input/digital output VI to perform keypad scanning are shown in Figs. 3.3.4.4 and 3.3.4.5. The block diagram shows the three types of the cases shown in Table 3.3.4.1 in the Case Structure. The default case shows a string indicator with the string "1" as an input, which is the encoded value for the decimal number 110. The string indicator was created using the Controls palette in the front panel (**Modern>>String & Path>>String Indicator**) and renamed "Keypad Encoder". The second case shows a local variable of the string indicator in the default case with the string "2" as an input. Section 1.4.14 shows how to create local variables. All other keypad symbols are treated in the same manner as the case showing the string "2". However, for the three rows in Table 3.3.4.1 that represent no key stroke, whatever value that is currently displayed in the string indicator in the front panel should not change. For these cases, nothing is placed in the case structure.

All functions that have been employed in this VI have been described in this chapter or Section 1.4, except for the Index Array, Build Array, and Boolean Array To Number functions. The Index Array function returns a row or column of an n-dimensional array at the specified index. The function can be found in the function palette under **Programming>>Array>>Index Array**. The Build Array function combines arrays into larger n-dimensional arrays. The function can be found in the function palette under **Programming>>Array>>Build Array**. The Boolean Array To Number function interprets a Boolean array as a binary pattern and converts the binary number to a decimal number. The function can be found in the function palette under **Programming>>Boolean>>Boolean Array To Number**.

The digital output pattern will be stored as logical elements in a 2-D array. LabVIEW requires a two-step process to store data in an array. First you must create an array shell. The array shell simply tells LabVIEW to set up an array structure for the variable. The second step is to tell LabVIEW what type of data exists in the array. Arrays can store numbers, logical (Boolean) values, character strings, etc. The logical array shown in Fig.

3.3.4.5 supplies update values to the digital output task, which will be used to scan the keypad.

Figure 3.3.4.4   Front panel of the digital input/digital output VI to continuously scan a keypad until stopped by a user

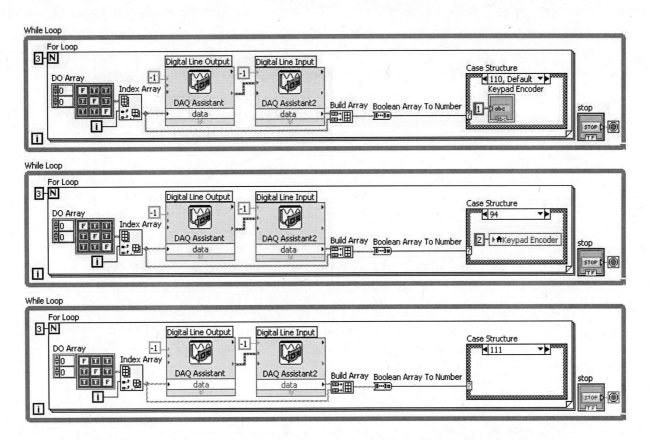

Figure 3.3.4.5   Front panel of the digital input/digital output VI to continuously scan a keypad until stopped by a user

The first step is to create an array shell. From the function palette, select **Programming>>Array>>Array Constant** and place the shell in the For Loop. Perform the second step by letting LabVIEW know that the array will be filled with logical values. From the functions palette, select **Programming>>Boolean>>True Constant** and place it inside the array box. Place the cursor over the index, right click, and select "Add Dimension" from the pop-up menu. Use the Position (arrow) cursor to enlarge the logical value box to view a three by three array. Place the position cursor over the constant box until the resizing brackets (stacked corners) cursor appears and then drag the box to resize. Right-click over the index, select **Visible Items>>Label**, and name the array "DO Array." Using the Operate Value (pointing hand) cursor, select the logical values shown in Fig. 3.3.4.5. The array will provide the pattern for the digital output function. However, to supply one row at a time, you must extract each row using the Index Array function.

The configuration of the digital output task using the DAQ Assistant is shown in Fig. 3.3.4.6. Note that "Line Output" was selected for the digital output generation task when the task was created. The output lines, DigitalOut_0 through DigitalOut_2, were selected as "port0/line4" through "port0/line6." Obviously, other appropriate digital output lines could be selected.

The configuration of the digital input task using the DAQ Assistant is shown in Fig. 3.3.4.7. "Line Input" was selected for the digital input measurement task when the task was created. The input lines, DigitalIn_0 through DigitalIn_3, were selected as "port0/line0" through "port0/line3," although, other appropriate digital input lines could be selected.

Fabricating and Testing

The hardware connections for the keypad and DAQ board are shown in Figure 3.3.4.3. The digital input and output lines are connected to the connector block terminals shown in Figs. 3.3.4.6 and 3.3.4.7. Use the device pinout diagram from the Measurement & Automation Explorer (MAX) to determine the terminal numbers on the terminal connector block. The +5 V excitation can also be provided by the DAQ board as long as the resistors are appropriately sized to keep the current below the maximum rating for the DAQ board.

Once the connections are made, the VI is ready to run. If your VI is working correctly, the keypad symbol of a pressed key should appear on the "Keypad Encoder" string indicator in the front panel and not change until another key is pressed. The VI continues to scan the keypad until stopped by the user. As a general practice, you should always ensure that the output voltage on the digital output lines is 0 V when you are done with the VI. One quick method is to open the digital output DAQ Assistant window and run a test of the lines with a logical low (0 V) signal, which is the default value.

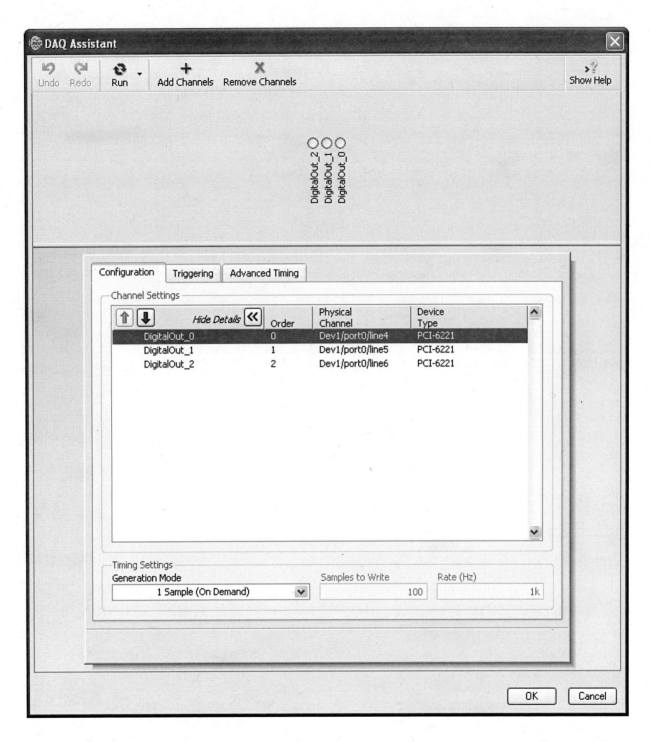

Figure 3.3.4.6   Digital output generation task configuration using the DAQ Assistant for the digital input/digital output VI to continuously scan a keypad until stopped by the user

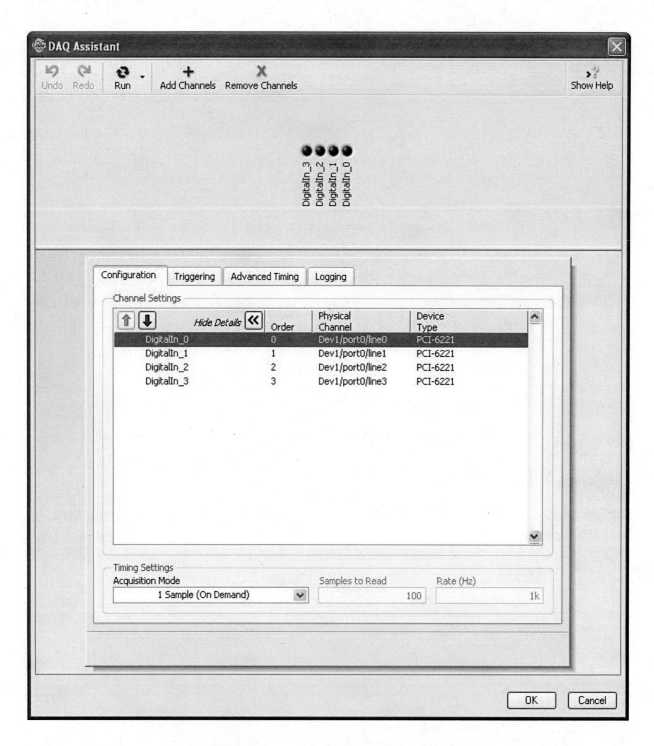

Figure 3.3.4.7   Digital input measurement task configuration using the DAQ Assistant for the digital input/digital output VI to continuously scan a keypad until stopped by the user

Discussion

As mentioned in the Introduction section, the keypad scanning technique works when the scan rate is faster than successive key strokes. The digital input and output tasks are configured for one sample, on demand. Therefore, the execution of these tasks is controlled by the software, that is, software timing is employed. As the VI is presented, LabVIEW will call the measurement and generation tasks as quickly as LabVIEW can execute the code, typically on the millisecond time scale. A Time Delay function could be added to the VI to have more control over timing.

It should also be mentioned that Case Structures can identify cases based on numeric, Boolean, or string scalar input. The Boolean array created after the Build Array function cannot be used as an input to the Case Structure since the Case Structure requires a Boolean scalar, not a 1-D Boolean array. Therefore, the Boolean array is converted to an equivalent decimal numeric scalar. The numeric values that appear in the selector label when the numeric scalar is connected to the Case Structure are 0 and 1 by default. These values can be changed to the decimal numbers in Table 3.3.4.1 using the Edit Text cursor.

Notes:

Chapter 4   Counters

4.1   Counter Basics

Counters on DAQ boards can perform many applications with Transistor-Transistor-Logic (TTL) signals. A TTL signal is a square-pulse wave where the voltage of the signal toggles between the low state (0V) and high state (5V). Applications include:

- measuring the duration (width) of a single pulse or multiple pulses
- measuring the semi-period(s) or period(s) of TTL square waves
- measuring the frequency of a TTL square wave
- measuring angular or linear position using encoders
- counting events (rising or falling edge of a TTL signal) or elapsed time between events
- generating a TTL pulse
- generating a finite or continuous series of TTL pulses, which is called a pulse train

Not all DAQ boards can perform the functions listed above. Consult the hardware specifications for your DAQ board's specific capabilities.

The low state and high state of a TTL signal are also referred to as phase 1 and phase 2, respectively, of the signal. The duty cycle of a TTL pulse is the fraction of time the pulse is in the high state. Since the period of the TTL pulse is the sum of the two phases, the duty cycle is defined as

$$duty \quad cycle = \frac{phase \quad 2}{period}.$$

The frequency of the TTL signal is the reciprocal of the period.

There are three basic terminals on a typical counter, which consists of a SOURCE (or CLK) input terminal, a GATE input terminal, and an OUT output terminal. The counter may include other terminals, like those associated with encoders or auxiliary input terminals, although they will not be discussed in this introductory chapter on counters. The counter also includes a count register, which stores the current count of the counter.

The edges of a TTL signal are the transitions from low-to-high or high-to-low states. They are counted at the SOURCE terminal and stored in the count register. Depending on the specific counter, the edge may be low-to-high or high-to-low. The resolution of the counter limits the maximum number of counts that can be stored in the count register, which is called the terminal count. For example, the terminal count for the M-series DAQ-STC2 counter, a 32-bit resolution counter, is 4,294,967,296 (2^{32}) counts. You must consult the hardware specifications for each board since the resolution of the counter is DAQ-board specific. An internal or external signal may be used as an input to SOURCE. If an external signal of known frequency is not connected to the SOURCE terminal, a signal based on an internal clock will be used. The time bases of the internal clock vary with each specific counter. For example, the DAQ-STC2 supports internal time bases of 100 kHz, 20 MHz, and 80 MHz.

The signal at the GATE terminal controls when counting occurs. Gating occurs during an active signal, which can occur based on the rising edge or falling edge of the signal or a high-level or low-level signal. For example, with high-level gating, the source signal is counted only when the gate signal is high.

This is how the pulse width of an unknown signal can be determined, for example. Let's say that gating occurs during the high level of a pulse. If a pulse of unknown width is connected to the GATE terminal, the SOURCE terminal will count the edges of the known high-frequency time base signal connected to its terminal only during the high state of the signal on the GATE. The high-level pulse width on the GATE is the product of the known time base period of the SOURCE signal and the number of counts obtained during gating. Obviously, the higher frequency time base provides greater resolution to measure the pulse width. However, an error will occur if the pulse width is greater than the maximum time that the counter can measure. For example, the DAQ-STC2 counter has an 80 MHz time base with a period of $(80,000,000)^{-1}$ seconds and a 32-bit resolution counter. The maximum time the counter can measure is the product of the maximum count (2^{32}) and the period (1/80,000,000 seconds) of the time base signal, which results in approximately 53.68 seconds. If it is anticipated that a pulse will have a duration longer than 53.68 seconds, a slower time base must be used.

Counters can generate both pulses and pulse trains using the OUT terminal. The shape of the pulse is determined by the pulse delay (phase 1) and pulse width (phase 2). The shape of the pulse train is determined by the frequency and duty cycle. Some counters also allow the option of choosing a high or low pulse polarity. If the pulse polarity is high, the initial state is low and the pulse is high. Likewise, if the pulse polarity is low, the initial state is high and the pulse is low. Some counters provide an additional means to generate a pulse train with limited options. For example, the E-Series, M-Series, and X-Series National Instruments DAQ boards have a FREQ_OUT pin that generates a pulse train with a single or limited range of duty cycles.

There are different types of counters in DAQ boards. The examples in this chapter were developed with the National Instruments M-Series DAQ-STC2 counter in mind. However, the examples in this chapter cover basic concepts and may work for other counters as well since LabVIEW supports a number of different types of counters. If you are using DAQ hardware with a different counter, LabVIEW 2012 also provides many example programs, for example, to generate a pulse or pulse train, count events or time, and measure frequency, period, or pulse width. These example VIs can be found in the following directories, which assumes default installation of the National Instruments software:

C:\Program Files\National Instruments\LabVIEW 2012\examples\DAQmx\Counter Input
C:\Program Files\National Instruments\LabVIEW 2012\examples\DAQmx\Counter Output

Skill-development examples are offered for one application of measurement and generation of digital signals using counters. The example in Section 4.2 shows how to use a counter to measure a pulse width. The example in Section 4.3 shows how to use a counter to generate a continuous TTL pulse train for devices that employ pulse width modulation control. Once you understand the general concepts behind the measurement and generation of digital signals using counters, it is a relatively simple extension to apply the concepts to other measurement or generation applications.

4.2   Counter Input

4.2.1   Introduction to Counter Input Applications

A brief description of some of the more common counter input applications are provided in this section. Each application may be run in single sample (on-demand or immediate) mode or in multi-sample buffered mode. Refer to your DAQ hardware manual to determine what capabilities are available on your DAQ board.

Counting Edges

Counting events, such as counting the number of boxes moving along a production line, is a common application of counting TTL edges. For example, a light source would be placed on one side of a conveyor and a solid state photodiode light detector aligned with the light source would be placed on the opposite side of the conveyor. Boxes, moving along the conveyor, would toggle the voltage across the photodiode between 0 V and 5 V as the boxes interrupted the light beam and created a pulse train. The number of boxes transported by the conveyor could be determined by counting the number of active (rising or falling) edges of the TTL signal across the photodiode.

The photodiode signal is connected to the SOURCE input terminal to count edges. Counting may go up or down. You may also connect a second, independent, signal called a pause trigger to the GATE input terminal. When the pause trigger is active (high or low), the counter ignores the edges on the SOURCE terminal.

Pulse Width Measurement

An example of pulse width measurement is to determine the speed of an object of known length like, for example, a ball exiting a tube. A light source would be placed on one side of the ball and a photodiode aligned with the light would be placed on the opposing side. A TTL pulse is created as the ball interrupts the light source. The ball's velocity can be determined since the length of the ball is known and the time it takes to pass through the light beam (pulse width) is measured.

The photodiode signal is connected to the GATE input terminal of the counter and a clock signal of known period (or frequency) is routed to the SOURCE input terminal. The clock may be internal, like the 80 MHz clock that comes with the DAQ-STC2 counter, or an external clock that you provide. A physical connection must be made between an external clock and the SOURCE terminal. No physical connection is required for the internal clock as the clock signal is internally routed. The number of TTL edges (rising or falling) from the clock pulses is counted when the photodiode signal on the GATE terminal is active (high or low). The duration of the pulse (pulse width) is the product of the number of edges counted and the known period between each clock edge.

Period Measurement

A common application for period measurement is to determine the rotational speed of a shaft with the aid of a magnet and a Hall Effect sensor. A Hall Effect sensor consists of a flat rectangular plate of a p-type semiconductor that has a continuous current passing through it. As a magnet is placed near the sensor, electrons and holes are displaced to opposite sides of the sensor creating a voltage difference across the sides. Typically, a strong magnet is embedded in a shaft, which sweeps past the Hall Effect sensor mounted in a casing causing a TTL signal with one period every rotation. The rotational speed of the shaft can be determined by the time it takes to complete one period of the TTL signal, which completes one revolution.

The Hall Effect sensor signal is connected to the GATE input terminal and a clock signal of known period (or frequency) is routed to the SOURCE input terminal. The clock may be an internal or external source. The number of TTL edges (rising or falling) from the clock pulses is counted between two active edges (either two rising edges or two falling edges) on the GATE terminal. The period of the Hall Effect sensor is the product of the number of edges counted and the known period between each clock edge.

Frequency Measurement

There are three separate techniques for measuring the frequency of a digital pulse train: low frequency pulses, high frequency pulses, and a pulse train whose frequency may vary between the low and high ranges. Since a wave frequency is the reciprocal of the period, the applications for measuring frequency can overlap with measuring the period.

For low-frequency pulses, the period of the signal of unknown frequency is measured using one counter. The signal of unknown frequency is connected to the GATE of the counter. An internal or external clock signal of known frequency (or period) is routed to the SOURCE input terminal. The period of a pulse is measured by counting the number of clock pulses on SOURCE that occur between the active edges of the pulse on the GATE input terminal. The frequency of the measured signal is the ratio of the frequency of the clock and the number of clock pulses. The total time of a user specified number of pulses on the GATE may also be measured to calculate an average period and, therefore, frequency.

The technique to measure high-frequency pulses is with the use of two counters. The first counter, COUNTER0, is used to generate a pulse with a known pulse width. Then route the output of COUNTER0 to the GATE1 input terminal of COUNTER1. The signal of unknown frequency that is to be measured is connected to the SOURCE1 input terminal. The number of pulses of the signal to be measured is counted on SOURCE1 during the time the active pulse width appears on GATE1. The frequency of the signal to be measured is the number of pulses on SOURCE1 divided by the known duration of the pulse width on GATE1.

The technique to measure frequency of a digital pulse train whose frequency may vary between low and high also uses two counters. The signal of unknown frequency is used to generate a pulse of relatively long duration. This is accomplished by connecting the signal of unknown frequency to the SOURCE0 input terminal of the first counter, COUNTER0, and generating a pulse width of a user specified number, N, of pulses of the signal that is to be measured. The pulse is generated on the OUT0 output terminal of COUNTER0 and connected to the GATE1 input terminal of a second counter, COUNTER1. A clock signal of known period is routed to SOURCE1 input terminal of COUNTER1. The number of clock pulses, M, on SOURCE1 is counted during the time of the active pulse width on GATE1. The frequency of the signal to be measured, F, can be determined from the known clock frequency, F_C, as $F = F_C(N/M)$.

Even though the technique for frequency measurement depends on the frequency to be measured (that is, low or high), there is no specific cutoff frequency that demarcates low and high frequencies. The technique of choice will depend on the internal or external clock speed and the level of uncertainty on the frequency measurement that can be tolerated by the project. In all of the techniques, the number of clock pulses is used to measure the duration of the pulse width or period of the signal connected to the GATE. However, since the active edge of the clock pulse on the SOURCE input terminal does not necessarily start (or end) when the pulse on GATE begins (or ends), the count of clock pulses is accurate to within ±1 clock pulse. Low frequency signals that are connected to the GATE require many clock pulses to measure the signal's period such that the uncertainty of ± one clock pulse does not contribute much to the overall uncertainty of the frequency measurement. However, as the frequency of the signal on the GATE approaches that of the clock, fewer clock pulses are required to measure the period of the signal on GATE and the ±one clock pulse can have a large impact on the overall uncertainty of the frequency measurement. The low-frequency technique is generally suitable for most applications although the user can estimate uncertainties based on anticipated frequencies of the measured signal to select the best technique.

Two-Signal Edge-Separation Measurement

One application of a two-signal edge-separation measurement is to determine the speed of an object of unknown length. A light source with an opposing photodiode is spaced a known distance apart from a second light source with an opposing photodiode. A TTL pulse is produced on each photodiode as the object moves past the photodiodes and interrupts the light beams. For example, the Society of Automotive Engineers (SAE) requires student teams to prove that crush zones on Formula cars will transmit less than a maximum force at a specified crash velocity. A weight, equal to that of the Formula car, is attached to the back side of the crush zone material, raised to a height that should create the specified crash speed, and released. A pair of light sources/photodiodes are separated by a relatively small known vertical distance and placed near the ground. The speed of the crush zone prior to impact is measured using the two photodiode signals since the time required for the crush zone to pass through a known distance is measured.

To make a two-signal edge-separation measurement, the first signal should be connected to the AUX input terminal of the counter and the second signal should be connected to the GATE input terminal of the counter. An internal or external clock of known period should be routed to the SIGNAL input terminal of the counter. The counter then counts the number of active edges (rising or falling) of the clock signal that are detected from when an active edge (rising or falling) occurs on the AUX terminal until an active edge (rising or falling) follows on the GATE terminal. The time between these two incoming signals is the product of the number of clock edges detected and the known period of the clock signal.

4.2.2 Skill-Development Problem: Continuous Measurement of a Digital Pulse Train's Period

This section describes how to write a general-purpose counter input program to continuously read and store the period of a digital pulse train for low-speed applications until stopped by the user. This section is structured so that you can develop the VI as you read the material. The idea is that it will be easier to learn and retain key data acquisition concepts by applying the concepts as you learn them. This program would be suitable for measuring a time-varying digital pulse train such as measuring the angular speed of a shaft. An example would be a rotating shaft containing a strong magnet embedded on the shaft's surface sweeping past a Hall Effect sensor. A digital pulse train is generated on the output of the Hall Effect sensor. The period of one pulse is the time that it takes the shaft to make one revolution. The shaft's angular velocity can be determined from the reciprocal of the pulse's period.

This VI employs period measurement of a digital pulse train with hardware timing and a circular buffer. The material discussed in this section assumes that LabVIEW Professional Version or Student Version software, NI-DAQ software, and a data acquisition board have been installed on your computer.

Equipment

1. A digital input source comprising a function generator or a digital device that outputs a TTL signal, such as a photodiode with a light source or a Hall Effect sensor with a strong magnet, such as an Earth magnet.

Goals

1. Become acquainted with some basic counter input data acquisition concepts using LabVIEW's configuration approach.

2. Develop the hardware-timed counter input VI shown in Figs. 4.2.1 and 4.2.2, which employs a circular buffer to continuously measure and store the period of a digital pulse train until stopped by the user.

Developing the VI

1. Beginning at the Start Menu, select **All Programs>>National Instruments>>LabVIEW 2012>>LabVIEW 2012.**

Figure 4.2.1   Front panel of the counter input example VI with hardware timing and a circular buffer

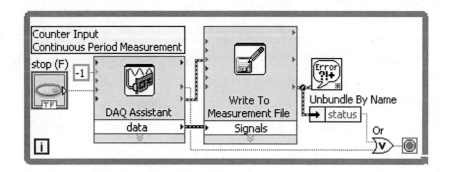

Figure 4.2.2   Block diagram of the counter input example VI with hardware timing and a circular buffer

Note: Read Section 1.3 if you need background on the LabVIEW environment.

2. Select "Blank VI" to open a new file.

3. From the Functions palette, select **Express>>Input>>DAQ Assistant** and drag it in the block diagram.

4. Click on "Acquire Signals", "Counter Input", and "Period" in the "Create New…" window as shown in Fig. 4.2.3.

5. Click on the hardware device to show the counters that are available to measure digital pulse trains on your DAQ board.

6. Select counter 0 ("ctr0") or other appropriate counter, as shown in Fig. 4.2.3.

7. Select "Finish" and the DAQ Assistant window appears.

8. Within the DAQ Assistant window, select a suitable range of periods for the input signal. A digital period between 1 and 0.1 seconds (corresponding to a frequency of 1 to 10 Hz), as shown in Fig. 4.2.4, was selected for this example anticipating that the signal may be manually generated using a sensor.

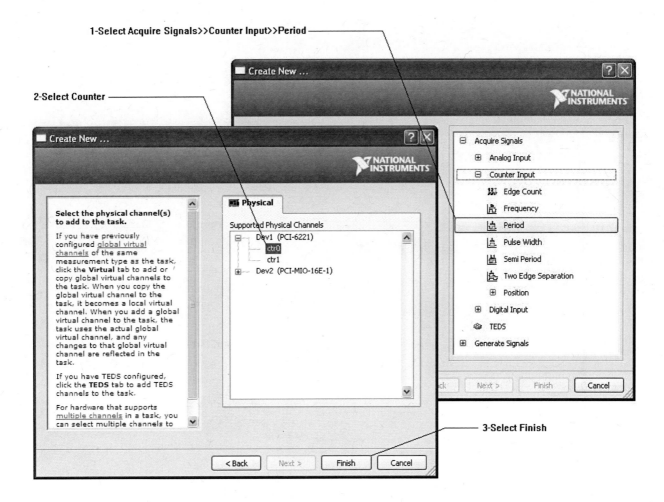

Figure 4.2.3   Steps to use the DAQ Assistant to select the counter for the counter input VI

Note: The default option of "1 Counter (Low Frequency)" is appropriate if you have selected a period between 0.1-1 seconds. If you plan to test this VI with an input signal that has a frequency close to the DAQ board's clock frequency, you may want to select "2 Counters (High Frequency)". Refer to the Frequency Measurement discussion in Section 4.2.1 for more details.

9. Select "Continuous Samples" for the acquisition mode and a manageable number of samples to read, like 10, as shown in Fig. 4.2.4, if you will be using a sensor to generate the TTL pulses.

Note: The acquisition mode "Continuous Samples" relies on hardware timing using the DAQ on-board clock. This mode continuously reads and writes samples from a circular buffer. See Section 2.3.1 for information on circular buffers.

10. Click "OK" in the DAQ Assistant window as the other default values are appropriate.

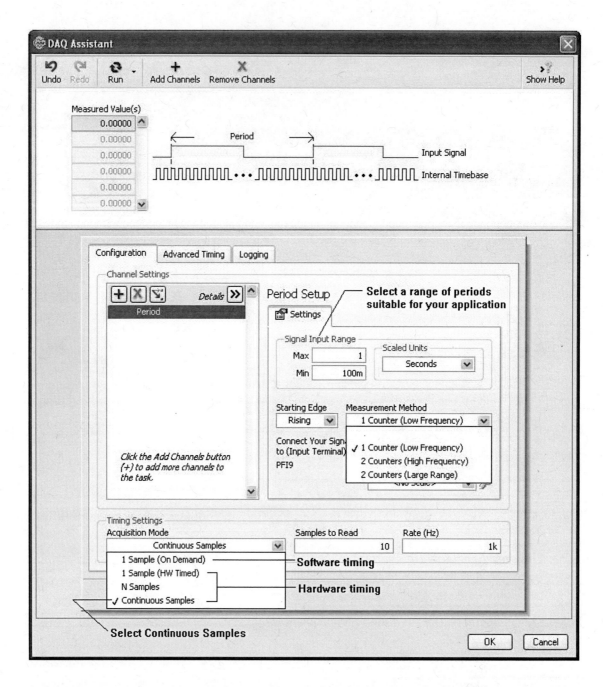

Figure 4.2.4   Counter configuration for the counter input VI using the DAQ Assistant

11. Select "Yes" when the "Confirm Auto Loop Creation" window appears.

12. Place the Position (arrow) cursor over the wire connecting the DAQ Assistant and the conditional terminal of the While Loop, right click the mouse, and select "Delete Wire Branch".

Note: The conditional terminal will be modified at a later time to stop if an error occurs or if stopped by a user.

13. From the Functions palette, select **Express>>Output>>Write to Measurement File** and drag the icon inside the While Loop and to the right of the DAQ Assistant. Resize the While Loop, if necessary.

14. Enter an appropriate filename if the default filename is not suitable, select the options as shown in Fig. 4.2.5 in the configuration window, and press OK.

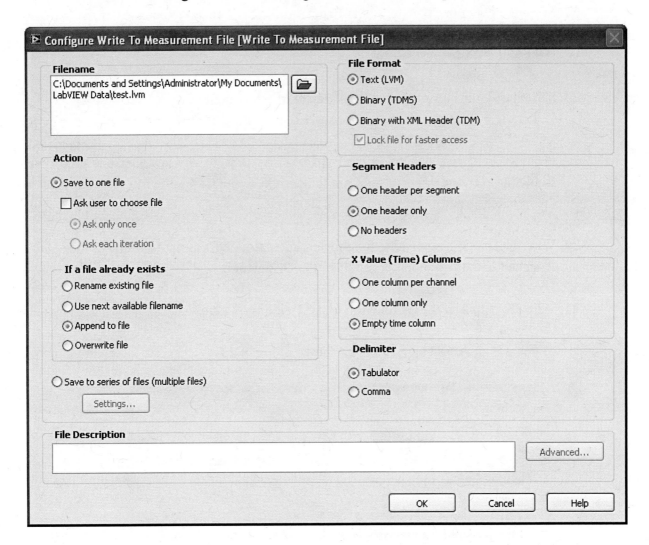

Figure 4.2.5   Write to Measurement File Express VI settings for the continuous counter input VI

Note: The file is created on the first iteration of the While Loop. Once the file exists, "Append to file" is selected since new data is written every iteration.

Note: "Empty time column" is selected because the number of each element in the data array is recorded, not the time the element is measured. Each iteration the element number restarts with one.

15. Wire the "data" output of the DAQ Assistant to the "Signals" input of the Write to Measurement File Express VI.

16. Wire the "error out" output of the DAQ Assistant to the "error in (no error)" input of the Write to Measurement File Express VI.

17. From the Functions palette, select **Programming>>Cluster, Class, & Variant>>Unbundle by Name** and drag the icon inside the While Loop and to the right of the Write to Measurement File Express VI

18. Wire the "error out" output of the Write to Measurement File Express VI to the Unbundle by Name function and observe that "status" appears.

19. From the Functions palette, select **Express>>Arithmetic & Comparison>>Express Boolean>>Or** and drag the function to the right of the Unbundle by Name function in the block diagram.

20. Wire the Unbundle by Name function and the "stopped" output terminal of the DAQ Assistant to the two input terminals of the Or function.

21. Wire the output of the Or function to the conditional terminal.

Note: The wiring should appear as that shown in Fig. 4.2.6.

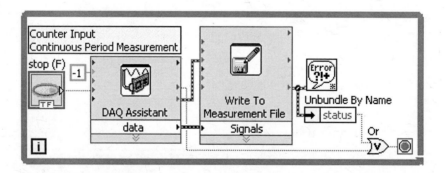

Figure 4.2.6   Wiring diagram for the counter input example VI

Congratulations! You have completed a VI to continuously measure the period of a digital pulse train using hardware timing and a circular buffer. Be sure to save your program using one of the save options on the "File" pull-down menu.

Testing the VI

To test the counter input VI, a digital output device, such as a function generator, a photodiode, or a Hall Effect sensor, must be selected to generate the digital pulse train. Since a common application of the counter input mode is to measure the angular speed of a shaft, the discussion in this section will focus on using a Hall Effect sensor. However, if you do not have ready access to a Hall Effect sensor, a function generator or other digital device may be used to generate a digital pulse train.

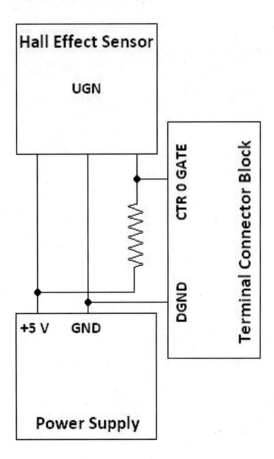

Figure 4.2.7   Diagram to connect a Hall Effect sensor to the DAQ board's terminal connector block for the counter input example VI

A typical connection diagram for a Hall Effect sensor is shown in Fig. 4.2.7. Consult the manufacturer's specifications of your Hall Effect sensor to ensure correct connections to the power supply. A typical resistance for the resistor shown in Fig. 4.2.7 is 1000 Ohms. It's beneficial to test the Hall Effect sensor before connecting it to the DAQ board since the sensor works with only one orientation of the magnet. This will ensure that any potential problem you may have measuring the period of the digital pulse is not due to the sensor output. Connect the output of the sensor and the ground to a multimeter or oscilloscope. The sensor output should be 5 V. Place one pole of the strong magnet close to the face of the sensor. Reverse the pole of the magnet if the voltage does not drop to 0 V. The magnet can then be affixed to a shaft that will rotate during testing, for example, a metal rod attached to a hand drill. If this equipment is not available, the magnet may be moved towards and away from the sensor by hand.

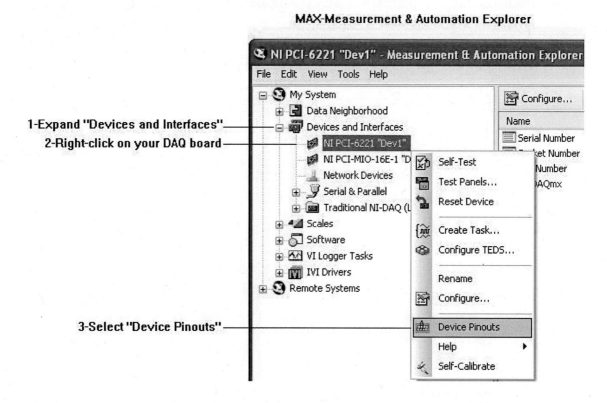

Figure 4.2.8   Using the Measurement &Automation Explorer utility to identify the pin connection for the counter input and digital ground terminals

Determine the counter input and digital ground pin numbers on the terminal connector block so that a set of leads may be connected to the digital output device. A device pinout diagram for your DAQ board can be found using the Measurement & Automation Explorer (MAX) software program, a National Instruments utility to manage hardware. Select "Measurement & Automation Explorer…" from the "Tools" pull-down menu. A window will appear like the one that is partially shown in Figure 4.2.8. Expand "Devices and Interfaces", right click on the DAQ board that was selected when you configured your counter using the DAQ Assistant, and select "Device Pinouts." Device Pinouts may also be selected in the toolbar at the top of the MAX window. The pinout sheet appears in a new window and the pin number for the counter gate and digital ground terminals can be identified using the "Default NI-DAQmx Counter Terminals" table below the pinout diagram. For example, the counter 0 input gate, CTR 0 GATE, is pin 3 and one of the digital grounds, D GND, is pin 4 on the NI PCI/PXI 6221 DAQ board.

The output of the Hall Effect sensor is connected to the counter's gate. The counter signal is referenced to system ground, which means that the power supply ground should be connected to the digital ground of the DAQ board. If a function generator is used instead of a Hall Effect sensor, the positive lead of the function generator connects to the counter's gate and the negative lead of the function generator connects to the digital ground of the DAQ board.

After the leads have been connected, the VI is ready to run. Each block of digital pulse periods is measured, stored temporarily in the circular buffer, and then recorded in the file specified in the Write to Measurement File Express VI. Execution of the VI terminates when the stop control in the Front Panel is set to true. Note, however, that there may be a substantial lag between when the stop control is pressed and when the VI stops running. After the stop control is pressed, the DAQ Assistant must continue to count the current number of periods (samples) specified in the "Samples to Read" input of the DAQ Assistant window and then complete the final iteration of the While Loop, which includes acquiring another block of samples. If you are generating the samples manually, you may have to wire a constant "-1" to the "timeout (s)" input of the DAQ Assistant to wait indefinitely, as shown in Fig. 4.2.2. The data can be viewed in the file specified in the Write to Measurement File Express VI.

Discussion

The continuous measurement of the period of a digital pulse train with hardware and software timing is compared and contrasted in Fig. 4.2.9 (a) and (b). The DAQ Assistant shown in Fig. 4.2.9 (a) is configured to take continuous period measurements using hardware timing with a circular buffer. This is the example counter input VI developed in this section. The DAQ Assistant in Fig. 4.2.9 (b) is configured to take a single period measurement on demand (software timing) and continuously measures periods of the digital pulse train through repeated calls of the While Loop. On the surface, the two VIs look very similar using the same Express VIs and the same structure with the same criteria for stopping VI execution.

The VI with hardware timing reads blocks of samples, whose size is specified by the DAQ Assistant "Samples to Read" input, temporarily stores the samples in a circular buffer, and periodically writes the samples into a permanent file. The period of every pulse in the digital pulse train is read.

The VI with software timing reads one sample when called by the software. Once the sample is read, the sample is written to the permanent file based on the principle of data flow. When the DAQ Assistant is called in the next iteration of the While Loop, another sample is read. However, even though the sub diagram within the While Loop executes as fast as it can be run by the software (no Time Delay Express VI was added), the period of every digital pulse is not recorded. Once one period is measured, the subsequent digital pulse that appears on the DAQ board terminal is not read because the previous pulse period is being written to the permanent file. At best, every other pulse period is recorded.

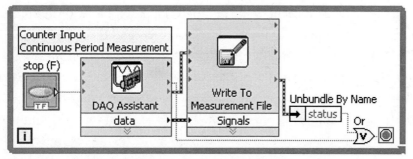

(a) Continuous period measurement using hardware timing

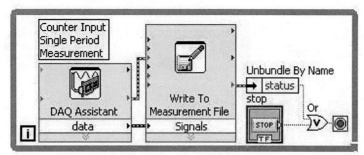

(b) Continuous period measurement using software timing

Figure 4.2.9   The continuous measurement of the period of a digital pulse train using (a) continuous buffered input with hardware timing and (b) a single measurement called repeatedly within a While Loop with software timing

4.3 Counter Output

4.3.1   Introduction to Counter Output Applications

A brief description of some of the more common counter output applications are provided in this section. Each application may generate a single pulse (on-demand or immediate) mode or generate a pulse train in buffered mode. Refer to your DAQ hardware manual to determine what capabilities are available on your DAQ board.

Single Pulse Generation

TTL pulses are commonly used for triggers to initiate other modes of data acquisition. TTL pulses are also used as gates, as described in Section 4.2.1.

The pulse appears on the OUT output terminal of the counter. You specify the pulse width and typically a delay can be specified. A pulse can be generated when called by software or when triggered.

Continuous Pulse Train Generation

A common example for pulse train generation is for the control of electrical devices through pulse width modulation (PWM). A pulse train is a signal that continually switches between the high (5 V) and low (0 V) state. Modulating a TTL signal is achieved by controlling the time the signal is in the high state versus the total period of the digital wave. As defined in Section 4.1, the duty cycle is the fraction of time the digital wave is in the high state compared to the period of the wave. PWM is used to control many inertial electrical devices, that is, devices that cannot respond to a rapid switching of the TTL signal between the high and low states. For example, PWM is used to control the position of servomotors and the speed of DC motors.

Pulse trains can be generated with software-controlled frequency and duty cycle. The pulse train appears on the OUT output terminal of the counter. The pulse train can be continuous or a finite number of pulses can be generated. Pulse generation can occur when called by software or when triggered. A pulse train with limited options for duty cycle can be generated with the counter's frequency generator, which is independent of the counter/timer modules, and the signal appears on the FREQ OUT terminal.

4.3.2 Skill-Development Problem: Pulse Train Generation and Pulse Width Modulation

This section describes how to write a general-purpose counter output program to continuously generate a digital pulse train and modulate its pulse width until stopped by the user. This section is structured so that you can develop the VI as you read the material. The idea is that it will be easier to learn and retain key data acquisition concepts by applying the concepts as you learn them. This VI would be suitable for controlling inertial electrical devices. The VI generates a pulse train with a frequency that is higher than the inertial electrical device can respond to the rapid switching between the high and low state of the signal. The power delivered to the device is controlled by the width of the high state compared to that of the low state or, in other words, the duty cycle. By modulating the pulse width, an analog electrical device can respond to a modulated digital pulse train in the same way it would to a time-varying analog output signal. Examples of the use of pulse width modulation of a digital pulse train to control an inertial electrical device include the intensity of an LED, the rotational speed of a DC motor, or the position of a servomotor.

This VI employs the generation and modulation of a digital pulse train with software timing. The material discussed in this section assumes that LabVIEW Professional Version or Student Version software, NI-DAQ software, and a data acquisition board have been installed on your computer.

Equipment

1. An oscilloscope to display the digital pulse train output signal or, if an oscilloscope is not available, a multimeter may be used for low frequency signals.
2. Optionally, an inertial electrical device, such as a LED or a DC micromotor may be used as long as the power requirements do not exceed the capabilities of your DAQ board.

Goals

1. Become acquainted with some basic counter output data acquisition concepts using LabVIEW's configuration approach.

2. Develop the software-timed counter output VI shown in Figs. 4.3.1 and 4.3.2, which employs software timing to continuously generate and modulate a digital pulse train until stopped by the user.

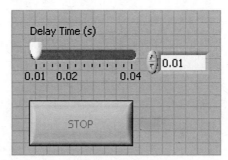

Figure 4.3.1   Front panel of the counter output example VI using software timing to generate and modulate a digital pulse train

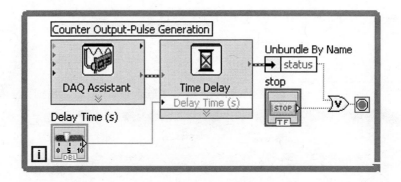

Figure 4.3.2   Block diagram of the counter output example VI using software timing to generate and modulate a digital pulse train

Developing the VI

1. Beginning at the Start Menu, select **All Programs>>National Instruments>>LabVIEW 2012>>LabVIEW 2012**.

Note: Read Section 1.3 if you need background on the LabVIEW environment.

2. Select "Blank VI" to open a new file.

3. From the Functions palette, select **Express>>Output>>DAQ Assistant** and drag it in the block diagram.

4. Click on "Generate Signals", "Counter Output", and "Pulse Output" in the "Create New..." window as shown in Fig. 4.3.3.

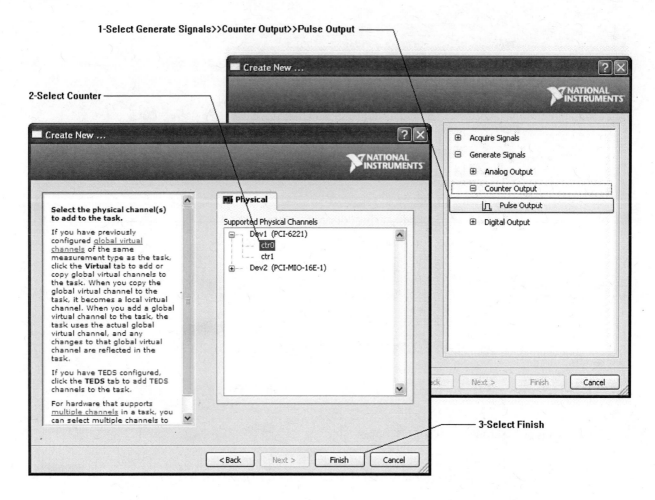

Figure 4.3.3   Steps to use the DAQ Assistant to select the counter for the counter output
example VI

5. Click on the hardware device to show the counters that are available to generate
    digital pulse trains on your DAQ board.

6. Select counter 0 ("ctr0") or other appropriate counter, as shown in Fig. 4.3.3.

7. Select "Finish" and the DAQ Assistant window appears.

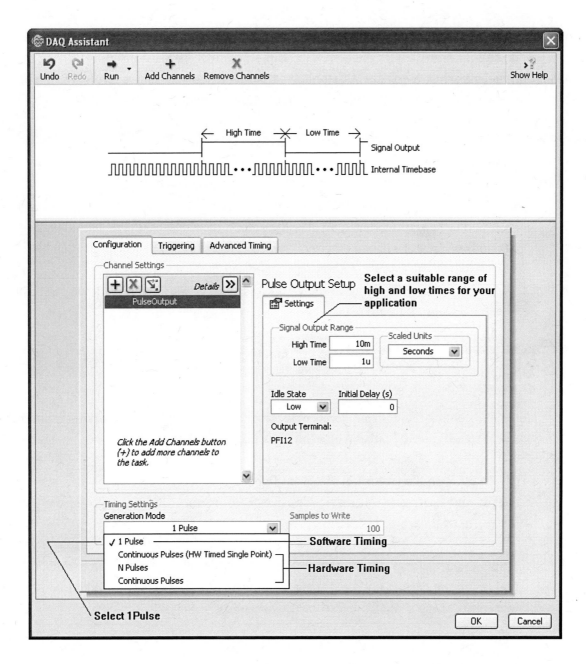

Figure 4.3.4   Counter configuration for the counter output VI using the DAQ Assistant

8. All default values in the DAQ Assistant window shown in Fig 4.3.4 are appropriate except for the signal output range. If you will be using a multimeter to display the signal, select a long high time, like 2 seconds or greater, to allow the multimeter to respond to the signal. For all other equipment, like an oscilloscope, an LED, or a small DC motor, you may keep the default high time of 10 milliseconds. Enter a small low time, like 0.000001 seconds (1 microsecond), for all applications.

9. Select "OK" to build the counter generation task.

Note: The generation mode "1 Pulse" generates only one pulse when called by the VI. The timing of the call is controlled by the computer's internal clock (software timing). It can generate pulses continuously when the DAQ Assistant is called repeatedly within a While Loop while using a timing subVI to control the rate at which the DAQ Assistant is called.

10. From the Functions palette, select **Express>>Execution Control>>Time Delay** and drag the icon to the right of the DAQ Assistant.

11. Click OK after entering 0.01 seconds in the Configure Time Delay window, unless you will use a multimeter to display the signal, in which case you should enter 2 seconds or greater.

12. Wire the "error out" output of the DAQ Assistant to the "error in (no error)" input of the Time Delay Express VI.

13. Right-click on the "Delay Time (s)" input terminal of the Time Delay Express VI and select Create>>Control from the pop-up menu.

Note: The control in the Front Panel will be replaced with a horizontal pointer slide to facilitate modifying the pulse width during VI execution.

14. Right click on the control in the Front Panel and select **Replace>>Express>>Numeric Controls>>Horizontal Pointer Slide** from the pop-up menu as shown in Fig. 4.3.5.

15. Unless you will use a multimeter to display the signal, in which case the default values on the pointer slide are acceptable, use the Edit Text (letter A) cursor to adjust the limits of the scale from 0.01 to 0.04 seconds.

16. Right click on the pointer slide and select Visible Items>>Digital Display from the pop-up menu to show the exact value of the time delay.

17. Select **Express>>Execution Control>>While Loop** and drag the structure over the objects in the block diagram from the top left corner to the bottom right corner.

18. Place the cursor over the wire between the "stop" control and the conditional terminal, right-click the mouse, and select "Delete Wire Branch" from the pop-up menu. Move the stop control to add space between the control and the conditional terminal.

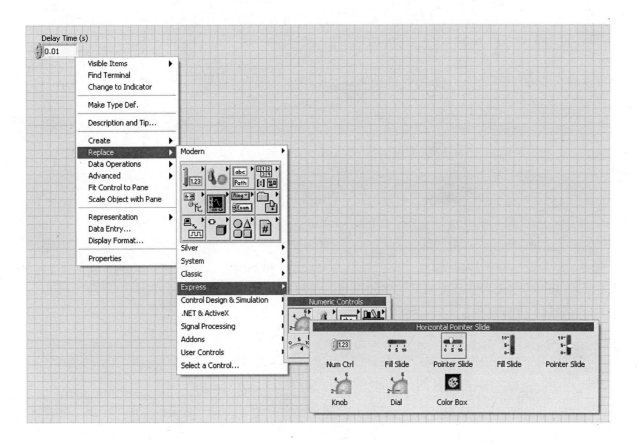

Figure 4.3.5   Procedure to replace the control with a horizontal pointer slide for the counter output example VI

19. From the Functions palette, select **Programming>>Cluster, Class, & Variant>>Unbundle by Name** and drag the icon inside the While Loop and to the right of the Time Delay Express VI

20. Wire the "error out" output of the Time Delay Express VI to the Unbundle by Name function and observe that "status" appears.

21. From the Functions palette, select **Express>>Arithmetic & Comparison>>Express Boolean>>Or** and drag the function between the Unbundle by Name function and the conditional terminal.

22. Wire the Unbundle by Name function and the stop control to the two input terminals of the Or function.

23. Wire the output of the Or function to the conditional terminal, if not done so automatically.

Note: The wiring should appear as that shown in Fig. 4.3.6.

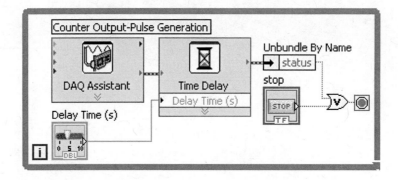

Figure 4.3.6   Wiring diagram for the counter output example VI

Congratulations! You have completed a VI to continuously generate and modulate a digital pulse train using software timing. Be sure to save your program using one of the save options on the "File" pull-down menu.

Testing the VI

To test the counter output VI, an inertial electrical device that can be controlled with pulse width modulation, such as a LED or a small DC motor, may be selected. A small DC motor will be used for this example VI. However, if you do not have ready access to an inertial electrical device, an oscilloscope or multimeter (if an oscilloscope is not available) may be used to display the digital pulse train signal.

Determine the counter output and digital ground pin numbers on the terminal connector block so that a set of leads may be connected to the input devices. A device pinout diagram for your DAQ board can be found using the Measurement & Automation Explorer (MAX) software program, a National Instruments utility to manage hardware. Select "Measurement & Automation Explorer…" from the "Tools" pull-down menu. A window will appear like the one that is partially shown in Figure 4.3.7. Expand "Devices and Interfaces", right click on the DAQ board that was selected when you configured your counter using the DAQ Assistant, and select "Device Pinouts." Device Pinouts may also be selected in the toolbar at the top of the MAX window. The pinout sheet appears in a new window and the pin number for the counter out and ground terminals can be identified. For example, the counter 0 output terminal, CTR 0 OUT, is pin 2 and one of the digital grounds, D GND, is pin 4 on the NI PCI/PXI 6221 DAQ board.

If you are using an oscilloscope or a multimeter to display the signal, attach the lead of the counter output (CTR 0 OUT) on the terminal connector block to a positive terminal on an oscilloscope or multimeter, if an oscilloscope is not available. Attach the digital ground lead on the terminal connector block to the negative (or common) terminal of the oscilloscope or multimeter. Note that the digital ground is used for the negative (common) terminal since a referenced single ended system configuration is used for digital I/O signals, which means that the output signal is referenced to the system ground on D GND.

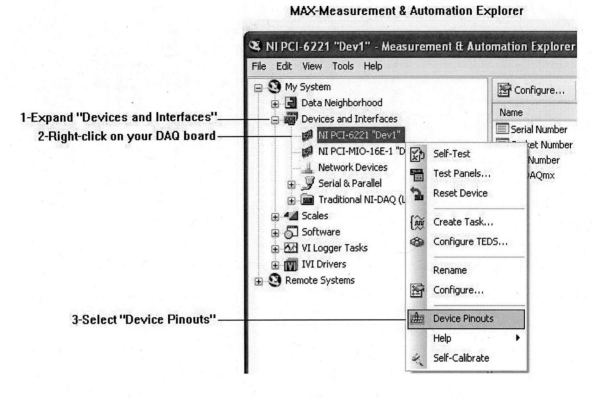

MAX-Measurement & Automation Explorer

1-Expand "Devices and Interfaces"
2-Right-click on your DAQ board

3-Select "Device Pinouts"

Figure 4.3.7   Using the Measurement &Automation Explorer utility to identify the pin connection for the counter output and digital ground channels

A DC micromotor is used in the current example and may be safe to drive using the DAQ board *under no load conditions*. A DC micromotor is commonly used in CD or DVD players or ROM drives. Specifically, a NI PCI 6221 DAQ board is used to drive a RF-300C-11440 DC brush micromotor in the current example.

Hardware specifications for the DAQ board and electrical device should be consulted before using the DAQ board to drive any device. This will ensure that you do not damage the DAQ board. National Instruments specifications for the PCI 6221 DAQ board show that the recommended maximum operating output current for a programmable function interface (PFI) channel, which includes the counter 0 output channel, is 16 milliamps. *Under no-load conditions*, the manufacturer's specifications show that the motor draws 18 milliamps when the motor runs at 3000 RPM with 3 V applied. Since the generated high pulse width is set at 0.01 seconds (specified in the DAQ Assistant configuration window shown in Fig. 4.3.4) and the time delay range is set from 0.01 to 0.04 seconds, the duty cycle cannot exceed 50%. Using a 5 V TTL signal, this ensures that an average of 3 V will not be applied to the motor and the motor will draw less than 18 milliamps. The connection of the RF-300C-11440 DC micromotor to the DAQ board is shown in Fig. 4.3.8.

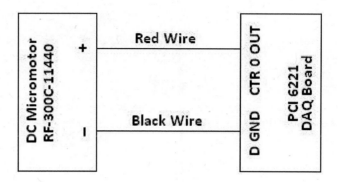

Figure 4.3.8   Wiring diagram to connect a DC micromotor to a PCI 6221 DAQ board

After the leads have been connected, the VI is ready to run. The high pulse width should be 0.01 seconds and the limits on the time delay pointer slide should be 0.01-0.04 seconds, unless you are using a multimeter. If a multimeter is used, the high pulse width should be 2 seconds and the limits on the time delay pointer slide should be approximately 2-6 seconds. Click on the Run button in the toolbar to begin execution of the VI. Vary the time delay and observe the change in the signal on the oscilloscope or the rotational speed of the motor. The VI will generate a digital pulse train continuously until the user selects the stop control in the front panel. As a general practice, you should always ensure that the output voltage on the digital output channel is 0 V when you are done with the VI, which is ensured since a low idle state was selected in the DAQ Assistant.

Discussion

The development of a pulse width modulation VI using only Express VIs provides an example how to modulate a digital pulse train but one that may not yield accurate control over the pulse train's frequency and duty cycle. Ideally, the pulse high and low times, or equivalently the frequency and duty cycle, would be the parameters varied to modulate the digital pulse train. Unfortunately, these parameters are not inputs to the DAQ Assistant Express VI icon. For illustration purposes, Fig. 4.3.9 identifies terminals for the DAQ Assistant. These include the timeout, error in, stop, and device name input terminals. The high time and low time are inputs to the DAQ Assistant only through the configuration window, as shown in Fig. 4.3.4, but not during its execution.

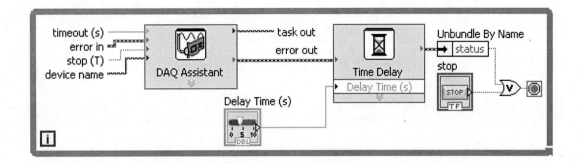

Figure 4.3.9   Block diagram of the counter output example VI showing labeled DAQ
                Assistant terminals

An approximate way to modulate the pulse width using only Express VIs is to include a time delay at the end of the pulse. The Time Delay Express VI icon has an input parameter, Delay Time, and, since it is inside the While Loop, it can be modified during any iteration. Because of the principle of data flow, the time delay follows the pulse generated when the DAQ Assistant executes. The generation of a single pulse begins with the high time and ends with the low time. Since the time delay is added at the end of the pulse, it effectively becomes part of the low time of the pulse. It seems intuitive to set the low time equal to zero when the DAQ Assistant is configured but the low time is required to be at least two periods of the sample clock or greater. Therefore, the pulse is configured in the DAQ Assistant to have a very short low time, 1 microsecond in this example, to effectively permit the low time to be controlled by the time delay. Of course, the low time could be subtracted from the time delay but it represents only a small error compared to other sources discussed in the next paragraph.

There are a couple of disadvantages to the method employed in this example VI to modulate the pulse width. Since the duty cycle of the pulse train is modulated only through the low time of the pulse, the frequency and duty cycle vary simultaneously. For example, the high time of the pulse is set at 0.01 seconds and the time delay varies from 0.01-0.04 seconds in the current VI. As the time delay varies from 0.01 seconds to 0.04 seconds, the duty cycle varies from approximately 50% to 20% while the frequency of the pulse train also varies from 50 Hz to 20 Hz. This is not a problem if the electrical device that is being controlled, like the DC motor in the current example, does not require a digital pulse with constant frequency and that the frequency of the pulse remains high enough that the inertia of the electrical device cannot respond to changes between high and low states. Another disadvantage to the current method is that the value of the duty cycle based on the high time of the pulse and the time delay are only approximate. The time delay is controlled by the computer's clock so that the actual time delay may be different from that specified. Likewise, the time it takes to check inputs to the conditional terminal of the While Loop is also added to the time delay. The uncertainty in the duty cycle is reduced by using larger high times and time delays but this approach is limited to digital pulse train periods small enough that inertial electrical devices cannot respond to changes between high and low times of the pulse.

Accurate control over the frequency and duty cycle of a digital pulse train requires developing a VI using LabVIEW's DAQmx approach. This approach allows the VI to be developed using the continuous generation of a pulse train using hardware timing and a circular buffer while continuously checking for any user-requested changes in the pulse train's frequency or duty cycle. Changes that are made to the pulse's high and low times are controlled by the clock on the DAQ board, which result in accurate pulse train frequencies and duty cycles.

4.4   Learn by Doing

The problems in this section are offered to help you work on developing proficiency using LabVIEW for data acquisition. The problems are often multi-function in nature and strive to show the practical application of LabVIEW to real-life problems. The presentation of material in this section assumes that you have worked the introductory LabVIEW example problem in Section 1.4, which helps you to learn some basic LabVIEW concepts, and the skill development problems in this chapter. The hope is that you will be able to complete the LabVIEW proficiency problems without the need of a guide…the next step to developing LabVIEW VIs on your own.

4.4.1   Proficiency-Development Problem: Inductive Proximity Sensor/Metal Detector

Introduction

An inductive proximity sensor is based on the principle that the inductance of a coil in an alternating magnetic field changes in the presence of a metallic object. A current flowing through a circular coil of wire will induce a magnetic field whose flux lines are parallel to the axis of the coil. A metal plate placed over the coil and perpendicular to the coil axis will induce a current in the plate called an eddy current. The eddy current will create its own magnetic field opposing the coil's field and lowers the inductance. The closer the metal plate is to the coil, the stronger the effect.

If the coil is a component of an LC oscillating circuit, the frequency of the oscillations increases as the inductance decreases in the presence of a metallic object. The change in frequency can be related to the proximity of the metallic object. Likewise, different metals have different effects on the magnetic field and thus the frequency of oscillations in the oscillator circuit. This forms the basis of one type of metal detector.

The schematic of the inductive proximity sensor used in the current example problem is shown in Fig. 4.4.1.1. The feedback from the first Schmitt trigger passes through the LC oscillator circuit. The frequency of the oscillator circuit changes as the inductance varies with distance of a metallic object from the coil. The second Schmitt trigger squares up the output wave. The frequency of the output signal of the circuit, V_{OUT}, is measured by the appropriate counter input channel on the DAQ board.

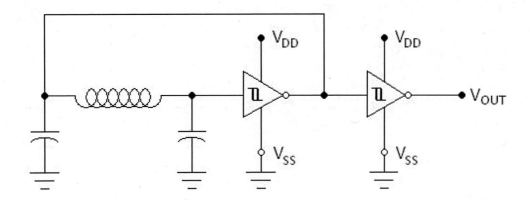

Figure 4.4.1.1 Schematic for the inductive proximity sensor proficiency problem

Goals

1. Develop proficiency with counter input data acquisition concepts using LabVIEW's configuration approach.

2. Develop a software-timed counter input VI to continuously measure the frequency of a digital pulse train until stopped by the user.

3. Build an inductive proximity sensor and test the sensor with different metallic objects at different distances.

Equipment

1. Motorola MC14584BCP Hex Schmitt Trigger or equivalent
2. Capacitor, 0.01 µF, Quantity (2)
3. Inductor, 35 mm diameter coil with approximately 100 turns of fine wire or equivalent wrapped around a wooden core
4. Breadboard
5. Power Supply
6. Plates of various metals (iron, aluminum, copper, etc.)

Developing the VI

The front panel and block diagram of the VI to measure the frequency of an oscillator circuit that is part of an inductive proximity sensor are shown in Figs. 4.4.1.2 and 4.4.1.3. All functions that have been employed in this VI have been described in this chapter or Section 1.4, except for the Simple Error Handler. This subVI indicates if an error has occurred and, if so, provides a description of the error. The subVI can be found in the functions palette under **Programming>>Dialog & User Interface>>Simple Error Handler**. Its use is optional. The gauge can be found in the Controls palette (**Modern>>Numeric>>Gauge**).

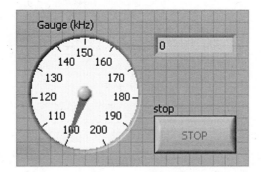

Figure 4.4.1.2   Front panel of the counter input VI to continuously measure the frequency of a digital pulse train until stopped by the user

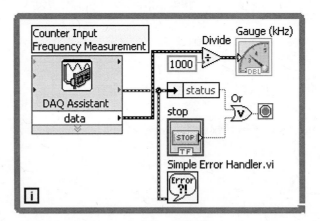

Figure 4.4.1.3   Block diagram of the counter input VI to continuously measure the frequency of a digital pulse train until stopped by the user

The configuration of the measurement task using the DAQ Assistant is shown in Fig. 4.4.1.4. The configuration values should be appropriate for your proximity sensor with the possible exception of the signal input range. The oscillating frequency of your proximity sensor will depend on specific values for your capacitors and inductor. This is discussed more in the next section on fabrication and testing.

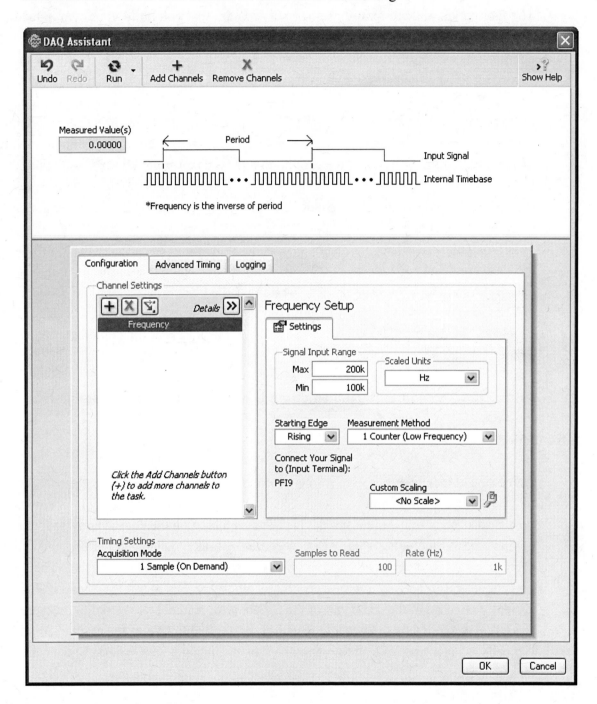

Figure 4.4.1.4   Counter configuration using the DAQ Assistant for the counter input VI to measure the frequency of one sample of a digital pulse train

Fabrication and Testing

The fabrication of the proximity sensor may require that you build your own inductor, which will approximate a short air-core cylindrical coil. Otherwise, the remaining components can be obtained commercially. Assemble the components on the breadboard according to the schematic shown in Fig. 4.4.1.1. Connect the breadboard to a power supply. Supply 5 V and 0 V (GND) to V_{DD} and V_{SS}, respectively, to power the Schmitt triggers and produce a TTL pulse train. Connect the output, V_{OUT}, of the second Schmitt trigger to the input terminal specified in your DAQ Assistant configuration window, like that shown in Fig. 4.4.1.4, and the ground to a D GND terminal on the DAQ board.

Once the connections have been made, the VI is ready to run. If the needle on the gauge in the front panel does not move, observe the digital display next to the gauge. It's possible that the oscillator frequency is outside of the range specified when configuring the measurement task with the DAQ Assistant. If so, change the minimum and maximum gauge values to an appropriate range. Next place the plane of a metal plate above the coil and perpendicular to the axis of the coil. Observe the frequency of the oscillator circuit change as the distance between the plate and coil vary. Repeat the demonstration with different metal plates.

4.4.2 Proficiency-Development Problem: Simple Engine Dynamometer Simulation

Introduction

An engine dynamometer is used to measure the torque or power of an engine. It consists of a power adsorption unit that is connected directly to the crankshaft of the engine. The power adsorption unit can be any device to place a load on the engine and dissipate the engine's power including a water brake, hydraulic brake, mechanical brake, and an electric motor. The power adsorption unit consists of a rotor and its housing. The rotor housing is constrained by a torque arm but is otherwise free to rotate. A load cell is typically attached at the distal end of the torque arm. A load cell is used to measure the force that is applied by the housing resisting the applied torque of the engine. A load cell typically is comprised of a strain gage or set of strain gages in a Wheatstone bridge arrangement.

The two principle measurements made on an engine dynamometer are the force of the load cell and the rotational speed of the crankshaft. The force of the load cell can be converted to a torque using the moment arm of the torque arm. The power developed by the engine can then be calculated as the product of the torque and the angular velocity, which is obtained from the rotational speed of the crankshaft. Other measurements may be made including fuel and air flow rates to calculate the air/fuel ratio.

The rotational speed of the engine is frequently measured using a strong magnet sweeping past a Hall Effect sensor. The Hall Effect sensor outputs a high TTL signal unless in the presence of a magnet, when it outputs a low TTL signal. One rotation of the crankshaft generates a digital pulse whose period can be measured to determine the rotational speed of the crankshaft. The continuous measurement of the period of the digital pulse train permits continuous calculation of the rotational speed of the shaft.

The VI in this section was developed with the purpose of simulating data acquisition for an engine dynamometer although it has general applicability. The VI may be used for any application that requires a counter to measure the frequency of a digital pulse train and analog signals from multiple channels.

Goals

1. Develop proficiency with multi-function data acquisition concepts using LabVIEW's configuration approach.

2. Develop a software-timed counter input VI to continuously measure the frequency of a digital pulse train and a multi-channel analog input to measure analog signals continuously until stopped by the user.

Equipment

Unless you are fortunate enough to have an engine dynamometer with permission to connect sensors to your DAQ board, the following equipment may be used to simulate the engine dynamometer instrumentation. A Hall Effect switch placed near a magnet on a rotating rod can simulate the measurement of the angular speed of the crankshaft. If that is unavailable, a function generator outputting a square wave may be used. An analog signal from a load cell would make the simulation more realistic but any sensor will provide the experience of testing the VI. If sensors are unavailable, a power supply may be used to provide voltages to read and record.

1. UGN 3030u Hall Effect switch or equivalent
2. Earth magnet or other strong magnet
3. Iron rod and a means to rotate it, like a hand drill
4. Function generator, if items 1-3 are not available
5. Load cell or other appropriate sensor

6. Power supply

Developing the VI

The front panel and block diagram of the VI to measure the rotational speed of a shaft and multiple analog sensors are shown in Figs. 4.4.2.1 and 4.4.2.2.

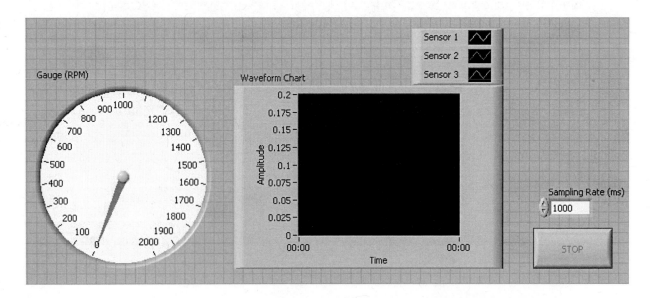

Figure 4.4.2.1   Front panel of the simple VI to simulate measurement of engine dynamometer inputs

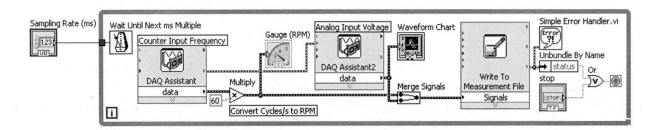

Figure 4.4.2.2   Block diagram of the simple VI to simulate measurement of engine dynamometer inputs

All functions that have been employed in this VI have been described in this chapter or Section 1.4, except for the following: Wait Until Next ms Multiple, Merge Signals, and the Simple Error Handler. When the Wait Until Next ms Multiple function executes, control of the VI resides in this function until the timer reaches a multiple of the wired input. The Wait Until Next ms Multiple function resides in the functions palette under **Programming>>Timing>>Wait Until Next ms Multiple**. Merge Signals merges two or more signals into a single output and can be found in the functions palette under

Express>>Signal Manipulation>>Merge Signals. The Simple Error Handler subVI indicates if an error has occurred and, if so, provides a description of the error. This subVI can be found in the function palette under **Programming>>Dialog & User Interface>>Simple Error Handler**. Its use is optional. The gauge can be found in the Controls palette (**Modern>>Numeric>>Gauge**).

The configuration of the task to measure the pulse train frequency using the DAQ Assistant is shown in Fig. 4.4.2.3. The configuration values should be appropriate for the simulation of data that would typically come from an engine dynamometer. However, the signal input range may need to be modified to accommodate the shaft speed in your test.

The configuration of the task to measure the analog input signals using DAQ Assistant2 is shown in Fig. 4.4.2.4. The configuration values should be appropriate for your sensors with the possible exception of the signal input range. The range will depend on specific values for your sensors. The VI is configured to measure the analog voltage from three channels, such as from a load cell, fuel flow sensor, and an air flow sensor, but the number of channels can be reduced or expanded as appropriate for your application.

The configuration of the file to store measurements is shown in Fig. 4.4.2.5. Enter an appropriate filename if the default filename is not suitable. "Append to file" is selected since the Express VI will be called repeatedly within the While Loop and new data will be appended every iteration. Time will be recorded in the first channel followed by the order in which the channels are merged. For this VI, the frequency will be in the second column and the analog input channels in subsequent columns. The analog input channels are listed in the order shown in the configuration window of DAQ Assistant2.

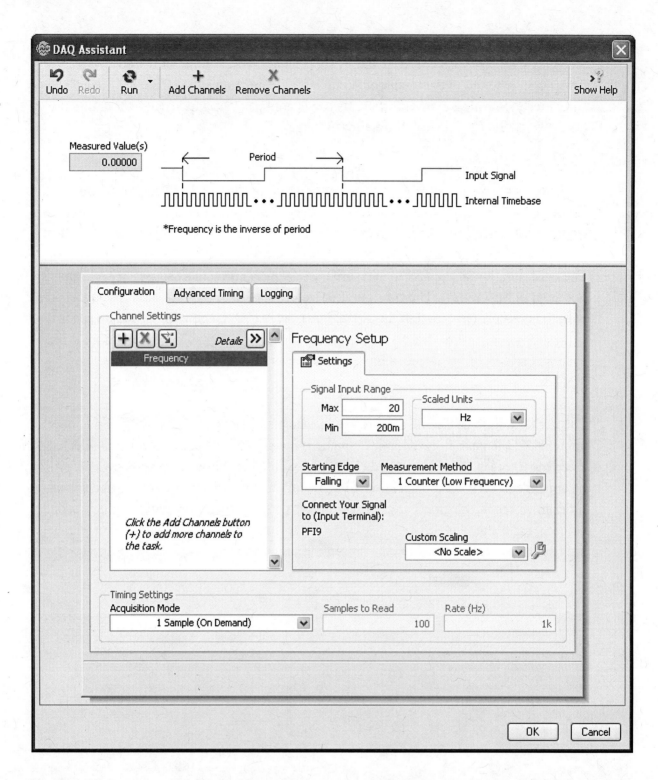

Figure 4.4.2.3   Counter configuration to measure the frequency of one sample of a digital pulse train using the DAQ Assistant

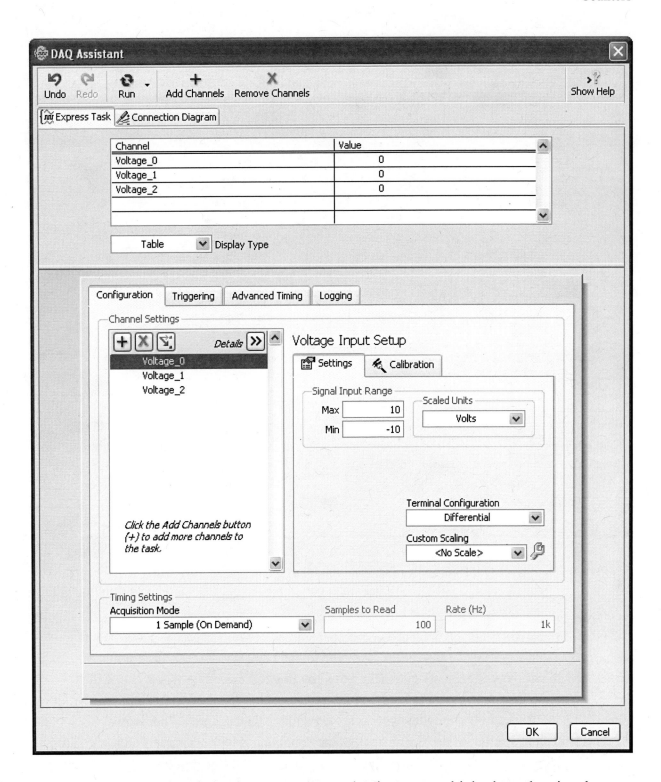

Figure 4.4.2.4   Configuration to measure analog input on multiple channels using the
                      DAQ Assistant

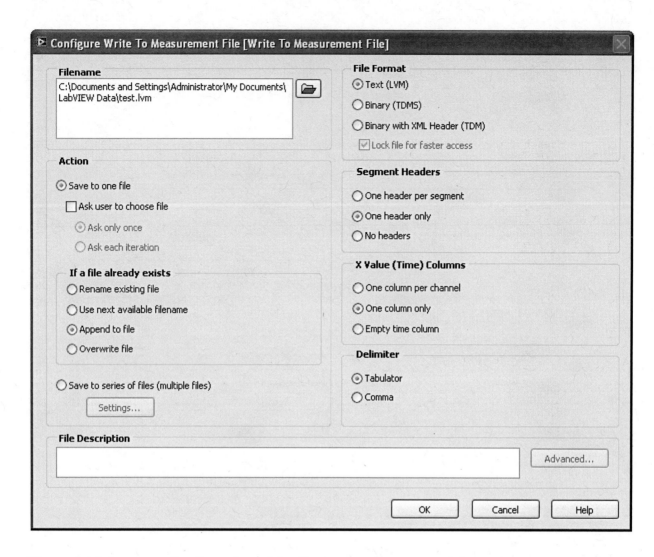

Figure 4.4.2.5   Configuration of the file to store the measured data using the Write To
                      Measurement File Express VI

Fabrication and Testing

If you will be using a magnet attached to a rotating rod sweeping past a Hall Effect switch to measure angular speed, first fabricate the Hall Effect switch circuit shown in Fig. 4.2.7 and follow the procedure outlined under "Testing the VI" in Section 4.2.2. Connect the output of the Hall Effect switch to the input terminal specified in the DAQ Assistant configuration window, like the one identified in Fig. 4.4.2.3 and the switch ground to D GND. If you are not using a Hall Effect switch, connect the function generator to the same two terminals to simulate the Hall Effect switch output. Use the device pinout diagram from the Measurement & Automation Explorer (MAX) to determine the terminal numbers on the terminal connector block.

Connect the leads from the sensors to the analog input terminals shown under the Connection Diagram tab in the DAQ Assistant window. If a power supply or other means to generate analog signals will be used instead of sensors, connect the leads of the power supply the same way as you would with the sensors, as shown in the Connection Diagram.

Once the connections have been made, the VI is ready to run. Measure the angular speed of the rotating shaft (or output from the function generator) and output from the sensors (or power supply) and observe the values on the gauge and chart in the front panel. Measurements will continue until stopped by the user. The shaft must continue to rotate until the completion of the frequency measurement before the VI stops. The output can be viewed in the file specified in the Write To Measurement File Express VI.

Discussion

The timing and order of measurements are controlled through the principle of data flow and a timing function, as shown in Fig. 4.4.2.6. According to the principle of data flow, analog signal measurements are made after the frequency of the digital pulse is measured because the analog measurement task cannot execute until the error code cluster is received from the counter input measurement task. Without the error wiring, the order of the measurement tasks is uncertain.

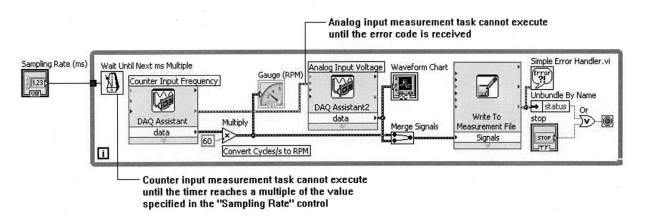

Figure 4.4.2.6   Block diagram showing how a timing function and data flow control the measurement of data

The VI is designed to take samples every interval specified in the Sampling Rate control (one second for this example), which is achieved through the Wait Until Next ms Multiple function. Without this function, measurements would be taken every other revolution at best, as detailed in the Discussion portion of Section 4.2.2.

Notes:

INDEX

U

Unbundle by Name function, 46

V

VI, 5
  Debugging a VI, 63
  Documenting VIs
    labels, 59
    VI Property window, 59
  Running a VI, 63
Virtual channel, 23

W

Wait Until Next ms Multiple function, 298
Waveform chart, 33
  Update mode
    scope chart, 34
    strip chart, 34
    sweep chart, 34
Waveform graph, 36

Express palette, 36
Graph palette, 37
  cursor movement tool, 37
  panning tool, 37
  zoom tool, 37
Modern palette, 36
Wheatstone bridge, 171
Wheatstone quarter bridge circuit, 181
While Loop, 18
  Conditional terminal, 29
  Creating, 30
  Indexing, 32
  Iteration terminal, 29
  Shift registers, 32
  Tunnel, 32
Wires, 38
  Broken wire, 42
  Removing broken wires, 42
  Tip strip, 39
  Tips for wiring, 40
Write to Measurement File Express VI, 24